KIAC
9/13

DRESSAGE FOR THE NOT-SO-PERFECT HORSE

Riding Through the Levels on the Peculiar, Opinionated, Complicated Mounts We All Love

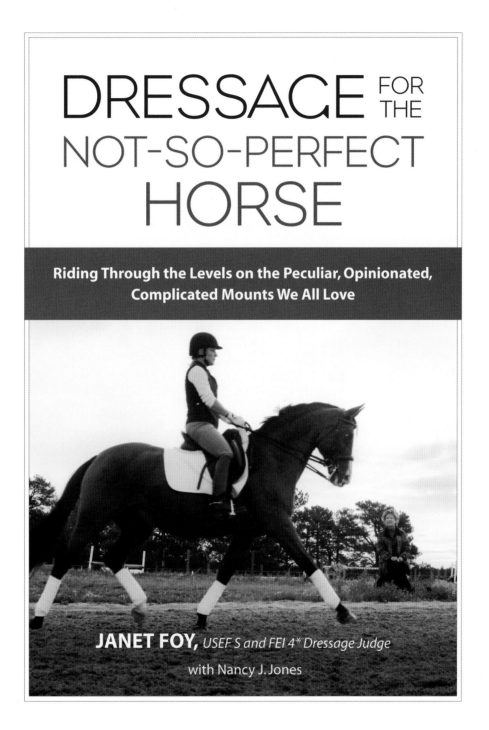

JANET FOY, *USEF S and FEI 4* Dressage Judge*

with Nancy J. Jones

TRAFALGAR SQUARE
North Pomfret, Vermont

First published in 2012 by
Trafalgar Square Books
North Pomfret, Vermont 05053

Printed in China

Library of Congress Cataloging-in-Publication Data
Foy, Janet.
    Dressage for the (not so) perfect horse : training secrets for the peculiar, opinionated, nonconformist, complicated mounts we all ride and love / Janet Foy with Nancy J. Jones.
      p. cm.
  Includes index.
ISBN 978-1-57076-509-4
1. Dressage. 2. Horsemanship. I. Jones, Nancy J. II. Title.
   SF309.5.F66 2012
   798.2'3--dc23
                            2012002722

Book design by Lauryl Eddlemon
Cover design by RM Didier
Typefaces: Myriad, Eagle

10 9 8 7 6 5 4 3 2

Front cover photo features Lisa Peterson on Willow

Dedication

To my family: my grandfather John Altrichter Sr, my parents John and Betty Altrichter, and my wonderful husband Michael Foy, who wanted me to write a book long before the vision took shape!

Contents

Rodeo Queen to Dressage Queen

First Lessons, First Horses

I grew up in Colorado Springs living next to a horse pasture so my sister and I naturally fell in love with horses. My Austrian grandfather, John Altrichter Sr., or "Papa" (my maiden name, Altrichter, means "old judge" in German...a sign perhaps?), was a true animal lover, and he made sure my sister Charlene and I got plenty of exposure to horses.

On Saturdays, Papa would take us to Mark Reyner's stables in Austin Bluffs (an area of Colorado Springs) where we would have a group Western riding lesson. Afterward we always lunched at Conway's Red Top, where the burgers were the size of soup plates.

Soon my sister and I convinced my mom and dad we must have a horse. Now up to this point, my sister and I were supplementing our Saturday lessons by going into the pasture next door with our jump ropes, putting them over a horse's neck, jumping on, and riding away. There was not much chance of being caught by the neighbors as the pasture was about 400 acres with hills, trees, and streams!

One of the horses in the neighbors' pasture was a little black Quarter Horse called Snakes who was for sale for $500. My sister and I had

Janet Altrichter, Girl of the West, 1971.

both secretly ridden him so we already loved him. However, once we were his owners, Snakes would not let us catch him. Now, instead of just jump ropes, we had to carry a halter and a bucket of grain. Snakes would put his head in the bucket, grab a mouthful of grain, and then spin and run away. (When we later sold him we had to hire a cowboy to chase him all over the pasture and rope him.)

Being sisters, we soon were fighting over Snakes. So Mom bought a pony, Cricket, for my little sister. He was a typical naughty pony. My friends and I enjoyed taking her and Cricket into the trees where to our delight he would find just the right height tree branch to knock her off.

Cricket the pony did not last long, especially when he dragged my Green Beret uncle through the garden. Chief, a very tall, kindly older Appaloosa became my sister's new mount.

About this time I started to do local gymkhanas, riding to and from the shows. Snakes did well and, of course, then I wanted to attend some larger shows, but we did not have a horse trailer. Next purchase—a horse trailer.

Mom and Dad would hook up the trailer behind the Oldsmobile Delta 88 and off we would go. The next problem was that Snakes was not good enough to do well at the bigger shows. So another purchase—a new horse.

We bought a blue roan Appaloosa named Popeyed Chief. "Pepper" and I had a great life together. We rode in the all-girls drill team, the Pikes Peak Rangerettes, whose highlight was always the performance at the National Western Stock Show in Denver.

I tried barrel racing him, but it made him crazy, so I ended up taking a lot of reining lessons and won quite a bit as a junior on the Appy Circuit. I still love reining and think the challenge of the sport set me up later to be a success in dressage.

The highlight of our career was for me to be chosen as "Girl of the West" for the Pikes Peak or Bust Rodeo in 1971. My two aides

My grandfather, John Altrichter Sr. ("Papa"), who instilled in me his love of animals and nature.

and I were the main promoters for the rodeo. We gave many speeches at Service Club breakfasts, lunches, and dinners. We also traveled to other rodeos within a four-state area, including Cheyenne Frontier Days. We appeared in parades and Grand Entries, and were featured in many print and television interviews, as well.

Pepper loved parades and galloping into the arena with me waving like mad at the crowds. He knew exactly where to stop and rollback. Then he would stand like a statue for the National Anthem.

College and England

Pepper was sold and retired to a great couple who owned a large ranch in Southern Colorado. I was horseless for the first time in 15 years. But college and growing up were ahead of me, and my parents could not afford to put me through college and pay for a horse.

I attended the University of Colorado in Boulder and quickly joined the CU Riding Club. I rode once a week with a hunter/jumper trainer, Colonel Nance. I have to say, I never really enjoyed this discipline, so I did not rejoin after my freshman year. I did not ride again for four years.

Then fate intervened. I married Ken Brown, and we moved to Oxford in England, where he was a Rhodes Scholar. Of course, I joined the Oxford Riding Club. I met another Rhodes Scholar wife named Virginia who was from Georgia and had been a hunter rider. We rode in the group lessons for about a month but were hungry for more. Virginia had a car, so off we went to the Talland School of Equitation in Cirencester for semi-private lessons.

After a few months, we still had no idea what

the instructor really meant, and he did not seem to want to enlighten us. So we bought a book, Lockie Richards' *Dressage: Begin the Right Way,* which had pictures to show us what we were supposed to be doing.

I did stay at Talland and passed my British Horse Society Assistant Instructor exams. We had to show jump, go cross-country, and ride a dressage test in order to achieve this. I also learned a lot about stable management and teaching techniques. But as far as true dressage riding, I was still in the dark.

My Own Horse (Again) and Training

Upon returning to the United States, Ken and I moved to Golden, Colorado. I had no plans to be a horse trainer, and got a job with American Salesmasters, a motivational film-production company. I was their public relations director and enjoyed this job immensely.

In the meantime, I bought a horse. I could not afford more than $1,000 so my first horse was a very skinny Thoroughbred mare Wide Awake (named after Lucinda Prior Palmer's great event horse.) It turns out once she became fit and fat, she lived up to her name. She was also in foal, having been pasture-bred prior to my buying her. Surprise! "Wakey" was not a dressage horse, but she was fun to event. She was also my entry into becoming a professional horse trainer.

I boarded her at Table Mountain Ranch in Golden, Colorado. The office secretary, Cariellen DeMuth, a tall, thin woman, saw me riding Wakey and asked me to train her daughter's horse, a darling gray Arabian named Tino. I accepted and my

career took off. Soon I had so many requests for lessons and training I decided this was my life's path. I still did not know very much about training horses, but I was determined to learn.

I had been on the longe line for two years in England. I had a good seat. I just did not know what to do with it. Lessons were always in a group setting and were more like traffic direction than real learning. "Ride prepare to walk." "Ride walk." Commands, but not much instruction on how to make things happen in the right way.

I remember asking one instructor how to put the horse on the bit, since he kept telling me to do it. The direction was "You squeeze until you are puce in the face." I tried that, and it did not seem to work very well either. But it sure wore me out. (I do believe that in the 1970s dressage was not very far along in England. The German influence had not yet arrived. Today it is very different.)

When I came back to the United States, I tried this method on my horse Wakey and realized that Thoroughbred mares don't like to be squeezed this hard with the leg. So I was learning, but more what not to do than what was correct.

Enter Bodo Hangen into my life, and just in time! Bodo was one of the trainers and instructors at Tempel Farms, Old Mill Creek, Illinois, and he had ridden at the Spanish Riding School in Vienna. Julie Sodowsky, a trainer at Table Mountain Ranch, brought Bodo in for instruction and training on a monthly basis. She generously allowed me to take lessons with him every month.

Tempel Farms is still a working Lipizzan training and breeding facility. Every summer there are wonderful shows open to the public. The farm is also famous for hosting the North American Young Rider Championships for many years.

Cariellen DeMuth became a student of mine in 1978, and she still rides with me twice a month.

Cariellen only had Arabians when we first met, and she liked to show in a variety of disciplines. Her lovely chestnut, Ta-Aden, was shown in Western, English pleasure, and dressage shows. Luckily, I understood Western training and tried to help the horses "sort out" which tack they had on that day.

Eventually, I convinced Cariellen to stick to just dressage. She bought a wonderful horse I had in training from McKinstry Arabians named Regal Bee. "Reggie" was an "8" mover, but only 15.3 hands—a bit small for willowy Cariellen. He and I did some serious winning in open competition in the dressage ring. The other competitors would say, "Oh no, here comes the little sucker." And off we would go with the blue ribbon.

Cariellen's daughter married a veterinarian from California who owns a Hanoverian stallion, so today my friend has a nice Warmblood mare that fits her height well. Cariellen did her Century Ride in 2010—a competitive ride at any level in which the combined ages of the horse and rider equal at least one hundred. Cariellen is still a dedicated student, and still learning new things after 33 years as my student!

Cariellen DeMuth, my first paying student, with Regal Bee, the horse I found for her.

Many of our noted trainers have worked and been educated there, including Karl Mikolka and George Williams.

My first lesson with Bodo showed me just how far I had to go. Bodo had obviously been told I was a graduate of the British Horse Society program, which at the time, did not impress the Germans very much! He watched me ride Wakey around (not on the bit either!) for a few minutes and then said, "You call yourself an instructor? You are shit." Having grown up in a household of German men, this did not shock me too much. I replied calmly, "Well, I may be shit, but I have paid my money, and it's your job to teach me how to ride real dressage." We were best of friends for many, many years.

Bodo taught me how to put a horse on the bit correctly. He addressed the issues of suppleness and contact. Slowly the first pieces started to fall in place. He was my main teacher for four years, helping me take another Thoroughbred mare, Hibernian Breeze, to Prix St. Georges (PSG).

Bodo was exceptional: he could help me with Thoroughbreds and also with my Anglo-Arabian mare, Bright Owl. He had a wonderful way with a hot, sensitive horse. At the same time, he was there to help me with my first Warmblood mare, Malene, as well as my first Lipizzan, Conversano Grandioso. Over my lifetime, I have worked with many instructors and trainers. Some can work with any horse, any personality. Others have one system, and if your horse doesn't fit into that system, working with that person can cause more harm than good. Bodo was one of those great instructors who looked at the horse's personality and kept the work and training within the horse's comfort zone.

During this time I also passed the exam for my American Horse Shows Association (AHSA) "r" dressage judge's license. I was able to judge quite a bit in a five-state area as there were few dressage judges in the Mountain States. I also judged several horse trials and events each year.

As with any learning process, I am sure I did not learn all that Bodo had to teach me. Sometimes it takes several teachers to help the pieces fall in place. When Bodo left Tempel Farms to start his own training business, he was not able to come and do many clinics. So, time to find my next mentor.

New Horses, New Mentors

I had started competing outside of my area in the early 1980s, taking my horses to California to compete at the AHSA Regional Championships and stay for a month of training. This gave me the opportunity to meet new instructors and trainers. It also made me realize that in Colorado I was a big fish in a small pond. In California, balance-wise, the First Level horses looked just like my Third Level horse.

The first trainer I worked with outside Colorado was Hilda Gurney. Hilda and I are now the best of friends and serve on many committees together. Back then she was the top dressage star, and she scared the heck out of me!

I had a new, five-year-old Thoroughbred gelding named Applause who had qualified at First Level. I took "Rocket" and "Breeze" to Hilda's. I have to admit I was in tears almost every day for a week. I really felt dumb. I thought I would never get it. It did not seem that I could do anything right! But each day I tried harder and each day I rode better. Hilda gave me one of her three-year-olds to start so I thought she was developing some confidence in me: Applause was the first horse I ever trained who won a USDF Horse of the Year Award—he ended up in tenth place at First Level.

During this time the AHSA divided dressage judges into "r," "R," and "I." To show you how things have changed, I was able to compete with two horses at the Regional Championships in Pebble Beach and also take my "R" judge's exam at the same competition. I passed and now was able to judge up through Fourth Level.

The most important piece that Hilda added to my career is that she let me have lessons on her Grand Prix horse. I was able to ride Ahoy and learn how many of the upper-level movements should feel. Also I was able to learn the correct aids. In this regard, Hilda has been very generous over her lifetime. I don't think there are many Grand Prix riders in California who did not have a few "Hilda lessons."

Hilda was kind enough to come to Table Mountain Ranch as often as she could manage. I still remember her telling me, "If you don't get your hands out of your lap, you will never be an FEI rider!" Thank you, Hilda! I made it! With Bodo's and Hilda's help, I won my USDF Bronze Medal Rider Award.

My Main Sponsor

About this time I met my main sponsor, Dr. Dennis Law. Dennis had walked into Table Mountain Ranch looking for a dressage instructor. He did not have a horse—he had never ridden—but he decided this was his new passion. I was lucky enough to be the first person he ran into. A surgeon, Dennis was smart and knew what he wanted. I started him on the longe line on a schoolhorse and began a search for the perfect schoolmaster.

I also had met Denny and Anne Callin in Pebble Beach at the AHSA Regional Championships. They had stabled next to me and I enjoyed getting to know them. At the time, Denny was riding an amazing Swedish Warmblood named Zenith. They were in the running for the Los Angeles Olympic Team. Denny was working with a Swedish Warmblood breeder in the importation of horses. I wanted to buy a young stallion and a nice three-year-old named Electus had just been imported. Denny had also found a Thoroughbred PSG schoolmaster for Dennis Law.

I flew out to California, decided to vet the young stallion, and called Dennis with the great news that I had found a wonderful schoolmaster for him. He asked what kind of horse the schoolmaster was and how much they wanted. When I told him he said, "There must be something wrong with this horse; he is too cheap. Is there anything else you saw that you would buy for yourself?" I told him about a wonderful five-year-old black gelding named Ballad. Dennis said "Buy him!" So I did, and Dennis wired the money. I was a bit nervous when Ballad stepped off the trailer as Dennis had just spent a lot of money on a horse he had never seen!

Dennis loved the horse and Ballad had a wonderful temperament. Both Electus and Ballad were wonderful additions to my show string. Dennis supported all of the show, boarding, veterinarian, and farrier expenses for Ballad. My part of the bargain was to train him and give Dennis one lesson a week. Dennis never did show himself. However, he enjoyed bringing his family, including his parents, to the horse shows and cheering us on. Ballad won quite a collection of ribbons and silver bowls for Dennis.

I showed him very successfully, earning an invitation to Insilco at First Level. (Insilco was the first USDF/AHSA head-to-head National Championships that was held for a few years in Kansas City, Kansas. The top six horses from the USDF Horse of the Year ranking list were invited to compete.) The dressage arena in the old indoor hall was a few inches short, and the stabling was on the lower level with the warm-up arena. This arena was a bit tricky because you had to navigate large cement pillars—as well as the other competitors.

Unfortunately, later on Ballad became cast in his stall and injured a hock. Although sound, he had difficulty with a flying change one direction and never could move up the levels. He finished his career as a mount for Dennis. My assistant, Janet "Dolly" Hannon (now a USEF "S" judge), also showed him at the lower levels in eventing.

Breeding Horses

While still working mainly with Denny Callin and Hilda, I started expanding my breeding operation. I purchased a young Holsteiner stallion named Constitution from Locksley and Emil Jung in Virginia. Emil was a former World Champion German four-in-hand driver and was associated with the German Holsteiner Verband. It was about the only place in the United States at the time where you could see 75 horses at one location.

Dennis came with me on one shopping trip, and we fell in love with a gelding named Lago. He was five years old and very powerful and stood about 16.3 hands. Again, Dennis bought him for me to ride and train, and we had the same deal as with Ballad. He could be a bit naughty, and Dennis never really enjoyed riding Lago as much as he did Ballad. However, Lago moved up the levels quickly and successfully with me, winning Regional Championships from First Level on up. He was also invited to Insilco at Second Level, the same year as Ballad.

At Insilco, I had the amazing experience of being in the same warm-up arena as an elite list of riders. This was the first time a head-to-head dressage championship for all the levels was held. Also invited that year were Carol Lavell, Jan Ebeling, Kay Meredith, Robert Dover, Lendon Gray, and Dennis Callin. This was truly a turning point for me in seeing what the top caliber of dressage was in the United States at the time. I also got to meet all the players.

After Insilco, I invited Robert Dover and Kay Meredith to come and give clinics. They came almost monthly to my new home at Capricorn Farms, just down the street from Table Mountain Ranch.

Capricorn was a much smaller facility and was strictly dressage. At Table Mountain Ranch we had dressage, hunters, jumpers, Western, and Arabian trainers. Saturday lessons could be quite interesting in the winter months when we were all in the indoor arena.

Capricorn brought much needed peace and a place with a breeding laboratory where we could collect the stallions and ship semen.

Robert was a stickler for precision. He made sure everyone had well-groomed horses, polished boots, and a professional appearance. He is right in that you won't make as much progress if you don't present yourself as a professional. I had just purchased another five-year-old Holsteiner gelding, Halloh, when I started to work with Robert. Both Lago and Halloh were incredibly talented and athletic. Both had little quirks about them. I am so glad I had Robert—someone so enormously experienced with many Grand Prix horses and different types—at this time in my life. Without him I don't think either horse would have made it to Grand Prix. As it was, both were doing a green Grand Prix at nine years old.

I picked up the ride on two of Capricorn Farm's stallions, Gaspadin and Raubritter. "Gus" was a son of Gaspari and looked just like his daddy—chestnut with four, high, white stockings and a white blaze. He was 16.1 hands and a great size for me. He was picked for a Sports Festival Team, which was ridden at Prix St. Georges and was like an All-American Pan Am Games and included all Olympic Sports. However, he was unable to go due to a kidney stone. He had a great piaffe and one-tempis but never really learned the passage. Raubritter knew most of the Grand Prix movements, but it was difficult for him to really "sit" enough, so we kept him in the small tour (PSG and Intermediate I), and he did quite well.

I worked with Robert for about eight years, even following him to Malibu for some extra training sessions. He taught me more than I can talk about in one book: the most important, I think, being what the half-halt was really about and how to accomplish one. Up until that point, I knew I still hadn't 100 percent "got it," but thought I was getting closer. Robert helped push me to the limit, and I will never forget all of his time and effort spent on my behalf.

While working with him, I earned my USDF Silver Medal Rider Award. Electus was seven years old and showing Prix St. Georges in California when Robert helped me find a new owner for him. Electus did not want to be a Grand Prix Horse; he found that much collection difficult, and even though he tried hard, there was too much tension in our performances. I sold him as a hunter, and he never lost an under-saddle class! He had a long and happy life with his new rider.

Learning How to Teach

Kay Meredith's contribution to my education was how to teach. I was not a natural rider. I had to be told (no doubt over and over again) what to do. "Feel" is hard to teach—you can teach the mechanics, but feel is not so easy.

Kay was so precise with every movement. She would tell me which seat bone to sit on—and why; which leg to use where—and why. None of this: "Just use more outside leg." Everything about every movement and every aid had a *why!* I still have the notebooks and drawings I did when I rode with Kay. I would leave my lesson and quickly go to write everything down so I would not forget.

To this day, I have so appreciated all of the wonderful teachers and mentors I had in my life. Kyra Kyrklund and Kay Meredith were masters as teaching and explaining the *why* and *how* of the aids. For a woman, there are many times when you don't have enough strength to argue with a horse. I always tell my students that the horse is stronger, and we are smarter. Both Kay and Kyra train and ride with their brain. They are very logical, and consequently, the horses are very clear in their understanding of the rider's requests. I still attend every Kyra Kyrklund seminar I can.

A Horse "Happy" in His Work

Moving back to Colorado Springs and Bara Farms in the early 1990s, I was able to ride with Denny and Anne Callin again and also participate in the wonderful clinics that Bara organized. I rode with Jo Hinneman and Gaby Grillo and began my relationship with Betsy and Uwe Steiner. I eventually took over as head dressage trainer and manager at Bara Farms. It was a beautiful facility—all solar-heated. At that time I also began managing recognized dressage shows, which is another hat I still wear.

Abracadabra, Steppenwind, Maroon, Halloh, Count Salah, Black Magic, Ravenwood Hairoy, and Easter were a few of the horses I now had in training. Swedish, Arabian, Trakehner, Hanoverian, Thoroughbred, and Holsteiner were included in their breeds.

Betsy and Uwe Steiner (no longer married) were a great team to work with. Betsy would come one month and Uwe the next. Betsy showed me how happy any horse could really be with his work. She, like Bodo, had a great ability to work the horse within his comfort zone.

Uwe would really raise our standards. He would work our fannies off, but push us up to the next level. He was a master with the piaffe, passage, and pirouettes. The clinics would last three days, and I would ride two to three horses per day, trying to get the most out of the learning experience. By Sunday, I would pop a few Advil and know that since I was so stiff and tired, my body was not fit enough.

This was the part of my dressage life when I learned it was also important for the rider to go to the gym. Even riding multiple horses a day did not make me *strong enough.* I had heard this advice from Robert Dover years before but not taken it. I did now!

Judging the World

Even though I had met the requirements for my "S" years before, I was busy concentrating on my riding and getting a horse to Grand Prix so I could win my USDF Gold Medal. With Uwe and Betsy's help, I finally accomplished this in the early 1990s and went ahead and applied for my promotion to "S"—after completing the apprentice judging, I was accepted.

In 1995 I received my FEI (Fédération Equestre Internationale) "C" or Candidate Status. This status allowed me to judge around the world and on panels for all CDIs (FEI classes) or International Dressage Events, such as Dressage at Devon.

Soon it became clear that I was going to have to make some changes. I was on the road so much I was losing my fitness and so were my horses.

I first sold my small tour horse Maroon. (The "small tour" consists of the Prix St. Georges, Intermediate I, and the Intermediate I freestyle. The "big tour" consists of the Grand Prix, Grand Prix Special, and Grand Prix freestyle. Intermediate II is not required at any games or championships.) Then I leased my Grand Prix horse Halloh to a student. I kept my young horse for while, but eventually he was sold too. And so the journey began as a clinician, trainer, and judge.

Writing Inspiration

For 35 years I had the chance to ride with many of the top American, Canadian, and European trainers. During this time, I rode and trained Thoroughbreds, Morgans, Arabians, Lippizans, Warmbloods, Quarter Horses, and Appaloosa Crosses.

I own and have owned a huge library of equestrian books. But the one thing I have discovered is that the books are all written for "perfect" horses. They tell you the classical aids, and—*voilà*—your mount should obey. In my experience, I found that did not always happen. I discovered that training horses was a bit experimental. The rider needed to keep in mind the horse's physical abilities and limitations, as well as deal with her own thought process.

Author's Note

In writing this book, I hope to share with you the lessons I have learned while working with horses that were less than "perfect" in any number of ways. All horses can have their physique and gaits improved through dressage, and training strategies can be adapted for different horses' temperaments. Each chapter ahead, therefore, discusses conformation and temperament challenges you may encounter, and I explain how to adjust your training exercises and techniques for your "imperfect" horse. I hope this book will help you in your journey through dressage.

This book is written as an easy reference for the reader. Each chapter deals with one topic or movement. The chapters start with a discussion of the imperfections and evasions your horse may test you with, and then "solutions" to these issues are offered in the form of exercises and "how to train" tips. You can find a complete quick-reference "index" of imperfections and evasions, with the corresponding sections where they are addressed, beginning on p. xix.

For ease of reading and clarity of intention, in this book all riders are referred to as "she" and all horses as "he."

Janet Foy

Imperfections and Evasions

If during your **warm-up** your horse is:

- hot and hard to settle at the beginning of your ride,
- lazy and hard to "rev-up,"
- high-necked and hard to get "through" and over the topline,
- low-necked and tends to travel on the forehand,
- a draft-type horse that tends to pull with his shoulders rather than carry weight behind,
- nervous and spooky and tends to focus on anything but you,

see chapter 3 (p. 19).

If during **half-halts and transitions** your horse:

- has trouble standing still,
- throws his head up in transitions, opens his mouth, or leans on the reins,
- gets crooked and struggles with transitions from one gait to another or with changes of pace within the gaits,
- changes canter leads behind or picks up the wrong lead,
- drops his neck,
- is late in responding to the aids,

see chapter 4 (p. 33).

If when you attempt the **"stretch circle"** your horse:

- curls up his neck,
- speeds up as if he is off to the races,
- stretches his neck out without lowering it,
- stretches without any contact on the reins,
- puts his head up,

see chapter 5 (p. 43).

If during the **leg-yield** your horse:

- drags his haunches,
- leads with his shoulders,
- lacks "crossing" in his legs,
- tilts his head,
- changes his tempo,

see chapter 6 (p. 49).

If during **lengthenings** your horse:

- has no natural lengthening,
- runs onto his forehand,
- takes shorter, faster strides,
- scores poorly on the transitions to and from or within the gaits and paces on tests,
- travels wide behind,
- breaks into canter during a trot lengthening,

see chapter 7 (p. 57).

If in the **walk** your horse:

- has rhythm issues, ranging from minor to severe,
- has a stiff topline,
- curls up,
- jogs or exhibits mental tension,
- likes to be a "tourist,"
- lacks suppleness in transitions to and from the paces of the walk,
- lacks freedom of the shoulders or has limited overstep,

see chapter 8 (p. 69).

If in the **shoulder-in** your horse:

- has too much angle,
- has too much bend in his neck,
- tilts his head,
- has haunches falling out,
- tends to let his balance fall to his outside shoulder,
- loses cadence and regularity,
- loses impulsion,
- has haunches falling in off the track,
- lacks control and thus the angle of the movement varies,

see chapter 9 (p. 77).

If during the **travers** or **renvers** your horse:

- allows his shoulders to leave the line of travel (in travers),
- allows his haunches to leave the line of travel (in renvers),
- has difficulty in the movements because his rider sits incorrectly,
- lacks angle,

- loses impulsion,
- lacks bend,

see chapter 10 (p. 83).

If in the **halt** or **rein back** your horse:

- resists stepping backward,
- does not step back in diagonal pairs,
- does not come to a complete halt or anticipates the rein back,
- drags his feet backward,
- is crooked,
- drops his neck and falls on his forehand,
- runs backward without your aids,

see chapter 11 (p. 89).

If during the **turn-on-the-haunches** or **walk pirouette** your horse:

- steps backward,
- has hind legs that "stick" or loses the walk rhythm,
- has a walk that becomes lateral in the turn or the preparation,
- lacks bending or lateral position,
- allows his haunches to fall out against your outside leg,
- ignores the turning aid,

see chapter 12 (p. 97).

If in **more advanced transitions or paces** your horse:

- changes leads behind, either at the beginning or end of medium or extended canter,
- has transitions that judges say are "vague" or "gradual,"

- lacks groundcover,
- loses his clear, three-beat canter rhythm,
- gets crooked,
- falls downhill,
- gets stiff in his back, neck, and/or topline,
- won't lengthen his frame,
- gets "earthbound,"
- shows no clear difference between the medium and extended paces,

see chapter 13 (p. 103).

If during **counter-canter** your horse:

- won't pick up the correct counter-canter lead,
- breaks into trot,
- loses his lead in front,
- loses his lead behind,
- leans in like a motorcycle going around a turn,
- does a flying change over and over (won't "hold" the counter-canter),

see chapter 14 (p. 115).

If in the **half-pass** your horse:

- leads with or trails his haunches,
- loses cadence or impulsion,
- performs with his forehand not on the line-of-travel,
- tilts his head,
- lacks submission to the bend,
- has limited lateral reach,
- won't go sideways enough,
- experiences confusion regarding the aids,
- goes too much sideways and lacks engagement,

see chapter 15 (p. 121).

If during **flying changes** your horse:

- runs away,
- throws his head up,
- is late behind,
- is late in front,
- has a canter that isn't forward enough,
- has a long stride with little suspension (an "earthbound canter"),
- performs changes that are unequal,

see chapter 16 (p. 131).

If in the **extended trot or canter** your horse:

- trails his hind legs,
- pushes with his hind legs instead of "carrying,"
- is crooked,
- is wide behind,
- shows a loss of rhythm,
- falls downhill or gets croup-high,
- falls in or out with his haunches,
- is short in the neck,
- breaks to canter (in trot),
- lacks energy,
- shows improved freedom but lacks groundcover,
- changes lead either entirely or just behind (in canter),

see chapter 17 (p. 147).

If in the **zig-zag** your horse:

- leads with his haunches when you change direction (the "changeover"),
- goes more sideways in one direction than the other,
- anticipates the movement,
- changes late (in the changeover),

- rides a figure that is incorrect,
- falls from one direction to the other,
- goes the incorrect number of strides due to a rider counting problem,

see chapter 18 (p. 157).

If in the **tempi changes** your horse:

- takes control or "gets strong," and the rider has no half-halt,
- starts throwing changes without any aid from the rider,
- changes late in front or behind,
- drifts from the line of travel,
- swings his hindquarters or becomes croup-high,
- gets excited or tense,
- changes shorter on one side behind,
- has a rider with counting problems,
- is late to the aid in one direction,
- loses impulsion and the changes get shorter and shorter,

see chapter 19 (p. 165).

If during the **piaffe** your horse:

- loses rhythm in the piaffe or the transitions,
- has uneven steps,
- moves with unlevel steps,
- loses straightness in piaffe or transitions,
- moves with grounded front legs and a bouncing croup,
- has hindquarters that don't lower and take enough weight.
- says, "No thank you, not today,"

see chapter 20 (p. 173).

If during the **passage** your horse:

- lacks cadence or elevation (trot-like),
- is too "free," lacking collection, or not "closed" enough,
- has unlevel strides,
- has uneven strides,
- shows resistance,

see chapter 21 (p. 183).

If during the **canter pirouette** your horse:

- performs a pirouette that is too small (or has too few strides),
- performs a pirouette that is too big (or has too many strides),
- loses rhythm,
- loses bend,
- "rears around" the movement (has topline issues),

see chapter 22 (p. 189).

PART 1

Building a Solid Foundation

1

The Rider

*The rider must think of every mistake
as a training opportunity.*

The rider has a major role in the training process: even with the perfect horse, she cannot present a correct training picture without the correct skills. Before you assume your horse is "imperfect," be sure you are doing your best to help him do the work correctly and happily. That's why before I begin to discuss your horse, I want to touch on the Rider Training Pyramid.

Just as the Classical Training Pyramid exists for the horse, I've produced a "training pyramid" for the rider, who must also build her foundation before ascending to the pinnacle. This isn't an "official" rider pyramid, but I would like you to think about your position in this way (fig. 1.1).

The foundation of this pyramid is the rider's seat and ability to move *with*, rather than *against* the horse. A correct "independent" seat will help you be able to develop a correct and elastic contact, allowing you to use the leg aids correctly, neither gripping nor banging the horse's sides.

Find an Instructor

No rider can achieve correct riding without "eyes on the ground." This is why even Olympic riders regularly ride with a trainer, coach, or colleague to provide feedback.

Trainer vs. Coach

A *trainer* will give you lessons but also ride your horse in training sessions. These sessions are designed to help your horse move up the levels and

Harmony, invisible aids, and a wonderful partnership

Effective rider with good influence and tact

Effective rider with fairly good influence

Rider has correct position but lacks correct influence (rider a bit of a passenger but does not inhibit performance)

Rider lacks correct position

1.1 The Rider Training Pyramid I like to use with my own students.

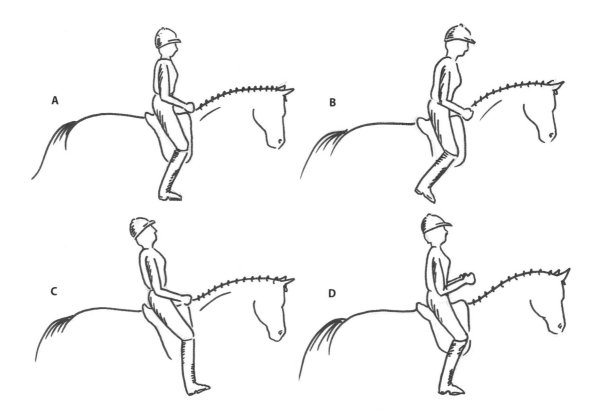

1.2 A–D Viewed from the side: correct alignment from shoulder through hip to heel and elbow through hands to the horse's mouth (A); lower legs too far back, upper body too far forward (B); lower leg too far forward, upper body too far back (C); hands too high (D).

come to a better understanding of the aids. The trainer will then put you back on your horse and teach you the correct aids, which the horse now understands. The worst scenario in any equestrian discipline is having a green horse and a green rider.

A *coach* is someone like myself who no longer rides and trains horses. A coach will work with you and your horse as a team. The coach's job is to provide information and exercises that will improve the horse's performance and develop the rider's skills.

It's very important that you take regular instruction from a knowledgeable, qualified instructor. Find someone with at least one of the following: 1) United States Dressage Federation (USDF) Instructor Certification; 2) USDF Rider Medals (Bronze, Silver, Gold); or 3) United States Equestrian Federation (USEF) judge's credentials. Remember that at each stage in your riding, you will need an instructor with more advanced credentials than you. A USDF instructor certified through Second Level or a Bronze Medalist (qualifying scores through Third Level) may be the perfect instructor to provide you with a good foundation to move up the levels, but as you advance, you will need to seek instruction from someone who has trained riders and horses in the upper level movements.

Collective Marks

You can evaluate your riding progress through the rider's scores your receive in the USEF dres-

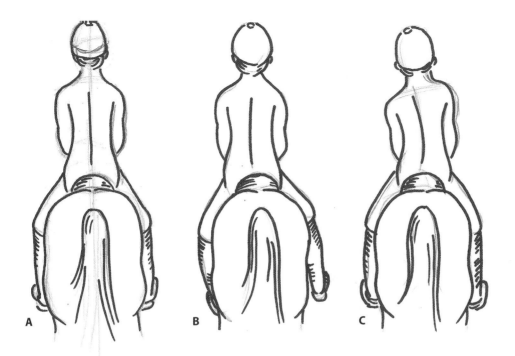

1.3 A–C Viewed from behind: correct alignment (A); rider crooked, sitting off to left (B); rider collapsed on the left side (C).

sage test. Called the Collective Marks, these scores are divided into *three parts,* with a maximum score of 10 points for each part. These scores relate to the Rider Training Pyramid.

1: Rider's Position and Seat

This score judges how you "look" on the horse. Can you sit in the middle of the saddle? Could a straight line be drawn directly down from your shoulder, hip, and heel so these parts are correctly aligned? Is there a straight line from your elbow and hand to the horse's mouth? Are you able to correctly sit the trot and not disturb the horse?

Deductions out of 10 are made when the rider's legs go too forward or too far back; when she leans forward or back; when she doesn't sit in the middle of the horse; and when she displays other faults, as well (figs. 1.2 A–D and 1.3 A–C).

One of my favorite games is to watch riders in the warm-up arena. I "disappear" the horse.

Where would the rider land without a horse beneath her? On her nose? On her behind? A good rider lands on her feet with her knees bent.

2: Rider's Correct and Effective Use of the Aids

This score is determined by how well the rider can prepare her horse for the movements required in the test. Does she understand the elements of each movement? Also reflected is whether the horse is responsive to her aids. The rider may be "whispering" but the horse may not be answering the aids.

Other deductions, for example, are made when the rider does not bend the horse in the correct direction for the turn-on-the-haunches.

Or, when the aids for the downward transitions are rough and not well prepared.

3: Harmony between Rider and Horse

The third score is for the presentation and the performance. I like to think a high score here from me means that I would like to ride your horse. There are many horses I admire, but I would not necessarily want to ride them. I can appreciate that a rider can be effective and that the horse may be difficult. But for the highest score here, the horse should look easy to ride and should bring a smile to my (or any judge's) face.

Mental or Physical?

There are two aspects to dressage riding. One is mental and one is physical.

Let's discuss the mental aspect first as I think it is the most often ignored. Steffen Peters and I do judge/trainer symposiums all over the United States. We often ask a trick question of the audience: "What is the most important part of your body when riding dressage?" The answer usually comes back with the majority saying "the seat." It's not. It is your brain. Dressage riders need to *think* more.

Dressage is hard because everything we would do instinctively is wrong in this sport. When we get nervous, we fall forward. When something happens, we pull on the reins. We usually correct a problem with our hands, rather than with our legs. Our reactions need to be retrained.

Making Mistakes

It is hard to convince a rider that when the horse makes a mistake, it is okay. Think of every mistake as a training opportunity. Here, we can learn from the world of dog obedience. Trainer Diane Bauman has a saying, "Wrong is wonderful." What she means by this is that if the dog performs correctly the first time, we have no idea whether it understood our request or whether its response was a happy accident.

Similarly, trainer Connie Cleveland distinguishes between "*effort* errors," in which the animal attempts to comply with our requests but does not understand, and "*lack-of-effort* errors," in which the animal is simply ignoring a command it already understands. Be sure before you assume that your horse is "imperfect" or disobedient that you are asking correctly and helping him to understand what you want.

Often, I tell the rider to *think first* before making a correction. Train your brain and body to react in the correct way.

Riders inadvertently punish the horse in several ways. They jerk on the reins, or bring the horse to an abrupt halt after a mistake. They often spur the horse or overuse the whip. Remember, we *all* must make mistakes in order to learn, but we as riders must direct our horse in the right way and teach him something from the mistakes he makes. When you halt and punish your horse, he will only learn to stop and shut down after each mistake.

In dressage, you also must be able to have impulsion and elasticity. When you lose that ability to go forward, you cannot do dressage. Keep riding forward through the mistake and feel free to reinforce the aid your horse was not listening to.

Here is an example: say the rider is working on a trot lengthening but the horse keeps breaking to canter. First the rider must assess if she is doing her job. Is she keeping the horse straight and supple? Is her weight equally over the horse? When the answer is yes, the next time the horse breaks to canter, make him canter forward into a lengthening instead of just bringing him back to trot and trying again. This way you are making the evasion more work than the work required. Your horse needs to understand that you want a bigger trot, not a smaller canter.

Here's another example: you are having trouble with your canter departs so when the horse just trots faster, you stop him from going forward. Then you try again—and again. But you are saying to the horse "Go—No, don't go." The horse is now confused. If you want him to canter when you use your aids you must make sure:

1 Your aids are being given correctly.
2 The horse is not falling in or out on the line of travel.
3 You put the whip in your outside hand and when you say "Go," you mean it. You may have to make your point once or twice.

Even if he picks up the wrong lead, praise him. He *must* canter when you give the canter aids, and you must be willing to *let him* even if he is a bit unbalanced for a few strides. If your seat is insecure and you feel you have to pull back and stop, then you need to have a professional sit on the horse and work out the problem.

How the Horse Learns

Many riders with green horses expect them to be able to read books! A green horse does not understand your aids. You must teach him the ABCs of dressage. This aid means "Go." This one means "Stop." This one means "Turn." Once he understands a few simple aids (for example, those for the turn-on-the-forehand), you can put a few of these aids together into "words." Then the words can become "sentences," then "books."

Horses learn early on to make the rider ask multiple-choice questions, which is not helpful: the horse doesn't respond to the first aid so the rider changes her question. As this goes on, soon the horse will be in charge with the rider always following and reacting to the horse. The horse must react to the rider. There is *one* aid, *one* answer. Period. Sometimes you must repeat this simple question—over and over. *One* aid. *One* answer. Good horse. The rider must teach the horse to come to her—not the other way around.

Remember that you must reward your horse often. Don't be greedy. When you get a good response, reward and move on. I see too many riders asking the horse for three lines of tempi changes. The first two are faultless. The third has mistakes, and the rider then corrects the horse for the mistakes. Why I ask, does the rider not reward the horse after the second line of changes and let the horse feel good about himself?

Horses also quickly learn to "volunteer" movements. Sometimes this can't be helped, and it is part of their learning process. Make sure you never punish your horse for something you want later. Once the horse has learned a movement and is confident, you can add some additional requirements and make sure it is your idea, not his.

Such additions could be necessary in a leg-yield, for example: Although the horse has already learned to move forward and sideways off your leg and weight, he is now going sideways too much. So you need to remind him this is a forward/sideways movement. Go several steps sideways and then stop the sideways and go several steps forward. Repeat the exercise until you reach the short end.

Feel

Okay, here is the elephant in the room. I can teach students all the "mechanics" of the aids and the movements of dressage *but*…I can't teach you *feel*. In clinics, I always hear myself say, "Can you feel the difference?"

Some riders have a natural feel. You can watch top dressage athletes and see this clearly. But often riders with a wonderful, natural feel cannot tell you *how* they do it. They just tell you to "Do it," as it is so easy for them. Many of the best instructors I ever had were riders like myself—who had to learn the hard way. These instructors have learned to verbalize and put into words the "feel."

When you choose an instructor, find one who will answer your questions and not just tell you to "Do it." She should be willing to tell you why you are "doing it" so that you can continue to work in the right way when she is not around.

I do think there are a couple of things you should keep in your head when riding, however, in order to get a better handle on the concept of feel. These are "clues" that tell you something is about to happen to your suppleness and/or your balance.

The horse:
- Goes faster or slower.
- Gets heavier or lighter in the contact.
- Falls in or out on the line of travel.

When you can "feel" these issues and react to them quickly, you can help to keep your horse "on the aids."

Using the Whip

The horse needs to learn how to react to your different leg aids, and the whip is there as reinforcement to help you teach him. Don't ever make your horse afraid of the whip or use it to punish your horse. The whip should never leave a welt or mark on your horse. Little short "tap-taps" are more effective than one smack. Never raise the whip above your head and hit your horse, and never hit your horse on the head.

There are specific ways in which you should know how to use the whip.

Behind Your Inside Leg
This reinforces the *go forward* aid. When your inside leg is one fist behind the girth and being used as a lateral moving aid, the whip reinforces the *go sideways* aid.

(*Note:* I discuss "inside" as meaning "inside of the bend," or when you are on a straight line, the inside of the shoulder-fore position (see sidebar, p. 9). Leg-yield is a special case with no bend in the body, but it requires lateral flexion of the poll *opposite* the direction of travel, so that side is the "inside.")

Behind the Outside Leg (Behind the Girth)

The whip in this position is reinforcement for either the *canter depart;* the *go sideways* aid in half-pass; or to *displace the haunches* in a head-to-the-wall leg-yield or travers (haunches-in). I also use the whip in the outside hand in canter pirouette work as sometimes using it in the inside hand confuses the horse and he will attempt to do a flying change.

On the Croup

This whip placement asks the horse to *sit* and lower the hindquarters. I like using this as a half-halt aid when the training is more sophisticated. Using the whip on the croup does not cause the hind legs to become unlevel as they might with normal whip use on one side of the body: often-times, when you keep the whip only in the hand that is comfortable for you and always use it on the same side, you can create a regularity issue with the hind legs.

On the Hock

When you have a horse that is always lazy with one hind leg, using the whip on the hock can be very effective by saying, *"Lift that leg and get active."* You do need to be careful when using the whip in this position not to make the horse's movement irregular or unlevel (referring to the height of the hind leg) by using this activation of the hind-leg aid too strongly.

Now that I've covered some rider basics, let's move on to your horse's basics.

The Very Useful Shoulder-Fore

I often refer to the shoulder-fore in the pages ahead. You may have heard it described as "position" left or right. It is a way to straighten the horse. If you think of a parenthesis as compared to the letter C, you have the idea of a shoulder-fore (it is the parenthesis, in this case). It doesn't have bend through the whole body like the C, but rather a slight positioning of the forehand in front of the hind legs to make the horse straight. If you were riding shoulder-fore right (on the right rein), your inside rein would slightly position the shoulders and front legs to the inside, making the inside front leg travel on the second track. The hind legs stay on the rail or line of travel.

Always So Basic

*If you take care of the basics,
the movement will take care of itself.*

Have you ever felt that perhaps you will never succeed in dressage because you don't have the "perfect" horse, the one with huge, floating gaits and seemingly perfect lateral and longitudinal suppleness? Have you struggled through a test in which you felt as if your horse suddenly "forgot" all the training you'd done? Have you ever wondered how to make better use of the judge's comments on your test sheets once you got back home?

Without the ability to ride your horse using the correct basics, you will undoubtedly find yourself frustrated with your progress—no matter what horse you ride and train. This chapter is the most important of all, the one without which none of the following chapters matters.

Many riders misunderstand the degree of balance and gymnastic train-

ing necessary to perform the movements at each dressage level—with harmony and ease. For example, just because your horse does flying changes, it doesn't mean he is a Third Level horse: he may not have the necessary degree of collection and extension for that level. I'll talk more later about how to determine whether your horse is ready to compete at a given level. (Hint: Read the test directives! They contain important information.)

The Horse's Training Pyramid

For now, let's start with the Classical Training Pyramid, also known as the Classical Training Scale. This pyramid originated in Germany and has long been the basis

Collection

Straightness

Impulsion

Contact

Suppleness

Rhythm

2.1 The Classical Training Pyramid.

of classical dressage training in Europe and else-where. It is also the basis of good judging. It is interesting that for a long time when I would do clinics, I would ask the students, "What is the first element on the Training Scale?" They would all yell, *"Forward!"* I am happy to say that with better education now in the United States, this doesn't happen very often anymore! There are many variations of the Classical Training Pyramid out there; some are more embellished than others. I am going to keep it simple.

I like to think of dressage as a finished jigsaw puzzle. The six steps of the Classical Training Pyramid are all pieces of the puzzle. The steps in the pyramid are the first pieces you should look for in training. The "basics" are like the "edge" pieces of the puzzle—you should find them first. With experience, you will know that the blue pieces are the sky and go on top and the green pieces are the grass and go on the bottom. Once the edges are in place, you can start to fill in the rest. You will never finish the puzzle and see the "big picture" unless you have correct basics.

Rhythm

This is the basis of dressage. Without correct rhythm of the walk, trot, and canter, you are not riding dressage in the classical sense. Take a look at the sidebar on p. 13 with the definitions and diagrams regarding rhythm from the USEF Rule Book.

2.2 Here I am riding the five-year-old Holsteiner mare Marburg in working trot, showing good contact and stretch to the bit during a First Level Test.

USEF Rule Book

WALK

1 The walk is a marching gait in a regular and well-marked, four-time beat with equal intervals between each beat. This regularity combined with full relaxation must be maintained throughout all walk movements.

2 When the foreleg and the hind leg on the same side swing forward almost synchronously, the walk has a lateral rhythm. This irregularity is a serious deterioration of the gait.

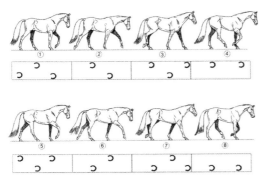

2.3 The walk is a gait in four-beat rhythm with eight phases (the numbers in circles indicate the beat).

TROT

1 The trot is a two-beat gait of alternate diagonal legs (left fore and right hind leg and vice versa) separated by a moment of suspension.

2 The trot should show free, active, and regular steps.

3 The quality of the trot is judged by general impression, i.e. the regularity and elasticity of the steps, the cadence and impulsion in both collection and extension. This quality originates from a supple back and well-engaged hindquarters, and by the ability to maintain the same rhythm and natural balance with all variations of the trot.

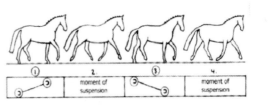

2.4 The trot is a gait in two-beat rhythm with four phases (the numbers in circles indicate the beat).

CANTER

1 The canter is a three-beat gait where, in canter to the right, for example, the footfall is as follows: left hind, left diagonal (simultaneously left fore and right hind), right fore, followed by a moment of suspension with all four feet in the air before the next stride begins.

2 The canter, always with light, cadenced, and regular strides, should be moved into without hesitation.

3 The quality of the canter is judged by the general impression, i.e. the regularity and lightness of the steps and the uphill tendency and cadence originating from the acceptance of the bridle with a supple poll and in the engagement of the hindquarters with an active hock action—and by the ability of maintaining the same rhythm and a natural balance, even after a transition from one canter to another. The horse should always remain straight on straight lines and correctly bent on curved lines.

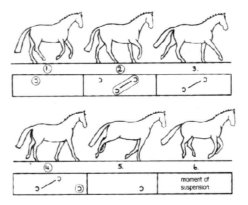

2.5 The canter is a gait in three-beat rhythm with six phases.

2.6 Gwen Blake riding a well-balanced working canter aboard Winsome during a First Level test.

When a judge looks at a horse, the *rhythm* of the gaits is the first priority. The *quality* is the second. Any horse can have his natural gaits improved with dressage. I will discuss this throughout the book. If you cannot afford a horse with an "expensive trot," then your training becomes even more important. And, if you do buy a top quality horse and your training is incorrect, you can ruin your horse's natural quality.

Suppleness

In my opinion, this is one of the most important parts of the Classical Training Pyramid. As a judge, I have never written on someone's test that the horse had *too much* suppleness. But what does this piece of the jigsaw puzzle really mean?

Horses do not volunteer suppleness; the rider must ask for it. Suppleness really is the section that discusses how a horse carries energy through the topline. Dressage riders are very picky about developing the horse's topline correctly. Without a strong and well-muscled topline, the horse cannot achieve the collection needed for the upper-level movements. This muscle development—a bit like a weightlifter's (whereas event horses have muscles more like a long-distance runner's)—also protects the legs from stress and damage.

Think of the hind legs as the power source. The power and energy comes up from the hind legs over the croup. The loin must then take the energy over the back. The loin is the part of the horse that is in charge of the elasticity and is often called the "bridge" that carries the energy forward. The neck muscles must also be supple, carrying the energy through both sides of the neck to the contact on the mouth.

The rider is then able to use the reins to "receive" the energy the horse's hind legs have created. This is what is meant by "throughness." (For more on this, see *Impulsion* below.)

Think of your horse's muscles as a two-lane freeway. When the highway is free of accidents or road blocks, the cars will travel smoothly from Point A to Point B. The horse's topline is like these lanes of traffic. When the rider is able to correctly influence the topline, energy from the hind legs flows smoothly over the back. When there is tension or a lack of contact or straightness, energy has too many detours.

Your goal is to develop an open freeway, which allows energy to come over the horse's back, through the neck to the bit. When you have this correct, supple connection—or "throughness"—then you have control of the horse's impulsion and balance.

Contact

When your highway is open with traffic flowing smoothly, the next step is for you to develop a supple contact with both reins. This piece of the puzzle requires the horse to stretch evenly into *both* reins. This is important because I see too many riders throwing away the inside rein while always holding onto the outside rein.

The reins must work together as a team. The inside rein is in charge of lateral suppleness. It positions the head and neck to the inside and also acts as a turning aid. This rein is almost 100 percent of the time used in the direction of the bend—in other words, it should not touch the neck. An *indirect rein of opposition* (where the inside hand goes to the rider's opposite hip) is rarely used in dressage because it holds the horse's shoulders out, and as you will read later, this is opposite of what you are trying to achieve.

How much weight should you have in your reins? Many riders mistake lightness on the reins as an indicator that the horse is light on the forehand. This is not correct. Many horses are heavier in the contact and yet very light in the shoulders. The term "lightness" should really be used only to describe the balance of the horse and elevation of his shoulders. I prefer to use the term "suppleness" or "elasticity" in the contact rather than the word "lightness."

I believe you should "have" 2 to 5 pounds in your hands. Some horses are lighter, some heavier, due to their breeding and/or conformation. This weight is fluid and like an elastic band attached to the bit. The rider should be able to follow the movement of the topline when necessary. (The horse moves his topline the most in the free walk, not much in the trot, and a little in the canter.)

These last two puzzle pieces—suppleness and contact—make up quite a lot of the submission score in a dressage test's Collective Marks.

Impulsion

In my opinion, it is dangerous to add too much impulsion before you have submission. The more impulsion you have, the more submission you need.

Impulsion is *not* speed. The horse should not be running so fast that he gets out of balance. Impulsion requires suspension in the gaits, which is why the walk does not have impulsion. If you do not have *suppleness* and an elastic *contact,* the horse will not have impulsion. When the horse is supple and going with an elastic contact, then the impulsion puzzle allows the horse to "lift" his back and stomach muscles, which creates a "circle of energy." This circle, which starts with the hind legs (the horse's engine), travels over the loins and through the neck to the elastic contact, then allows the horse to arch his back and lift the abdominal muscles. The energy will thus flow back to the hind legs. When this circle is complete, the rider will feel she has a horse that moves more on his own in self-carriage.

When a horse is "rigid" in his back or neck, speed is the result, not impulsion.

Straightness

Straightness is another totally misunderstood area of dressage. As mentioned, the Classical Training Pyramid (Scale) originated in Germany. German has many one-word "horse" terms. Some of these one-word terms actually take several sentences in English to completely define them. A German friend of mine asked me to help him with judging in English. He would give me one word in German, and I would give him three sentences. He said, "Oh, it is hard to judge in English."

I like to think of *straightness* as the line of travel. Only in travers (haunches-in) and half-pass is the *forehand* on the line of travel. Every other movement requires the *haunches* to be on the line of travel. Most movements have the horse's shoulders slightly displaced to the inside because the horse is wider behind than in front.

I like to think of the horse as a three-car, choo-choo train. I imagine one hinge in front of the saddle and one behind it.

Think of this train going around a curve. It is like the horse on a circle. The horse can be a "C" (or a "c" when the circle is smaller), and on a straight line his body should be like a parenthesis—that is, in shoulder-fore or position-left—or right. (Eventually, when you work on lateral suppleness of the poll, the poll must still stay a part of the neck train car.)

If the horse does not follow the line of travel, the train will derail, and when he is crooked, you will not have the ability to go to the next piece of the puzzle.

Only in piaffe, passage, one-tempi flying changes, and rein-back can the horse be like an "I" —a lower case "L." In these movements the horse is carrying weight on both hind legs equally and must be *absolutely straight* or he will lose his balance.

The word "straightness" means the *lateral suppleness* of the horse—the ability to conform to the line of travel—whereas the suppleness portion of the Classical Training Pyramid refers to the *longitudinal suppleness* (see p. 23).

Collection

Collection is the last piece of the horse's pyramid, and if you have correctly applied all of the pieces of the puzzle, you will begin to see the big picture. Collection is relative to the horse's level of dressage training. At Second Level, we are just developing collection, and we like to see an

2.7 Caryn Bujnowski and Preston showing a good collected canter with uphill balance and good basics.

"uphill" *tendency*, meaning it may come and go. At the Grand Prix Level, the utmost self-carriage and collection should be maintained.

If you are having issues with balance in regard to any level of collection, you must go down the "food chain" and discover the hole in your training. Perhaps your horse is not straight—that is, he is not following the line of travel and the haunches are falling in as the shoulders fall out. Perhaps he is still laterally lacking suppleness, not accepting contact with the bit, or tight over the back? Any of these issues will need to be addressed right away. Do not move on and start working on movements. Discover the missing piece of your puzzle and then address the big picture!

As I work through the following chapters, I'll be looking at specific issues as they relate to the Classical Training Pyramid.

The Warm-Up

*Wherever the horse wants to
be by nature....change it!*

In any athletic adventure, the warm-up is of the utmost importance. Without the correct stretching and warming up of the muscles, the body is prone to injury.

I am not a "the horse must be deep" or the "horse must be ridden up" type of person. For me, the horse needs to be ridden in a position where the warm-up can do him the most good. I often see people trotting around with their horse's head up in the air preparing for a lesson. I ask them why? They always tell me it is too hard on the animal to ask him to come on the aids too early in the lesson. I wonder in which book they read this? It must be a popular book as I hear this a lot!

I ask students if they were going to run in a marathon would they only warm up their arms? They finally get it. I tell them about how the horse works. That the topline muscles must be stretched and loosened correctly in order to carry the energy from the hind legs to the contact. I also discuss the belly muscles; if the back is pushed down, so are the belly muscles. The

horse needs to lift his back and belly muscles in order to use the "engine" (the hind legs) in a correct way.

Now, how do we make this happen? Each horse needs to have a warm-up tailor-made just for him. Why? Horses have different types of bodies, necks, balance, and of course, temperament. This may sound like strange advice, but "wherever" your horse likes to be physically speaking… well, you need to change it to warm him up. If he wants his neck high, it should be low. If he wants it low, keep it higher. If he is lazy, make him hotter. If he is tense and fast, slow him down. In other words, whatever the horse wants to do by nature, change it!

Imperfections and Evasions

This chapter will help you plan the perfect warm-up. Here are six strategies for warming up your horse when he is:

High Society ("Hi-C") was a Holsteiner mare who came by her "spice for life" via her mom. Her dam was Abracadabra, a Swedish mare who had a lot of Arabian (Urbino) blood in her. Abra was fifth in the country at Training and First Level for the USDF Horse of the Year awards. She was only 15.3 hands, a chestnut, and usu-

ally "on fire." Hi-C's dad was a stallion I owned named Constitution. Condo was 17.2 and Holsteiner bay. He was my favorite stallion of all the ones I owned and trained. He had a great attitude and loved to show. I told him he would "get more girls" if he won his class. He usually obliged.

Having had my patience tested by Abra, I was ready for Hi-C. I relied on quiet slow work, trying to relax her as best I could. Riding her deep and low made her more nervous. With Abra, the battle had also been the spook-

3.1 A & B Here I am on Abracadabra, a liver chestnut, but complete with "redhead"-hot qualities nonetheless (A)! Her daughter, High Society (Abracadabra x Constitution) was firey like her mom (B).

ing. At least Hi-C did not inherit this trait. I found with both mares that they had an incredible work ethic and worked very hard to try and please me. Too hard in fact. Half the time they did not wait for my aid. Lots of movements were "not my idea." Experience taught me that if they were punished for all of their great ideas, they would get more tense. So patience, repetition, and reward finally got through to them.

I caution anyone with this type of horse to be careful! Punishment doesn't work. If you don't have patience yet, you will after you get this one trained. Try to think of each of the horse's mistakes as a training opportunity. Often, when a horse is learning, there is tension. The horse may be trying to understand the desires of the rider. However, he often gets confused. If the rider freely deals out punishment at this time, especially with a high-spirited horse, the horse's mental tension will increase, and he'll be unable to progress.

An example is when a young horse takes the wrong lead. The horse does not yet understand your aids. He will only understand he is getting punished for the canter, and the canter will become tense and unrideable.

1 Hot and hard to settle at the beginning of your ride.

2 Lazy and hard to "rev-up."

3 High-necked and hard to get "through" and over the topline.

4 Low-necked and tends to travel on the forehand.

5 A draft-type horse that tends to pull with his shoulders rather than carry weight behind.

6 Nervous and spooky and tends to focus on anything but you.

Cures and Solutions

1 **Problem: My horse is hot.**

This horse wants to be "on the go" right from start of a workout. This will be a desirable trait in the long run, but in the beginning of the training session, it is necessary to tone down the tension. Speed control is a priority.

It is a terrible mistake to warm up this horse with no contact. He will just "run" out of balance and become more and more tense.

Put the horse into the roundest frame you can and work with a lot of transitions to help improve the half-halt. A lot of lateral bending also helps the muscles to relax and stretch. Increase and decrease the circle while using your lateral bending. When you prepare for trot-to-walk transitions, sit a few strides in the trot and think of making three half-halts. It is easier if you shorten the stride a little prior to the transitions, especially for a horse with a long trot stride who has more difficulty balancing in the transitions.

You may find voice aids helpful here, and when you ask for the walk, remember to use alternating seat bones and alternating legs as aids to influence the walk. To get the rhythm of this, allow your horse to walk and don't use any leg. Feel how the motion of the walk will put you first on one seat bone and then the other. Keep this motion going. You cannot drive the horse more forward with your seat, as walk has no impulsion—that is, no suspension. (You can, however, slow the tempo down with your seat by following more slowly.) Feel the horse's rib cage swing into your calf: first one leg then the other as the belly swings back and forth in the walk. As you feel the belly move into your leg, this is when you squeeze back. First one leg and then the other. This correctly influences the hind leg that is coming under the body.

Mental relaxation and physical suppleness are the goals here. Using smaller circles or some of the collecting movements such as shoulder-in, travers, renvers, half-pass or counter-canter can help in the warm-up just to "slow" the horse down a bit.

2 **Problem: My horse is lazy.**

Too often riders ride around and around, trying to make the horse want to go "forward." This type of horse will never "think" forward from this type of riding. The rider needs to concentrate on getting the horse's brain to connect more quickly to the legs. The process of your aids to the horse's brain to his legs is too slow.

Sometimes the lazy horse does not need to be ridden as deep and round as the hot horse. When the lack of energy is mental, keep the horse more in a working frame and make lots of quick transitions. Reactions are important. Change the gaits—and paces within the gaits—frequently. Don't be boring. Your goal is to get the horse to react quickly off the lightest possible aid and do more of the work on his own. If he doesn't react to a light aid, ask more insistently and get a quick response. Then try again with a light aid until the horse responds to that. Whenever I hear someone say that her horse is "dead to the aids," I know her training has gone off track. It's *your* job to make your horse responsive.

In addition, make sure there are no "blockages" in the topline. Sometimes, the horse could think more forward but there is a stiffness preventing this from happening. When your horse is stiff and "locked up," work on suppling him by flexing him briefly to the outside, then to the inside. This does *not* mean "wagging" his neck back and forth (like a dog's tail). The process should be done over a few strides, allowing the horse time to respond to your aids.

3.2 Here I am with Halloh and my corgis, Bear and Puffin.

Personal Story

Halloh was a five-year-old Holsteiner that I bought in Germany from Rosemarie Springer. His registered name was Ronaldson. He was the most expensive horse I had ever purchased. Halloh (named for Rosemarie Springer's barn Gut Halloh), could be either hot and "exiting the arena," or lazy.

In the beginning he was hot. I remember a show in Sun Valley, Idaho, at Parry Thomas's farm, with former Olympian Hilda Gurney judging. Halloh was put off by the noise coming from a plastic kickboard being hit by sand near the show arena. We left the arena three times. Hilda finally came out of the booth and told me "to get that stallion back in

the ring." First I told her he wasn't a stallion, and then I added that if I could stay in the ring, I certainly would!

About the time we reached Prix St. Georges, Halloh decided that lazy was better than foolish. He thought all the upcoming Grand Prix work was too demanding. Luckily, I had good instruction during this time. Olympian Robert Dover and German trainer Jo Hinneman both gave me lots of good exercises to keep Halloh sharp and on the aids. One of the best exercises was to ride him forward out of every corner for about 12 meters and then begin an exercise. This really helped in the show ring as he was already geared up to "go."

Avoid doing a lot of movements in the beginning that slow the horse down. In other words, use lots of straight lines; do not do small circles or too many collecting movements in a row. Ask for transitions and look for reactions!

3 Problem: My horse is "high-necked."

Some horses have a very high and uphill neckset. Perfect, right? No! A "high-necked" horse's tendency will be to contract his neck up and back toward the rider all the time. This will prevent the horse from correctly using his back and can lead to his developing the wrong muscles on the underside of the neck, while there is a lack of development in the loin area.

This is the type of horse that needs to be ridden deep and round in the warm-up. He must really stretch over his back, through his neck, down and out to the bit. Lateral bending may help encourage the horse to stretch.

Remember, the horse does not *offer* suppleness; you must *ask* for it. There are two types of suppleness: *longitudinal* and *lateral*. Each is worth 50 percent. When the horse is reluctant to stretch longitudinally over the topline, he may be willing to bend nicely latitudinally. This will encourage 50 percent submission laterally, which helps toward achieving the other 50 percent longitudinally. Or, maybe if you get longitudinal submission, it will help with the lateral submission. This is one instance where you *do* want to do whatever is easiest for the horse. *Do not* try to attack the suppleness the horse most wants to resist first; be sneaky, and use one type of suppleness to help the other.

4 Problem: My horse is "low-necked."

This type is just the opposite of the horse above. Riding him too deep and low in the warm-up can encourage him to go onto the forehand and stay there. Some experimentation may be needed to find the right position for the neck. There must be enough stretch down-and-out through the neck to encourage him to stretch the *back out.*

5 Problem: My horse is a "draft type."

The draft-type horse is bred to pull with the shoulders. I never put this horse too deep and low in the warm-up as it is then difficult to bring him up.

6 Problem: My horse is "spooky."

This horse will spend an entire lesson spooking and trying to get out of work if you let him. Take a lot of time warming up this one! If you are in a hurry, don't ride. Time is your best friend. Before you mount, walk the horse around the full arena in both directions. This will give you an idea prior to mounting where the horse is going to spook.

You can try kicking and spanking the horse each time he spooks, but in my opinion you will get nowhere. The horse will just be more afraid of the object or area in question, and you will teach him to fight rather than work. Then the behavior becomes learned and a way for the horse to avoid work altogether. This reaction can be dangerous for the rider, too.

This horse must learn that the line of travel is sacred. When you can keep the horse on the line of travel, you will win. It doesn't matter right now what gait you are in.

Poll-Suppling

Many horses that I judge are still stuck or lacking suppleness in the poll. I used to wait until the horse was a bit more mature before working on this issue, until I was coached by Bodo Hangen from Tempel Farms (see p. 138). He gave me several great exercises that I would like to share with you. I also encourage you to work on this area of stiffness sooner rather than later.

The horse needs to be able to stretch or lengthen his short side (the side he likes to bend toward) and shorten his long side. If the horse likes to bend left, we call this horse *"left-side-short and right-side-long,"* or "Hollow to the left." A horse that likes to bend left is like a person who is left-handed. The left side will be more coordinated and the right side will be stronger.

I am right-handed. I do the delicate work with my right hand, and when I need strength I use my left hand. Think of peeling potatoes. I hold the potato firmly in my left hand and use delicate wrist movements with the peeler in my right hand to get the job done. Try doing this the other way around! It will give you an idea of how hard it can be to change your strong or coordinated side. Remember, however, we keep insisting that the horse be equally supple in both directions. I believe as riders we should be able to use either side of our bodies equally as well (see chapter 1, p. 5).

If the horse is *right-side-short,* he will bend well to the right, but want to fall a bit left into his strong side. To the left, it will be difficult to bend him left or shorten the left side of his body. Make sure you have worked on the choo-choo train exercise and can get your three-car train aligned on a 20-meter circle (see p. 16). This will help with the following poll-suppling exercises.

Poll Suppling Exercises
On the Ground

From the ground, stand in front of your horse and take the bit near the reins into your hands. First ask the horse to yield to the left, then the right. The lower you can get his neck right now, the easier this exercise will be.

Try to supple him slightly first in one direction and then move him slowly into the other. In the beginning, he will lift his head

3.3 A & B
Willow supples her poll to the left (A) and to the right (B).

A

B

and neck up when you move him toward the stiff direction. Be careful you do not put your chin over his poll—in the event that he raises his head, he might hit you in the chin.

Eventually, you will be able to loosen the big muscles over the top of his neck and actually see them "roll" back and forth over the crest of the neck. As the horse becomes more supple the large muscles in the neck will be able to quickly lengthen or shorten as the horse changes his bending.

Success is when your horse's mane starts to stand straight up and bounce a bit rather than lie flat on one side. The horse by nature will wear his mane on one side or the other of the neck. Just observing this characteristic in a young horse will tell you which side is his stiff side—he will "wear his hair" to the supple or hollow side of the neck.

On the Horse

Once your horse will loosen his poll a bit on the ground, try the same exercise at halt while mounted. If you just pull the neck back and forth, he will only get supple at the base of the neck, not the poll. I see a lot of riders pulling the horse's nose to their knee with only one rein. That is not what this exercise is about.

Both reins must work together. The outside rein will keep the neck attached to the shoulders, and the inside rein will bend and flex the poll to the inside.

Remember this: the use of the reins in a tactful and elastic way creates this last bit of suppleness through the neck and poll. The rider must keep the contact playful without being too busy and should never have a stiff or resistant hand.

Use the inside rein low and toward the direction of your inside knee to turn the head and neck. Do not lift your hand and do not pull back as this will only shorten the neck. Remember you are working here to *stretch the outside of the neck*. The outside rein acts as a supporting rein to keep the neck attached to the shoulders. Think about your choo-choo train (see p. 16): you do not want the horse to learn to separate the "neck car" from the "shoulder car." The shoulders and neck must remain one piece.

Also, note your horse's ears. If your horse always carries his inside ear higher than the outside ear one direction, you have a poll-suppleness issue. The inside ear should be level with the outside ear. It is also okay to have the inside ear a slightly bit lower that the outside ear.

Stretch Circle

Use this exercise in your warm-up to supple the poll. Remember, it is easier for the horse to let go of the poll when the neck is down (low). While on your circle, put the horse's stiff (or long) side to the inside. Use your inside rein balanced by the outside rein to loosen the poll. He must stretch the outside of the poll area and you should see a hollow right behind his inside cheek bone. Try to hold this for a few strides to get a really good stretch. Then release as it will be a bit uncomfortable for the horse, at first.

Bring Your Horse's Frame Up

When you return to your working frame, you can use a few counter-flexing half-halts to still work the stiff side of the poll when it is to the outside. Think a little renvers (haunches-out) and you will have the idea, but don't ask for too much angle.

When your horse is in his working frame and you are feeling stiffness again in the poll area, then repeat the stretch circle again. Don't be afraid to use the stretch circle several times during your work to regain the suppleness you need. Eventually your horse will be able to "flip" his mane in the working frame.

3.4 Paula Helm on H.S. Wrapsody, a Hungarian Warmblood. Wrapsody was a very spooky horse and Paula could not get him around an arena. However, with patience and logic they are now winning at Third Level!

This is where you must *take away impulsion* in order to gain submission. Once you have mounted, walk around the arena both ways again. No doubt the horse will spook at something. Quietly halt and allow the horse to look. Pat and encourage him rather than punish him. You will feel the "brain return to the body." Often he will audibly breathe. At this point you are able to influence the horse again. Put your leg on and encourage a step or two forward. It may take a while in

order to get past the "ghost." But he must go past on your line of travel, even if it takes 10 minutes with two steps of walk and halts in between.

When you have gone around the arena both directions at walk, start on a circle at either end—or perhaps in the middle of the arena. Pick the place where the horse has the most confidence. Using your lateral bending, work to get the horse stretching longitudinally over the back as well. By using the inside bend you will help get the horse

Warming Up at the Show Grounds
Strategies and Etiquette

How should your warm-up change when you are at a horse show? It shouldn't. Try not to change your routine, if at all possible.

If you need to longe your horse, find the designated longeing area. Do not disrupt the warm-up arenas with longeing. I suggest longeing your horse early in the day and then untacking him and letting him have a break. Then, prior to your first class, he should be ready to work. Longeing and a warm-up all at one time can tire your horse out, and you may not have enough "gas" left for your class.

When you enter the warm-up arena, walk quietly around both directions on a long rein *off* the rail. The rail is needed for those already further along in their warm-up. Walking horses should always have the lowest priority. Keep your eyes up and try to stay out of the way!

Once you are ready to begin, pick up your reins and start on a circle. The curved lines will help you achieve the relaxation you need. I don't think anyone should practice every movement in the test they are going to ride. If you feel you should do that, you may not be ready for the level at which you are showing.

Make sure you can move the horse forward and back into and out of your lengthening—or mediums or extensions—if you have them in your test. You will need to find out how long it will take to get to the medium and how many strides to get back. You may find this will take a bit longer at the show than at home. Then you must remember this in the ring. You cannot "train" anything now. Don't try or you will only make things worse.

Work on your transitions and your reactions. Ride a few transitions to halt. You want your horse sharp but not tired, and also not too wound up. This takes a bit of time and mileage to know what your horse will need. The weather (hot or cold) and also the venue (calm or flags flapping) will also either add or delete time to your warm-up.

There always seems to be one "arena hog" at a horse show. This rider thinks no one else should be there and she will try to bully you into avoiding a good warm-up. Talk to the warm-up steward and don't be afraid to ask for help from the USEF Technical Delegate (TD). We all need a level playing field.

If your horse kicks, put a red ribbon in the tail. If your horse is nervous with other horses coming at him, you may need to find another arena or a grassy area to warm up. You must be careful, however, that you are not acting like you are trying to "hide" something from the warm-up steward or the TD. When you arrive, asking the show manager to help you is a good idea.

Whatever happens during your test, have a good time and enjoy your ride. The judge will want to reward you with higher scores when your horse looks easy to ride and you are a harmonious team. Trying to force your horse to do something will not be appreciated by the horse or the judge. Remember that every show ride is also a training experience for the horse. He will either remember an enjoyable experience, or he will learn to hate showing.

I trained a lovely Swedish stallion named Gaspadin ("Gus") for Capricorn Farms. I had qualified him for the AHSA Regional Championships in Prix St. Georges. This was the first year I had trained and competed him, so I had only shown him in Colorado shows. The warm-up arenas in Colorado had always been very civilized and not full of traffic.

I found out the hard way that California warm-ups can resemble California freeways. Watch out! It was a long walk from the barns to the warm-up area, so when I arrived I was ready to start our trot work. This went well, until more and more horses arrived. Soon Gus started acting very nervous. This was not his usual style, and I was not sure what was going on with his mind. I soon found out!

He let out a huge squeal and started running backward, cow-kicking like mad. I was totally out of control. Let me tell you, that warm-up cleared out fast. I soon had the entire arena to myself. I had never been in a situation with that many horses and so did not know he was totally insecure

in such a scenario. For the rest of the week, I made sure I had a nice quiet warm-up location with little traffic.

The highlight of our show weekend was a Pas de Deux that we did with Anne Callin riding Laylock who was owned by Peter Lert. Laylock was Gus's son. Our Pas de Deux was ridden to "Thank Heavens for Little Girls" as both were chestnut stallions with high white stockings. Natalie Lamping was one of the judges. She gave us a 10 for similarity as a pair as she could not tell us apart! We ended up second in a very large class.

3.5 Here I am on the Swedish stallion Gaspadin.

Our Pas de Deux was unusual in that we had to do mirror-image choreography. Just as Gus was not happy with too many horses in a warm-up area, he did not tolerate anyone riding with him as a "pair."

As long as I showed Gus, I always told the show manager that I had a warm-up problem and asked for a "safe haven" in which to work. I never had an issue because I made my concern known at the onset of the show.

more obedient to the inside leg. Once your circle is relaxed and obedient, start making it a bit larger at each end. Slowly work the circle until the horse is quietly going around the entire arena.

Using a shoulder-in will help immensely as horses usually do not spook about something in the interior of the arena, and by taking his vision away from the rail in shoulder-in, you are taking the horse's line of sight away from the spooky objects. This also gives you more control with your inside leg for the line of travel. The horse needs to think your aids are more interesting than anything he might see outside of the arena. When he is busy thinking about your requests, he is not focused on spooking.

If you have a place where the horse still spooks, quietly walk past that point, reward him, and then trot on. Eventually you will be able to trot by that spot. Allowing the horse to spin and twirl with you kicking and spanking will only increase the frequency of the naughty behavior.

Repeat the same circle exercise the other direction. Don't forget the horse usually spooks more on his stiff, long side than on his supple, short side (see p. 24). Just because the left eyeball thought all was okay, doesn't mean the right eyeball feels the same way!

Repeat the circle exercise at canter.

You will note after a month, the horse will still be looking but will allow you now to keep the line of travel. You may not always have the same degree of impulsion, but this, in time, will get better too.

In a dressage test, now you can keep the mistakes to one movement only, whereas before, this bad behavior influenced several marks.

Rider's Aids

Let's review the thinking of your horse as a three-car, choo-choo train: the neck and shoulder car; the dining car; and the caboose. In the warm-up, your train might get derailed. Remember the five basic aids:

1 Inside rein
2 Inside leg at the girth
3 Outside leg behind the girth
4 Outside rein
5 The seat

Inside Rein

The inside rein is the turn signal. It turns the horse's head, neck, and shoulders and indicates direction. It is also a lateral bending aid.

Inside Leg at the Girth

The inside leg is the gas pedal. When rising at the trot, the rider should squeeze the horse forward as she goes up in the post as that is when the inside hind is in the air coming under the body. This is also the time your weight is off the horse's back, which can also encourage a horse to lift the back or relax the back a bit more and allows the hind leg to come further under the body. The inside leg also pushes (or holds) the "dining car" in your choo-choo train out.

Outside Leg behind the Girth

The outside leg behind the girth controls the "caboose." Use this leg as a barrier to keep the haunches from falling out (a lateral bending aid, see p. 50).

Longeing as a Means of Warm-Up

There are many good books on longeing your horse. I don't want to go in depth into technique, as you can find this in the *USDF Lungeing Manual* edited by Gerhard Politz, as well as *Lungeing* by the German National Equestrian Federation (FN). (Note: Most publications in the United States use the French word "longe" rather than "lunge," which is commonly used in other parts of Europe.)

First, let me say, I do not believe in longeing without any sort of side reins or Vienna reins (see below). I think allowing the horse to race around with tack on gives him the wrong message. When your horse needs to blow off steam at home, put a set of good boots on him and turn him loose in the arena or in a turnout area. Allowing him to race around on a circle with his head up can cause quite a bit of damage to his legs and joints and can be unsafe for other riders and horses sharing the arena. Turning him out may not be possible at a horse show as space is usually limited. At the show, you will probably have to find the designated longeing area.

In my opinion, longeing is training, and training is about submission. I want my horses to know that when they have tack on, I am in control—not them—and this is all about work.

When dealing with a very high-headed horse—with or without tension in the back—side reins are probably not the best attachment to use. He can learn quickly to "set" his neck in a nice, round "pose" and never really develop suppleness and "throughness." I've always liked German longeing reins, which run from the surcingle, through the bit, and connect to the center of the girth between the fore-legs. I had a good leatherworker make me a pair for my horses in the 1970s. Now you can buy this same system in most tack stores marketed as *Vienna reins*. They encourage the horse to stretch forward and downward and round his back. They don't allow the horse to "curl up" as much as side reins.

If you have a horse that takes quite a while to warm up, sometimes it is easier to longe him for 15 minutes and get him to stretch the correct muscles *before* you get on. Then, once mounted, he will be more willing to work the muscles that are already warmed up.

I have also tried longeing with a *German neck stretcher* and this works well on some horses, too. This device puts pressure on the poll, but also encourages the horse to stretch forward and downward into the contact.

I do not like the *chambon* that only has contact with the poll. While it does lower the neck and release the back, it does so without any contact on the bit, so the horse can learn to wag the nose (like a dog's tail) quite a bit.

If you do prefer side reins, be sure you have some with a little donut or elastic inset. New studies show that horses will take 3 to 6 pounds of weight in the reins on their own while working. This contact is not static and changes as the phase of the gait changes. So, elastic allows the horse to find a contact and yet still not be rigid in this contact.

Side reins are helpful for a horse that is quite stiff to one side, and by shortening the inside side rein two holes, the horse can be encouraged to loosen and let go of the stiff side. The horse's brain seems to think if you are on the ground he is not fighting you, he is only fighting himself, and he tends to "give up" and release and relax the muscles a bit sooner.

Try a bit of longeing when you are having difficulty suppling your horse easily in the warm-up.

Outside Rein

This rein has two jobs. One is to slow the horse down—or be used as a brake. The second job of the outside rein is to control the horse's longitudinal suppleness—his suppleness from back to front. The height and length of the neck is also influenced by the outside rein.

The horse will be "on the aids" when he is submissive to the four aids I have just discussed. If the horse will bend and step toward the outside rein (from the inside leg), then the outside rein can have a positive influence on the horse and the half-halt. If the rider does not allow the horse to stretch toward (or lengthen the *outside* of his body through bending) the outside rein, and only holds tension on the outside rein, the horse will slow down and his neck will get shorter as the rider's arms get stronger.

The Seat

The seat influences the direction the horse moves by your shifting weight. It can help to collect the horse by being more still, and influence the horse by allowing a longer stride. Think of your lower leg as the gas pedal and your seat as the gear shift. All your movements should have the same "rpm," with your seat helping to direct the horse in using this energy.

Your warm-up should be used as a test or checklist of the five main aids. These are the simple aids needed to influence one part of more difficult movements. If you find one of the aids I've listed is not correctly influencing the horse, then you must stop here and correct the problem. Once you and your horse are warmed up, you are ready to begin the training portion of your riding session.

Half-Halts and Simple Transitions

When evasions change, you should be happy!
Your horse is learning and your training is progressing.

Half-halts and transitions are the building blocks of dressage training. In this chapter, I'll discuss how to use these tools to rebalance your horse and prepare him for a change of gait or a change within the gait.

In basic dressage, transitions are quite easy, and they progressively get more difficult as the horse moves up the levels. This chapter is about working with a green or young horse and teaching him the basic concepts of balanced transitions and the beginning of the half-halt.

The half-halt is developed through simple transitions. In other words, there is a walk-halt transition, which later becomes "half" of a "halt"—or a "half-halt."

Horses are not instinctively born with the ability to half-halt. They are born to flee. They are born to lift their neck to catch their balance. As their teacher, you must be able to teach them what you want—something that is in many ways against their nature—in a kind and patient way.

First, let's look at some issues that may come up when training half-halts and transitions.

Imperfections and Evasions

Your horse:

1 Has trouble standing still.

2 Throws his head up in transitions, opens his mouth, or leans on the reins.

3 Gets crooked and struggles with transitions from one gait to another or with changes of pace within the gaits.

4 Changes canter leads behind or picks up the wrong lead.

5   Drops his neck.

6   Is late in responding to the aids.

I'll discuss how to "fix" these evasions from your imperfect horse later in this chapter (see p. 41). First, however, it's important to know how the USEF Rule Book defines transitions (see sidebar).

Now, just how and why should you work on transitions? Think of transitions as the building blocks of your half-halt and future collection. Transitions are also where the learning and strength-building occurs. Robert Dover once said, "Most riders ride from movement to movement; good riders ride from half-halt to half-halt." So, frequent transitions must be part of your everyday training. This work and frequent changes of direction will keep your horse reactive to the aids and interested in his work.

In Training Level, the transitions are between the letters in the arena, and this allows you more time for preparation. The transitions are also mostly on curved lines, which are much easier for the horse to stay in balance. Later on, transitions are required to be accurate and prompt. In the Grand Prix Special, for example, the rider must make transitions from passage to extended trot to passage, as well as show transitions from passage to piaffe to passage. All must be done smoothly and without an interruption of rhythm.

Horses by nature use their neck to balance themselves. When they are insecure they put their neck up. In dressage, you are working to have the horse learn to balance himself on his hind legs instead.

How to Ride and Train

Using the Aids to Ride Half-Halts

A simple way to think about a half-halt is this: it is the perfect combination of the driving and bending aids, and the outside rein. Too many instructors make this too difficult. Keep it simple. As you progress up the levels, the half-halt will get a bit more complicated with the addition of the seat aids. But at this stage, your seat should only be allowing the horse to move more forward with larger strides with an opening in the "swing of your hips," or it should ask the horse to shorten and think of coming back under the seat by closing the "swing of the hips" in the moment of half-halt. Here are the basic aids:

1 Inside rein
2 Inside leg at the girth
3 Outside leg behind the girth

USEF Rule Book
TRANSITIONS

1 The changes of gait and pace should be clearly shown at the prescribed marker; they should be quickly made yet must be smooth and not abrupt. The cadence of a gait or pace should be maintained up to the moment when the gait or pace is changed or the horse halts. The horse should remain light in hand, calm and maintain a correct position.

2 The same applies to transitions from one movement to another for instance from the passage to the piaffe and vice versa.

4 Outside rein

5 The seat

To ride an effective half-halt, you should always think in this order:

1 First, is the topline supple?

2 Next, are the hind legs active?

3 Now, I can apply the aids for the half-halt.

If you just use the reins for the transitions and the horse is not supple in the contact and is stiff, his only reaction will be to shorten the neck and put the hind legs out behind him more. And, if the hind legs are not active, the horse might only slow down rather than make an active and balanced transition. So to repeat the steps just listed: First, you must check to make sure the horse is supple. Second, you must make sure the hind legs are active. Then, you can make a half-halt.

DOWNWARD TRANSITIONS

Rider's Aids

If you have correctly worked with your horse on the longe line (see p. 30), he will understand simple voice aids. He will also understand the driving aids from your voice and the longe whip, and he will understand and accept the bit from his work in the side reins or the Vienna reins. This makes the rest of the lessons much simpler because you can associate your voice aids with your seat and leg aids: As the "go" aid, use your leg and your cluck or "trot" voice aid at the same time. For "slow down," use your "Whoa" voice aid and your outside rein, close the "swing of your hips" through your seat, and use more upper thigh.

Walk to Halt

This transition is the most simple of all, as there is little impulsion. The horse must learn to halt and stand still. It is not important at the beginning for you to keep the horse on the bit or to be sure the halt is square. Those come later. First, make sure your horse understands that the reins are saying, "Whoa." Once the horse halts, "give" the reins and relax your legs. He should stand quietly without any contact. This may take some time and practice. Once the horse has mastered this lesson, you can move into more advanced aids for the halt.

The halt will be more balanced when the horse is a little bit positioned in shoulder-fore, which will allow a bit of room for the inside hind to step under and also allow you to have a clear outside rein.

Work at getting the hind legs to square up first. You can do a little groundwork to teach the horse to move his hind legs when you touch him with the whip. When you are mounted, on the side you want him to move his hind leg, use your leg slightly behind the girth and ask him to step up. Always reward when the horse responds.

Then you can teach the horse on the ground to move a front leg with a tap near the shoulder. After your groundwork is successful, you can use the same aid while mounted with a touch of your leg near the shoulder. Be sure to always give a bit and allow the horse a reward for responding to your aids.

Trot to Walk

Try to work on your transitions on curved lines, as working on straight lines adds difficulty. For this one, sit a few strides in the trot and think of making three half-halts—think little, more, most—

4.1 Kathy Davidson on M.A. Genie in working trot at First Level. To transition to the walk she will sit several strides and think of making three half-halts with graduated intensity.

prior to the walk. It is easier if you shorten the stride a little prior to the transitions, especially for a horse with a long trot stride, as he will have more difficulty balancing in the transitions. Voice aids are helpful again here. When you ask for the walk, remember to use alternating seat bones and alternating legs.

Prior to going back to trot, make sure your horse is calm and supple in the walk. If there is tension, keep walking until the horse relaxes so he learns to relax in every downward transition and not anticipate the new upward transition.

Trot to Halt

When your trot-walk transitions are going well, stay just a bit longer in your half-halt and ask the horse to halt. Remember, it is okay for a step or two forward to balance and square up. If you are having problems, use a bit of bending on your circle and leg-yield a bit to the outside of the circle (pushing the inside hind more under the body and more toward the outside rein) prior to the halt.

Make sure your horse is remaining supple and submissive to the bend. Most transitions that don't work, which I see as a clinician and judge, are ridden very straight in the neck and body. This allows the horse to stiffen and fall on the shoulders quite easily. When the horse falls down on both shoulders, we call this being "on the forehand." However, horses also fall sideways on either the inside or the outside shoulder.

If you have trained the horse with your voice on the longe line, then you can use your voice to associate the stopping of your seat (be sure not to sit heavier, just more still) and close your upper legs a bit. The horse will eventually associate these aids with your body, and you won't need your voice anymore.

Canter to Trot

I try to teach my horses that my going back onto both seat bones— that is, making my weight equal—is the cue to return to trot. I prepare the horse in canter with a little suppling, making sure that he is not falling to the outside. I slightly counterflex and push him a bit up off my outside leg. This is important to make sure the horse does not change his lead behind during the transition. Once I am sure my horse is supple and upright (in balance), I go back to both seat bones and relax. The horse is quite willing to learn this; I use my voice with a little "brrr" noise for trot so he learns to associate with my aids what he has learned via my voice cues on the longe line.

Always remember that once the horse trots, you will need to rebalance the trot with a half-halt as soon as possible!

UPWARD TRANSITIONS

Rider's Aids
For upward transitions, I like to use my seat aids

first, along with my voice, and then reinforce these aids with my leg. In trot, my seat bones work together, much as if I were in a rowboat with a sliding seat. In walk, my seat bones alternate. In canter, I weight my inside seat bone more and use it as if I am in a swing and want the swing to go higher.

Halt to Walk

Once your horse has settled into the halt, use a bit of a cluck and relax your seat, and begin to use your alternating seat and leg aids to ask for the walk.

Halt to Trot

Again, using your voice will be helpful. Use a bit of inside leg and both seat bones moving forward for the aid. Your outside leg needs to remain as a barrier so the horse does not misunderstand and move sideways rather than forward. Working these exercises along the rail can be helpful if you are having problems with the horse falling out. Make sure your horse is not lazy in his reaction to your aids.

Walk to Trot

Be sure you are clear with your walk aids (alternating seat and legs) and make sure your horse is supple. Create a bit of lateral suppleness on your curved line and then ask for the trot.

Trot to Canter

This is the most difficult transition for the young horse. If the horse is a big mover, bring the trot back a little (narrow the base of support) so that you make the transitions easier for him. Work on your circle. In his stiff direction you will need

4.2 Rebecca Blake rides a canter lengthening on her German riding pony, Hollywood.

to bend the horse a bit more to the inside and push him a bit toward the outside rein prior to the canter. In the other direction, he will want to fall out and take the wrong lead. In this direction, you will need to counterflex him a bit, and push him a little in with your outside leg to make sure you can correctly influence the outside hind leg. Remember the left-lead canter starts on the right hind leg and vice versa.

Be clear with your aids. I see many riders doing what I call a "progressive transition" by putting the aids on one at a time. This confuses the horse. Ride your half-halt in trot as described on p. 34, and then move to your inside seat bone and use your seat as if you are in a swing and want it to go higher. At the same time, your inside leg moves a bit more forward and the outside leg goes back.

For me, once the horse has a bit more training and is ready to move into Second Level work, I stop using the outside leg as an active leg, as I want my horse to know this aid will now indicate "move your haunches in" when it is active. So I use my outside leg as the barrier leg, but the canter depart is achieved with my inside seat bone and inside leg.

Change of Lead through Trot

If your horse anticipates this movement, ride to X, and do a 10- to 12-meter circle in the direction of the lead at X, then trot on this same circle. Upon returning to X, circle in trot the other direction, asking for the new lead on this circle before continuing on the diagonal.

Canter Lengthenings

When riding canter lengthenings, I never go the entire long side when schooling. I work a lot on a circle, as unlike the long side, a circle never ends. I will lengthen a few steps and then go back to working or collected canter a few steps. The horse learns to stay balanced and submissive. The slight bend of the circle helps keep the horse in balance.

Once I start the lengthening on the rail, I only lengthen about 12 meters before coming back to working or collected canter. I also find a 10-meter circle at the end of the lengthening helps the horse to understand that he needs to come back and rebalance in the corner. A horse that wants to be strong after a lengthening will benefit from this exercise because he will anticipate a circle and already start coming back on his own.

Trot Lengthenings

In this work, often the horse will confuse the "lengthen-trot" aid for a "go-more-forward" aid and will break into canter. I have found that just bringing the horse back to trot and trying again doesn't really make your point. I think that making the evasion more work than the work required is a good solution. When the horse canters instead

of lengthening at the trot, I ride him more forward in a lengthening canter around the arena once, then go back to trot and try again. Make sure the horse is not crooked and you are not sitting more to one direction. Young horses often try to give you a "little" canter rather than a bigger trot, because it is less work.

Once you are sure you have a true lengthening in trot, you may begin the transition back from trot lengthening. I like to school these with

Personal Story

Abracadabra ("Abra") was a hot little chestnut mare (see p. 20 for more about her). She had a lot of Arabian from her grandsire Urbino. She was only 15.3 but she moved like she was 17 hands. She was always in overdrive and was convinced she knew exactly what was required without any assistance from her rider.

Abra did not like the change of lead through the trot at all. She knew what was coming, and there were rarely any trot steps, mostly just a quick change of lead, which the judges did not really appreciate. I was at my wits' end with her and had just about decided to get out of First and Second Level as this movement was creating too much tension in my horse. She already was started in the flying changes, so why not? I could get a "4" for the change as easily as I could for Abra's version of the change of lead through the trot.

Former Olympian and FEI 4* judge Hilda Gurney helped me with this challenge—in training, I only rode my diagonals from trot to canter with the addition of the circles I describe on this page. At the show, Abracadabra would think she had to do those boring circles and so wasn't anticipating a change of gait. Because she was "waiting" for my aids, the new canter aid was accepted easily!

a little shoulder-in at the end, so again, I don't want to pull on the reins to bring the horse back, and I use the shoulder-in to help the suppleness and balance.

Increase or Decrease the Circle

This is a great exercise and can be done at shows in the warm-up arena when you don't have a lot of room as all you need is a 20-meter circle. You can either spiral down onto a smaller circle with the same bend, or counterflex and leg-yield down to a smaller circle. Go once or twice around the smaller circle and then leg-yield out to the larger circle. This can be done in trot and canter. This exercise will improve the horse's balance and suppleness. It's also great for a horse that wants to fall either in or out. When you prepare with this exercise and then lengthen a few steps, you will help to ensure your horse is really straight and is not leaning against either leg.

Remember, that any mistakes in these exercises should be considered a training opportunity. Horses need to make mistakes in order to learn, just as we do as riders and trainers. The key is to teach them something from the mistakes—and not to reinforce the mistakes!

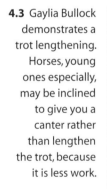

4.3 Gaylia Bullock demonstrates a trot lengthening. Horses, young ones especially, may be inclined to give you a canter rather than lengthen the trot, because it is less work.

Cures and Solutions

The exercises below help "fix" the transition problems listed under Imperfections and Evasions on p. 33.

| Problem: My horse won't stand still.

Dealing with this takes time and patience. The more you kick your horse for moving, the more confused he will be. Here I agree with the cowboys: "Whoa means whoa." The horse needs to learn to "hang out." He should stand in one place all day if you ask.

But remember, first the horse needs to learn to stop from the reins and stand still without them. Keep using your voice with a touch on the reins, and then drop them. You can work on the ground with this issue as well, if needed. Use a little tug on the lead rope and say "Whoa." I find that horses that have been shown in hand are much easier to work with, so a little groundwork goes a long way!

Again, the first goal is that the horse stands still. Later, you can raise your standards and work on the squareness of the halt and maintenance of contact, but you cannot do it all at once.

2 Problem: My horse throws his head up, opens his mouth, or leans on the reins.

When the horse loses balance he will either throw his head up to regain his balance or look to you for support from the reins.

Go back to your circle and make sure you can bend the horse and push him toward the outside rein. If your horse resists staying laterally supple for the transition, see the next evasion.

3 Problem: My horse becomes crooked and struggles with the up or down transitions.

Both of these evasions usually stem from the rider's lack of preparation for the transitions. You must make sure the horse is supple, both laterally and longitudinally (see p. 23). Remember, circles are used at the lower levels for a reason: bending helps the horse stay in balance. Straight lines are harder. Go back to your circle, do some leg-yielding in and out on the circle (increase and decrease the circle—see p. 40) to check and see where your horse is leaning. He might be falling in, he might be falling out. Usually a young horse will fall in on one direction (the stiff side) and fall out on the other. In others words, the horse will push toward the strong side no matter what.

As mentioned earlier (see p. 24), if your horse does not like to bend left, we say he is "stiff to the left," "hollow to the right," or "strong to the left." In essence your horse is right-handed; he is more coordinated to the right and stronger to the left. Think of how you use your hands. If you are right-handed, you use the right for delicate work and left for opening jars that have lids stuck.

Your horse is the same. He will fall to the strong side to catch his balance. Your job in training is to make sure that he will learn to carry the same weight on both hind legs and be able to equally stretch (lengthen) each side of his body while shortening the opposite side. When your horse is stiff to the left, he will not want to shorten the left side and stretch the outside of his body, which is on the right.

We must make our horses "ambihoofdrous"! So in your transitions, you must be aware that the horse will always want to push himself or fall in the direction of his strong side. You must take care of this prior to the transition and make sure you have him framed in and upright in his balance.

4 Problem: My horse changes his lead behind or picks up the wrong lead.

When your horse changes his lead behind in the transition from canter to trot, first check and make sure you are not using the reins first. Then make sure your horse is not pushing into your outside leg. You may need to go back and check there is no tension in the horse's back.

When the horse picks up the wrong lead, usually he is falling out. Be sure to counterflex a little, even push the horse in a bit off the outside leg prior to the depart. Remember, if this is not a trained horse, you will also need to ask him for the canter when his outside hind is coming under his body. A trained horse will take the correct lead even if you ask at the wrong time.

5 Problem: My horse drops his neck.

The rider is usually to blame for this imperfection and has allowed the horse to lose alignment and fall on his shoulders. Work your transitions in more of a shoulder-in or renvers position. You may have to try both to see which works the best.

6 Problem: My horse is late in responding to the aids.

When your horse is late to canter, put the whip into your outside hand and when you ask for the depart, give him a little tap as he needs to react quicker. For trot or walk, put the whip into the inside hand. You may need voice aids again to help the horse understand.

As you ride these exercises and think about your horse's imperfections and evasions, remember that the most important part of your body when training your horse is your brain. You must learn to react in the correct way. What your brain tells you by nature is not always correct. If you are not sure, don't do anything. Think about what happened.

Did the horse break out of canter because he was lazy? In this case, you must put him back into canter quickly. However, if he broke out of canter because he was falling through the outside aids and you try to quickly put him back into canter, you will just get the wrong lead and create more problems. If he was leaning out, simply counterflex him and leg-yield him back in a few steps, then canter again. You may need to make these little corrections as he is cantering in order to help keep him in balance.

Stretching the Frame on the Circle

The most important part of this movement is that the horse releases his back and shows a forward and downward stretch into the contact.

The USEF test movement for Training and First Levels reminds us to ask the horse in a 20-meter trot circle to be "allowed to stretch forward and downward," while the directive ideas call for "forward and downward stretch over the back into a light contact, maintaining balance and quality of trot; bend; shape and size of circle; smooth, balanced transitions."

I dubbed this movement the "stretchy, chewy circle" when it first arrived in our national tests. All the other verbiage seemed to me to confuse the issue. Now, everyone on our USEF Test Writing Committee has picked up this vernacular. I think I have also bequeathed it to the USDF L Faculty!

Since this has been in our Training and First Level tests for about 12 years, more and more riders are doing it well. However, I think it is still one of the most confusing movements for judges and for riders.

The most important part of this movement is that the horse releases his back and shows a forward-and-downward stretch into the contact (figs. 5.1 A–F). How far down the horse stretches is not the issue. When the nose is at the same level as the shoulder, in my opinion, the horse is low enough. The rider should also keep an elastic contact to the horse's mouth. The horse should relax—not speed the tempo up—and show some bending on the circle.

This movement must be trained like any other one and do not expect that on the first day your horse will show you the maximum stretch. You must be patient and allow him to get a bit lower and longer day by day. In perhaps a month, you might have the finished product. "Throwing the reins away" will never work.

5.1 A–F In A, the horse shows stretch both out and down with his nose in front of the vertical. The question would be does this represent the horse releasing his back, or is he stiff? That can't be answered without a moving horse!

In B, the horse is definitely stiff in the back while showing an outward and upward stretch.

The horse has dropped his neck and curled up in C, showing no inclination to stretch outward toward the contact.

In D, the horse has shown some outward stretch but lacks the downward inclination.

The horse in E is showing both an outward and downward inclination, with his nose slightly behind the vertical. However, if the neck was elevated, the nose would come in front of the vertical, so this is still okay. Compare it to D. In a moving horse, this type of stretch would most likely show suppleness in the back.

In F, the horse is showing an incorrect contact, with the middle part of the neck being the highest point, the poll very low, and the nose behind the vertical. It is doubtful that, were this a live situation, the horse would show any suppleness over the back.

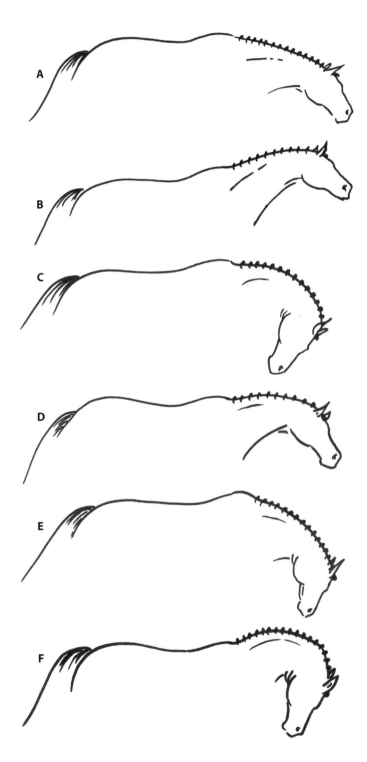

Imperfections and Evasions

When you attempt the "stretch circle," your horse:

1 Curls up his neck.

2 Speeds up as if he is off to the races.

3 Stretches his neck out without lowering it.

4 Stretches without any contact on the reins.

5 Puts his head up.

I'll discuss the solutions to these imperfections beginning on p. 46. Meanwhile, read the USEF definition for the movement (see sidebar).

How to Ride and Train

Rider's Aids

1 Inside rein: Bends the horse and encourages the horse to stretch the outside of his body. Also shows the direction around the circle.

2 Outside rein: Half-halts against the inside bending rein to keep control of the horse's speed. After the half-halt, slightly lengthen the outside rein and encourage the horse to lengthen his frame. How much you lengthen the outside rein will tell the horse how much stretch and lowering of the neck he is allowed. The outside rein also works with the inside leg at the girth (see below) to keep the horse from falling in on the circle.

3 Inside leg at the girth: This keeps the impulsion and helps to support the bend by keeping the rib

cage to the outside; it also keeps the horse from falling in on the circle, along with the outside rein (see above).

4 Outside leg behind the girth: This is a supporting leg to keep the haunches from falling out on the circle.

I like to teach my horses this movement in the following manner. First, I teach them (as do the cowboys, I might add) that when I use the inside rein at halt, they must bend and lower their neck. They must then repeat this exercise at walk and trot.

Once they understand the inside rein, I will then use the outside rein as a half-halt against this bend. The outside rein should make the neck lower. As soon as I feel this small reaction, I give and lengthen both reins a small amount and reward the horse. The horse must stay balanced in this frame before I ask again for more lowering, and eventually he should "follow" the inside rein down as I slowly lengthen the outside rein, which allows the horse to lengthen the frame.

Some horses, because of incorrect prior training, are not very willing to perform this move-

USEF Rule Book
STRETCHING THE FRAME

The horse gradually takes the reins, stretching forward and downward with light contact, while maintaining balance, rhythm and tempo, and quality of the gait.

ment. In this case, it will affect your warm-up. With a horse you are retraining, you may have to warm up in more of a "working frame," or a frame that allows you to connect the horse to the bit, even if the frame isn't what you want in the future. Once this connection has been established, you can then try to lengthen it a bit each day. This process may take a few weeks. Be patient!

JUDGING TIP

On the "stretchy, chewy" 20-meter circle, as a judge I allow the rider the first quarter of the circle to establish the stretch. Then I like to see the stretch maintained for half a circle. The rider can use the last quarter of the circle to pick up the reins. Be sure to keep the lateral bending as you pick up the reins or the horse might stiffen and raise his neck too quickly.

Cures and Solutions

1 Problem: My horse curls up.

When the horse curls up (showing no forward inclination), usually the rider has lost the bend. Remember the horse will not curl when you have one side of his entire body bending with the outside of the body lengthening and stretching toward the outside rein.

A horse can learn to curl in an attempt to avoid contact due to a severe bit, too strong rein contact, or incorrect use of draw reins. Sometimes, due to poor conformation of the neck or incorrect muscling, a horse will curl up on his own. When you have a horse curling for any of these reasons, you may first have to actually make the neck *shorter* in order to establish the correct connection. Once you have a connection from the leg to the hand, you can work on lengthening the neck a bit at a time.

Do not expect it to happen overnight. You can ride with long reins in the hope that the horse will at some point stretch to the bit, but I can tell you it won't happen!

2 Problem: My horse speeds up.

This horse is a bit out of balance. Try not going so far down for a while and keep riding half-halts with your seat or using your voice to slow the tempo down. Work a bit more with a little stretch for maybe half a circle and then bring him up for the other half. Remember, the horse is used to bringing the head and neck up to balance himself, not depending on the rider to help. You must encourage the horse to trust that you will

5.2 Even a Grand Prix horse should be able to show a good stretch circle! Caryn Vesperman shows us how as she warms up Salope.

help him and allow him to understand that he can maintain his balance and still lower his head and neck.

3 **Problem: My horse stretches his neck out without lowering it.**

I call this the "swallow-the-telephone-pole stretch." The horse is lengthening his topline but in a stiff way, while his back is not staying supple and round. Again, check to make sure you have lateral bend. This will encourage longitudinal suppleness. The other possibility is that your horse is not supple over the topline to begin with. Go back to your warm-up session and check to make sure your horse will allow you access to his topline, as well as willingly bending (see p. 25).

4 **Problem: My horse reacts by stretching with no contact on the reins.**

This is known as a "gravity stretch." The rider just "throws" the reins at the horse, and the horse's head only goes down because it weighs a lot. This is really a rider issue and the rider must be taught the correct aids for this movement.

5 **Problem: My horse's head goes up when I ask for the stretch.**

This horse has not achieved the suppleness necessary to perform his work. The rider needs to go back to the warm-up and work on loosening the horse's topline muscles correctly. Again, this type of horse might benefit from correct longeing (see p. 30).

A final question with regard to the stretchy, chewy circle is: Should the horse be allowed to come behind the vertical or not? This issue is always under discussion among judges. The consensus is that coming behind the vertical while stretching is *not* a problem *as long as you can visualize* the neck being raised into a working frame and the nose in front of the vertical (see fig. 5.1 E, p. 44).

CHAPTER

Leg-Yield

*Riding a leg-yield at the beginning of the warm-up
is the perfect exercise for a horse at any level of training
to test the horse's reaction to your lateral moving
(sideways) aids. Keep in mind that you must always
test your aids or your horse will test you.*

The leg-yield is the first movement called for in dressage tests that asks the horse to move forward and sideways at the same time. Generally, it is helpful to train the turn-on-the-forehand prior to training the leg-yield.

Imperfections and Evasions

Your horse:

1 Drags his haunches.

2 Leads with his shoulders.

3 Lacks "crossing" in his legs.

4 Tilts his head.

5 Changes his tempo.

Before I discuss how to train the turn-on-the-forehand and leg-yield, and then address these imperfections, look at the USEF Rule Book definition for the leg-yield (see sidebar, p. 51).

The leg-yield is part of a pyramid of increasingly difficult movements that require the horse to move both forward and sideways. Here is what you should master at each level of what I call the "Pyramid of Lateral Movements" before progressing to the next level (fig. 6.2):

1 Turn-on-the-forehand
2 Simple leg-yield (on the diagonal)
3 Leg-yield tail-to-wall and head-to-wall
4 Shoulder-in
5 Travers (haunches-in) and renvers (haunches-out)
6 Half-pass

How To Ride and Train

Turn-on-the-Forehand

I prefer to always teach my horses turn-on-the-forehand before introducing the leg-yield. This teaches them to move away from the leg without having any impulsion or forward movement and is the first lesson in the inside-leg-to-outside-rein connection. I use this simple exercise all the way up through the levels to reinforce the horse's reaction to the "move sideways" aid.

Even though it is said that horses doing dressage are only doing what they do by nature, I don't believe I have ever seen a horse running sideways in the pasture, "naturally" performing a half-pass or a leg-yield. I do think that teaching the horse to move sideways and still a bit forward at the same time, which encourages him to cross his legs, requires a bit of time and suppling.

Rider's Aids

When performing a turn-on-the-forehand off your *left* leg, first halt the horse on the rail, with your left hand and leg against the rail.

1 Inside rein: Flexes the horse's poll slightly toward the rail or to the left (the "inside" is in the direction of the lateral bend—in this case, the left).

2 Outside rein: Keeps the horse from walking forward—in other words, keeps the front legs in the same spot.

6.2 The Pyramid of Lateral Movements.

3 Outside leg: This is not necessary behind the girth. You want the horse's hindquarters to step to the right, so you might need to move your outside leg forward toward the shoulder to help support the outside rein and act as a barrier to keep the entire horse from moving to the right.

4 Inside leg: This leg now becomes the lateral moving leg and therefore moves about 3 inches behind the girth. This is the active leg.

5 Seat: Sit in the middle of the saddle.

With the horse halted next to the wall, flex him slightly in the direction of the wall. Use your leg (the one closest to the wall) just behind the girth and, with a gentle pressure, ask the horse to move one step *sideways*. The opposite rein (the one furthest from the wall) will be the "Whoa" rein. If the horse moves *forward*, halt again. He must understand that the outside rein says "Stop. Don't move forward." Reinforce this aid and then "give"—let the horse stand a few seconds. Then ask the horse to move sideways again, away from the leg nearest the wall.

Walk forward a few steps and repeat the movement. Always make sure the horse is equally responsive off each leg. Also, be sure to allow an "action/reaction" with your aids. In other words, when you use your lateral moving leg (action) the horse should quickly step away from it (reaction). This is followed by the reward (praising, petting the neck,

Half-Pass

Travers/Renvers

Shoulder-In

Leg-Yield Tail-to-Wall and Head-to-Wall

Simple Leg-Yield

Turn-on-the-Forehand

sugar, voice, relaxing aids). Do not allow the horse to just do the exercise on his own without your aids.

Turn-on-the-forehand is also the beginning of the lateral bending aids. The "dining car" and the "caboose" of your choo-choo train will move outward away from the leg. Later, when you ask the horse to bend correctly, your outside leg behind the girth will "catch" the caboose. For now, allow both "cars" to move out!

Leg-Yield

Once the horse understands the turn-on-the-forehand, you can begin to sequentially train the *three* types of leg-yield:

1 On a diagonal line
2 Tail-to-wall
3 Head-to-wall

On a Diagonal Line

Rider's Aids

Begin by leg-yielding off the left leg to the right, away from the wall. Note that the horse's left side is his "inside" since his poll is flexed slightly toward the wall. The horse is on four tracks, which means that if you stand in front of the horse, you can see all four of his legs.

1 Inside rein: Keeps the horse flexed in the poll slightly to the left.

2 Outside rein: Controls the speed as well as helps to support the horse's balance by not allowing him to fall on the outside shoulder.

USEF Rule Book
LEG-YIELD

The horse is almost straight, except for a slight flexion at the poll away from the direction in which he moves, so that the rider is just able to see the eyebrow and nostril on the inside. The inside legs pass and cross in front of the outside legs. Leg-yielding should be included in the training of the horse before he is ready for collected work. Later on, together with the more advanced movement shoulder-in, it is the best means of making a horse supple, loose and unconstrained for the benefit of the freedom, elasticity and regularity of his gaits and the harmony, lightness and ease of his movements.

Leg-yielding can be performed on the diagonal in which case the horse should be as close as possible parallel to the long sides of the arena although the forehand should be slightly in advance of the quarters. It can also be performed along the wall in which case the horse should be at an angle of about 35 degrees to the direction in which the horse is moving (figs. 6.1 A & B).

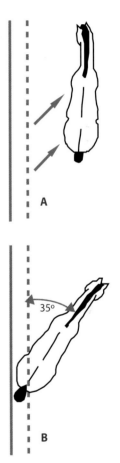

6.1 A & B Leg-yield on the diagonal (A) and along the wall (B). Note that leg-yield along the wall can be either tail-to-wall or head-to-wall (see p. 53).

3 Inside leg: In this direction, your left leg is the lateral moving leg, positioned 3 inches behind the girth. This is also the active leg.

4 Outside leg: You may use the outside leg (in this direction, your right leg) behind the girth when the horse's haunches are leading. Use this leg near the shoulder to help support the outside rein when the horse is falling over the outside shoulder. And, when the horse is going sideways *too* much, you can use this leg as the active leg for a few strides in order to encourage the horse to move more forward and less sideways.

5 Seat: Sit in the direction of travel—in this case, to the right.

Here, the horse's body stays *parallel to the wall.* This is the easiest way to begin the leg-yielding as it requires the least amount of suppleness and crossing of legs. In addition, start by asking the horse to move *toward* the wall from the quarterline so you ask him to do something he likes—most young horses like to stay near the wall, as it gives them confidence and a place to find their balance.

Once the horse is more proficient at leg-yielding and has more lateral reach, the angle of the leg-yield can be increased to add more difficulty. You can then begin to ask to horse to move *away* from the wall toward centerline.

For this first type of leg-yield, turn onto the quarterline and walk straight ahead. Be sure the horse understands he must *go straight first* and that he doesn't begin to fall sideways in anticipation. He must wait for your leg-yield aids. Then, use a little outside rein to "close the front door" a

bit, put your inside leg slightly behind the girth, and move your weight in the direction you want the horse to travel. The movement must be a forward and sideways one. The horse should remain flexed or positioned *away* from the direction of travel, but I find it helpful to change the flexion a bit to keep the horse supple in both reins.

Once the horse understands the aids for the leg-yield on the diagonal, you can move into trot. Again, start from the quarterline or centerline and move *toward* the wall first. When the horse is proficient in this exercise, leg-yield at the trot *away* from the wall to the quarterline or centerline, as well.

The Stair Step Exercise

When you find the horse starts to fall sideways out of balance, there is an exercise to solve this problem. If you review the aids I've described for leg-yielding on the diagonal (see p. 51), you'll see that your outside leg can also be used up near the horse's shoulder. Also note that when one leg sends the horse sideways, your other leg is either the *holding* leg or the *"forward-sending"* leg.

In leg-yield, the horse should be moving away from the *inside* leg ("inside" the bend), but when he falls through the outside rein and leg, you can correct the problem by changing the active leg: use the *outside* leg to send the horse a bit forward and straight ahead. So, go sideways from your inside leg a few strides, and then use your outside leg to send the horse straight ahead for a few more strides. It is what I call the "Stair Step Exercise." The horse needs to learn which leg is in charge of what job.

Tail-to-Wall

Rider's Aids

Begin with a leg-yield on the right rein, moving away from the right leg (inside).

I Inside rein: Leads the forehand off the wall and flexes the poll slightly to the right.

2 Outside rein: Controls the speed as well as helping to support the horse's balance by not allowing him to fall on the outside shoulder.

3 Inside leg: The right leg will be your active and lateral-moving leg—positioned about 3 inches behind the girth.

4 Outside leg: Can be used behind the girth if the haunches fall too much to the left, or may be used closer to the shoulder to help support the outside rein.

5 Seat: Sit in the direction of the movement—in this case, to the left.

Again, this type of leg-yield is on four tracks. The inside hind and inside front legs will cross over the outside legs (see fig. 6.1 B, p. 51). This is a good way to start the "idea" of shoulder-in (a movement on three tracks—see p. 77).

Be sure to start at the walk. You will lose a bit of angle in the trot and of course until the horse becomes supple, you will also lose some impulsion. Be sure to only do about 12 meters at first and then straighten and reward the horse. Don't keep going until you have no impulsion left, or until the horse gets fed up with the exercise.

Head-to-Wall

Rider's Aids

Begin with a leg-yield off your left leg (the "inside" leg).

I Inside rein: As in turn-on-the-forehand (see p. 50), the inside rein will slightly flex the horse's poll to the left. The inside rein also helps the horse understand that the forehand should be positioned to the left, away from the direction of travel.

2 Outside rein: Controls the speed as well as helping to support the horse's balance by not allowing him to fall on the outside shoulder.

3 Inside leg at the girth: This is the left lateral-moving leg, positioned about 3 inches behind the girth. It's the active leg.

4 Outside leg: Can be used behind the girth if the haunches fall too much to the right, or used closer to the shoulder to help support the outside rein.

5 Seat: Sit in the direction of the movement—in this case, to the right.

This type of leg-yield is also on four tracks. The horse's head and shoulders face the wall and the outside front and outside hind legs cross over the inside legs.

This exercise is the beginning of travers, renvers, and half-pass (see pp. 84, 85, 121). It teaches the horse to displace his hindquarters from your outside leg behind the girth. It also teaches the horse not to throw the "caboose" of your choo-

Applause (real name Rocket Launcher) was an unbroken three-year-old purchased by me as my first "really good horse." He was 16.3 hands and a half-brother to Bruce Davidson's famous event horse, J.J. Babu. Applause finished in twenty-first place in the USDF Horse of the Year awards at First Level one year. Little did I know that his registered name was actually a fitting one.

Our early training on the longe line went smoothly. However, it turns out Applause was a bit cold-backed. Once he was mounted, he would either quietly walk forward or start bucking like a saddle bronco. Even having someone lead me forward wasn't safe— at least for the person trying to lead him. You could never really tell which decision he would make. I remember not

really wanting to get on…I had to just hope he would outgrow the habit, which he did, thankfully. And I never did hit the dirt!

Our next obstacle was leg-yield. I was out at Keenridge preparing for the Regional Championships, and in a lesson, Hilda Gurney thought it was time for Applause to learn head-to-wall leg-yield. My horse was not happy with the idea of crossing his hind legs and found his family eventing history handy as he jumped out of the dressage ring and raced through the walnut orchard. I told Hilda that head-to-wall really should be taught with an actual wall in front of the horse…not an 18-inch fence.

6.3 Here I am on Applause, a young horse I trained. During one early lesson he decided leg-yielding head-to-wall did not hold his interest!

choo train to the outside of the circle when asking for lateral bending.

In this exercise it is important for you to move your weight into the direction of travel. This aid will then be established when you add bend in the more difficult lateral exercises. The horse must move away from your leg, under your weight.

JUDGING TIP

The difference between a "7" and a "10" in leg-yield in a test is that while both horses go from Point A to Point B correctly, the horse that receives the higher score takes fewer strides to get there. Later in training you can use the leg-yield to increase the lateral reach in the half-pass.

Cures and Solutions

1 Problem: My horse drags his haunches.

This is usually a lack of responsiveness to your lateral-moving leg aid. Go back to turn-on-the-forehand (see p. 50) and use your whip if you need to reinforce your leg aid. The horse must answer your quick and light aid to be successful later in the half-pass.

2 Problem: My horse leads with his shoulders.

This is a bit like when the horse drags his haunches (see above). Remember, once the horse is leading with the shoulders, you cannot make his hind legs go faster. You will need to slow the shoulders down. You can stop going sideways for a few strides and get your alignment (see the

Stair Step Exercise on p. 52). You can also counter-flex the horse a bit in the direction you are going. This will help "stand up" the outside shoulder.

3 Problem: My horse lacks "crossing" in his legs.

As mentioned in the Judge's Tip at left, the difference between a high score and a modest score from the judge is really the amount of lateral reach the horse can show. From Point A to Point B, your horse may be able to do it in ten steps, but another can do it in eight steps. Some horses, by nature, have quite a lot of lateral reach—but since the horses reading this book are *not* perfect, they will need a bit of work here!

You may have to feel that you are actually pushing the horse sideways out of balance in order to increase his lateral reach. The horse must really open up the angles of his shoulders. Don't ride leg-yield at home as you would at a show. Your job in training is to raise your standards and develop more lateral reach and suppleness than you would need in competition. If your horse can easily do a leg-yield at home with energy and ease, then when it comes to show time and the requirement is easier, he will be a star!

Try counting the number of strides it takes you to get from Point A to Point B. Do this in both directions. One direction will take more strides because the horse will be less supple this way. First, work on this more difficult direction until it matches the other side. Then, when both sides are equal, start working again on improving overall lateral reach. You should be able to take out a stride or two each direction.

4 **Problem: My horse tilts his head.**

This is caused by the horse not staying even in both reins. You will need to change the flexion in the poll to keep the horse supple. Your goal in the show ring is to maintain flexion away from the direction of travel, but in training the suppleness and even contact is more important than maintaining flexion in one direction.

5 **Problem: My horse's tempo changes.**

This is a balance issue. For a high score in the show ring, the tempo must be the same. In schooling, work first toward a good response to the leg aid and good lateral reach. At each show you can then find the exact balance that works for your horse on that particular day.

Begin the Pendulum of Elasticity— Trot and Canter Lengthenings

*Make sure you don't make the horse afraid of the whip.
It is an important aid for this part of your training.*

The Pendulum of Elasticity

This chapter deals with the gymnastic muscle development and strength your horse will need as he moves up the levels. You must first start the horse within his comfort zone and make sure you have developed his working or natural gaits in the correct way using the Classical Training Pyramid (see p. 11).

What a lot of riders do not understand is that the horse has natural gaits, some more expressive, balanced, and ground-covering than others. However, no matter how gifted your horse may be, you still must be able to develop muscle and strength in order to create the "paces" that are needed at the upper levels.

What are paces? These are the different types of trot, for example. The *working trot* is the natural gait. The *lengthened stride* at trot (see USEF description in sidebar, p.59), the *collected trot, medium trot,* and *extended trot* are all paces within the gait of trot. *Piaffe* and *passage* are also within the trot rhythm, but have a different quality and tempo.

The same process applies to the canter, where the horse must first learn to *lengthen* then proceed on to *medium* and *extended canters*. The collected canter, *"very collected"* canter, and *pirouette* canter are also canter, and are also developed through correct gymnastic training.

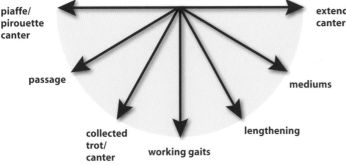

piaffe/
pirouette
canter

passage

collected
trot/
canter

working gaits

lengthening

mediums

extended trot/
canter

7.1 The Pendulum of Elasticity, beginning in the middle with the pendulum hanging straight down—your horse's working gaits. As you swing left you work up through the collected trot and canter, the passage, to the piaffe and pirouette canter, and as you swing right you progress through lengthenings, medium trot and canter, to extended trot and canter.

Now, I'll discuss the "Pendulum of Elasticity," which I hope will help you understand the different paces you need to develop and how to develop them. Without collection, there cannot be extension. Look at the drawing of the pendulum on this page (fig. 7.1). Remember, some horses are more talented, but *all* horses need to work on this pendulum in order to progress successfully up the levels.

USEF Rule Book
LENGTHENING OF STRIDE

In some tests, "lengthening of stride" is required. This is a variation between the working and medium trot (or canter), in which a horse's training is not developed enough for medium trot (or canter).

When the pendulum is hanging straight down, we'll say that is where Mother Nature has put this horse's working gaits. As you begin gymnastic training (approximately when a horse can score about 65 percent in a USEF Training Level Test) you will slowly start to swing this pendulum. As you swing slightly to the *left,* you move slowly to collection, or shorter and higher strides. As you then swing slightly to the *right,* you'll move slowly to the lengthenings in trot and canter (longer more ground-covering strides).

Remember, I said the horse must develop his topline and muscles in the right way. Think of how a long-distance runner's body looks compared to a weight lifter. The event horse should look more like the long-distance runner as the demands of the sport are quite different from those of Grand Prix dressage. Our Grand Prix athlete looks like a weight lifter, with good development of topline muscles.

Working on this pendulum every day as part of your training will not only help develop the correct muscles but also help the horse become more responsive to your forward-driving aids and your collecting halt-halts.

At First Level, the pendulum only swings a tiny bit. It goes to the left for the trot, which will have to become a bit more balanced in order to perform the transition back from the lengthenings, the 10-meter circle, and to be able to go more into the corners. The pendulum goes to the right in order to perform the trot and canter lengthenings.

As you progress up the ladder of the levels, you can see how the pendulum will need to swing more to the left and to the right as the different paces are incorporated into the training.

Required Gaits and Paces in Dressage Tests

Training Level
- Working trot
- Medium walk/free walk
- Working canter

(One trot, one canter, two walks.)

First Level
- Working trot/lengthenings
- Medium walk/free walk
- Working canter/lengthenings
- Transitions

(Two trots, two canters, two walks, transitions to and from trot/canter lengthenings.)

Second Level
- Collected trot/medium trot
- Medium walk/free walk
- Collected canter/medium canter
- Transitions

(Two trots, two canters, two walks, transitions all with uphill tendency to and from trot/canter mediums.)

Third Level
- Collected trot/medium trot/ extended trot
- Medium walk/extended walk
- Collected canter/medium canter/extended canter
- Transitions

(Three trots, two walks, three canters, transitions all with collection and carrying power between collected trot/medium trot, collected trot/extended trot, collected canter/medium canter, collected canter/ extended canter.)

Fourth Level
- Collected trot/medium trot/ extended trot
- Collected walk/extended walk
- "Very collected" canter/ collected canter/medium canter/extended canter
- Transitions

(Three trots, two walks, four canters, transitions all with increased collection and carrying power between collected trot/medium trot, collected trot/ extended trot, collected canter/ medium canter, collected canter/extended canter, collected canter/very collected canter.)

Prix St. Georges/Intermediate I (Small Tour)
- Collected trot/medium trot/ extended trot
- Collected walk/extended walk
- Pirouette canter/collected canter/medium canter/ extended canter
- Transitions

(Three trots, two walks, four canters, transitions with established balance and suppleness to easily shift between the paces. Additional transition from collected canter/pirouette canter.)

Intermediate II/Grand Prix (Big Tour)
- Piaffe/passage/transitions
- Collected trot/medium trot/ extended trot
- Collected walk/extended walk
- Pirouette canter/collected canter/medium canter/ extended canter
- Transitions

(Six trots, two walks, four canters, transitions all with harmony, athleticism, suppleness. Additional transitions walk/piaffe, piaffe/ passage, passage/piaffe.)

7.2 Michelle Albertus riding Troy shows the self-carriage required in collected trot.

Your horse becomes stronger and more elastic in his gaits as he is able to transition from the working to the collected and extended gaits. The supreme evidence of this elasticity, for example, is demonstrated by Grand Prix riders and their horses as they transition directly from extended canter into a lovely and balanced canter pirouette in their freestyles. Steffen Peters and Ravel demonstrate this in their freestyle with a wonderful and difficult transition from extended trot to piaffe to extended walk.

Recall that in order to show above Training Level, you need to be able to develop the horse's gaits in the various paces required in the tests.

You can find a list of the various gaits and paces each level will require in the sidebar on p. 59.

Moving Toward Collection

As you move toward collection, remember that everything you take away in length you should add in height. So the extended gaits are those that go the most *over* the ground. They also lose some of their height as they have maximum groundcover. The passage is the trot that has the most height but has less groundcover than the medium trot.

This concept is very important, as many riders think that collected trot is only a shortened, slower version of working trot. Collected trot will have a shorter stride, *but* it will also require the horse to *bend the hind legs more actively*, and will have a bit more *power, lift,* and *expression* than the working trot. My students are often surprised when I say "There, that is your collected trot!" They are amazed and are really thinking that the trot feels a whole lot like medium! I also tell them that if the collected trot feels "divine," and it is easy to sit, it is no doubt wrong.

Another important point to remember is that the pendulum can only swing equally in both directions. So for our purpose, you will only have as much extension as you have collection. Extension is never trained by running the horse across the diagonal over and over again.

This strength (or pendulum) training should start in the horse's fourth or fifth year or as soon as he has mastered the exercises in Training Level.

How to Ride and Train

Pendulum Training: Beginning Half-Steps

What are half-steps? These are the slightly shorter and higher (or more active, quicker tempo) strides that you need to develop in order to get the pendulum swinging more to the left. Remember, if you can move the pendulum more to the left, it will also move more to the right. You are now at the point where a medium trot and canter are going to be required, as well as a collected trot and canter. To accomplish this, the horse will need more strength.

7.3 The Trakehner stallion Raubritter, owned by Capricorn Farms, and I demonstrate medium trot.

These half-steps can be used in many ways: in a corner; prior to a medium trot; and after a medium trot to show a clear, downward transition. Remember that the pendulum is a gradual movement, so allow your horse a few strides to collect and a few strides to develop the lengthening. As he gets stronger you will be able to make

7.4 Medium canter shown by Gwen Blake and Tjesse 400.

7.5 J. J. Tate works with Mary Hanneman from the ground to help encourage Phoebus to use his hind legs in a better way—a tap on the hind legs from the whip, along with a cluck from the ground person and a brush from the rider's legs encourages him to increase the activity and speed up the tempo of the hind legs.

quicker and more prompt transitions without losing suppleness or rhythm, which is a common problem in the trot.

Remember you train the horse via association. You start with the longe line when you use your voice aids to get a reaction. Then when you mount, you use your voice as well as your body aids for the same aid so the horse can associate one with the other.

First, I try this with the horse in the cross-ties. I take a dressage whip (a longer driving-type whip might be a good idea if your horse is "kicky") and tap the horse on the hock. I use a light aid first, then a stronger tap if nothing happens. Once the horse lifts the leg, I pat him and give him some

sugar. I repeat this several times with both hind legs. After about a week, the horse should be lifting both legs up in the air for an equal amount of time with a little tap and have no tension as a result of this exercise.

Since horses are stronger on one hind leg and want to have a longer suspension phase on one leg or the other, the next exercise is equally as important.

I now ask the horse to lift the leg with the whip and then use the whip on the back of the cannon bone to encourage the horse to hold this leg up in the air. I repeat with the other hind leg. You will find the horse will like standing longer on one hind leg or the other. Keep working until you can have the horse hold both legs up in the air for an equal amount of time.

Next, go into the ring. With a rider now in the saddle, repeat the exercise using a little clucking in addition to the whip. I ask the rider to put her legs back and lightly brush the horse's sides as I cluck. Only ask for a quick response of several steps. Then, give lots of sugar. Don't get greedy and ask for too much. The most important part of the exercise is the horse's reaction. You don't want to "whip train" your horse so that by the time you reach piaffe, he will only perform the movement with use of the whip.

Some horses learn this better out of the walk, others out of the trot. You may have to experiment to find the right way to teach your horse. You can also try tapping lightly on his croup, or on top of his tail; sometimes just on top of the gaskin is also effective. If your horse stops and plants his front legs and bounces his croup up and down you are not doing the exercise correctly. Stop. Get help.

The idea at this juncture is not to teach a finished piaffe but merely to teach a *reaction* from the horse that will help "mature" the half-halt. Your goal is to have a horse that understands that the "front door" will be closing momentarily, but that the hind legs are going to get quicker and more active at the same moment. In other words, we are working our pendulum.

Developing the Canter

Now you will need to address how to work on your pendulum in canter. You may find that your horse will have more talent or will understand the collection better in either the trot or canter. Don't worry, this is normal. Use the gait he prefers to

help him understand and strengthen his muscles. Then take your time to teach him what you want with the other gait.

How will you use this new canter you'll have access to? Again, use it in the corners, before and after your lengthening. Remember how a pendulum works. You cannot expect the horse to move in one stride from your slightly more collected canter to a big lengthening and come back in one stride. Think of allowing the horse a few strides to "develop" the lengthening—sort of like a spring slowly uncoiling. Then allow him a few strides to come back, or to recoil the spring.

As the horse gains strength and confidence, your transitions will become quicker and more prompt without being abrupt or stiff.

Losing the lead behind at the end of a lengthening or medium is a common problem because the rider is not thinking about how a pendulum works. Take your time. Create confidence within your horse. Work in his comfort zone.

In my experience, two exercises most helpful in collecting the canter are the simple changes of lead and the counter-canter. When you begin collection, most horses do not understand a half-halt to collect the canter; they just think it is an aid to trot.

Simple Changes

When you work with the simple changes, expect that you will have a few trot steps at the beginning. You must make it clear to the horse, however, that you want walk. So, even if you have a trot step, make sure you *walk*. Do not let the horse just keep trotting as then he will think he is doing the right thing.

Using 10-meter circles will help you col-

Lago was a five-year-old Holsteiner gelding that was purchased for me by my sponsor, Dr. Dennis Law. I had heard that in Europe, trainers tried the piaffe, passage, and changes with every young horse, and if one movement proved difficult they would sell the horse to the United States! This was certainly the case with Lago.

He was an exceptional horse with amazing balance and three good gaits. Hilda Gurney saw him and said, "Well, if he isn't Horse of the Year, it won't be the horse's fault!" Lago won many Rocky Mountain, Regional, and USDF National awards, from First Level through Grand Prix, in his career. He was the first Grand Prix horse I trained myself, and I loved him dearly, even with his quirks.

The first quirk I discovered was his fear of a person with the whip on the ground. Dianna Mukpo (the first woman to ever be accepted by the Spanish Riding School) was training at Table Mountain Ranch in Golden, Colorado, the same time I was. She and I used each other as a ground person. We decided it was time to begin the half-steps with Lago. Dianna walked up behind me with a whip—and Lago was in the next county at warp speed.

It took two weeks with Lago in a surcingle and side reins, and me in front with a stud chain and lead line, for him to finally relax. Dianna would touch him with the whip, and we would stop and give him sugar. Lago eventually accepted Dianna, but it took a while longer for him to trust men on the ground.

Lago also was a bit learning-challenged with the flying changes, in one direction only. I had lessons from the best around and one side was always half-a-stride late. Then, suddenly one day it was clean and there was never a problem from that day forward. I wish I knew what finally got through to him!

7.6 Here I am on Lago, a horse with great balance, three good gaits, and a great fear of the whip.

lect and shorten the horse's canter stride. This allows the horse to take more weight on the hind leg and shorten the base of support, which makes it easier to walk. A little haunches-in (travers) on the circle also will help. I am also more than happy to use my voice aids again and say "Whoa" or the "Brrrr" noise. Make sure you take time in the walk to allow the horse to relax. Establish the walk. Don't be in a hurry to get the upward transition back to the canter. For collecting the canter it is the downward transition that will help you create a collecting half-halt in canter.

Counter-Canter

The counter-canter will help the horse achieve a better balance and more suppleness. Work a little counter-canter, then come across the

diagonal and ask for the walk. If your counter-canter is correct, you should feel more collection and balance as a result.

Getting the Horse to "Sit"

You can also start a little of the "very collected" also known as "pirouette" canter on a circle by pushing the haunches in for a few strides. This will help the horse take more weight on the inside hind leg. If you feel the canter getting too short or "hoppy," then go forward again. The medium canter will help put the inside hind leg back under the center of gravity. The horse must learn that you want him to "sit," not just shorten and bounce up and down.

In the beginning of this work, the tempo of the canter may well slow down. This happens because the horse is spending more time on the inside hind leg. Accept this for a while until the horse gets stronger and really understands the aid. Once he is stronger, you can ask for a bit more activity from the hind legs while he sits.

Imperfections and Evasions

Your horse:

1 Has no natural lengthening.
2 Runs onto his forehand.
3 Takes shorter, faster strides.
4 Scores poorly on the transitions to and from or within the gaits and paces on tests.
5 Travels wide behind.
6 Breaks into canter during a trot lengthening.

Cures and Solutions

Problem: My horse has no natural lengthening.

To develop a trot lengthening, it is helpful to work this type of horse over ground poles first and then raised cavalletti. With certain breeds you may have to realize you will never get more than a "7" on a lengthening in trot or canter. The important information here is to realize this and not try for a "10" and make the score a "4" because you have created balance and regularity issues (regularity implies there is no unevenness in the gaits).

If you can work with in-hand schooling, you should be able to teach your horse to lengthen a bit and show more freedom. Sometimes, this is all you can do. You may not be able to have increased groundcover without the horse falling out of balance or "running." This groundcover is a function of elasticity and airtime. If your horse does not have this by nature, you need to accept his limitations.

For the canter lengthening, I begin on a 20-meter circle. It is helpful as a circle never "runs out" (ends), and the horse stays in a better balance than on a long side of the arena. I canter the horse a little forward on the open end (the end toward the middle of the arena) of the circle and then transition back to working canter on the closed end (the end against the wall). Some horses have much more scope in the canter and you can expect better results here, especially if there is a lot of Thoroughbred blood in your horse. Keep working with the collecting exercises described earlier (see p. 61). Remember, the more collection you have, the more extension you can show. You need to be able to show a clear difference between the paces.

2 Problem: My horse runs onto his forehand when I ask him to lengthen.

This can be either a strength issue or a straightness issue. Make sure you are not trying to do too many steps of either trot or canter lengthening. The pendulum work is the best exercise I know to help strengthen your horse. You will need to keep this in mind as you move up the levels. Each level requires more strength and balance. The pendulum work will never end; it is an ongoing process.

Be careful not to "throw your horse away" in front by releasing all contact on the reins. I know the test does say you should lengthen the frame. I am pleased that the test-writing committee finally made a distinction here in the directives from "modest lengthening to utmost lengthening" of the frame. At First Level, in my opinion, few horses can lengthen the frame without falling on their face. Your horse may need a bit of support from you in the beginning. Don't be afraid to "help" your horse with his balance through a series of half-halts and releases. Remember, however, you cannot hold him up and become the horse's "fifth leg." Eventually the horse must use his own muscles to hold himself up, not yours.

3 Problem: My horse takes shorter, faster strides when I ask him to lengthen.

Again, these are due to balance issues, perhaps coupled with the horse's natural way of going. Check again the suppleness of the topline. No horse can stay elastic with a tight back or a short neck. Check the straightness. A crooked horse will run, get wide behind, or break into canter. I recommend you work more with transitions and perhaps cavalletti.

4 Problem: My horse scores poorly on the transitions to and from, or within gaits on tests.

This is a twofold issue. You may be too vague or gradual with the aids. Many riders just coast in and out of transitions and this system does not score well with the judge. If you can collect more, it will look like your lengthenings are greater. I often have students with horses that are a bit limited in their lengthening, but are talented in the collection. So, we show the judge more collection than is needed prior to the lengthening and after the lengthening, which shows a clearer difference between the paces. Perhaps the lengthening still only scores a "6" or "7," but the transitions are usually scored a "7" or "8," as judges are used to see the "coasting" version. So, when judges see a real attempt to prepare the horse and bring the horse back, they give high marks!

JUDGING TIP

There must be a relationship between the transitions and what happens in between. Do not expect an "8" on transitions if you only score a "4" on the lengthening. The judge will give you credit for what happens either before or after a mistake, however. So, if in the test, for example, your horse breaks into a few canter strides, quickly come back and try to show a few strides of trot lengthening.

5   Problem: My horse travels wide behind.

This happens often with stallions and short-coupled horses like Arabians. When the horse goes wide behind, it is because he cannot get his front legs out of the way in time for the hind legs to step through. The horse is smart enough to not want to hit himself. First, make sure your horse is not out of balance or falling on his shoulders. You may have to ask a bit less and keep the horse in a better balance for a while until he gets stronger. Once the horse learns this habit, it is not easy to get rid of it, so be careful in the beginning of your training.

6   Problem: My horse breaks into canter during trot lengthenings.

This is usually a crookedness, line-of-travel issue. The horse comes out of the corner, drifting in one direction. When more impulsion is added, the balance is lost, so he falls into canter. Let's say your horse leans into your left leg. If you approach the diagonal on the left rein, you will have better luck, as you have the ability in the corner to bend and move the horse more off your inside leg. I would suspect he canters more often when coming out of the corner on the right rein. If you bend him too much right and move him more off your right leg, you are just pushing him more into the left side. Then he is drifting left already on the diagonal so it is easy for him to canter.

Here, the correction is simple: When approaching from the right rein, in the corner, counterflex the horse and move him off your outside leg. In other words, he must stand up or be upright as you come onto the diagonal line.

JUDGING TIP

Remember, at First Level, if you choose to post the lengthening trot, you do not change your posting diagonal at X. I would also start posting in the corner if you have been sitting rather than surprising the horse once he is on the diagonal. It is too easy to cause a balance issue.

CHAPTER

8

The Walk

*The rider must create a reason
for the horse to let go.*

You may be surprised to find a separate chapter on the walk in this book. Perhaps, like many riders, you have been told that the walk is the easiest gait to ruin. While this is true, unfortunately, rather than learn how to train the walk correctly, many riders avoid the walk altogether and then wonder why they get low scores in their dressage tests. The walk is an important part of dressage, not simply a "vacation" between the trot and canter.

There are a number of common problems the not-so-perfect horse can be prone to in the walk, which may have discouraged you from learning how to train this important gait.

Imperfections and Evasions

Your horse:

1 Has rhythm issues, ranging from minor to severe.

2 Has a stiff topline.

3 Curls up.

4 Jogs or exhibits mental tension.

5 Likes to be a "tourist."

6 Lacks suppleness in transitions to and from the paces of the walk.

7 Lacks freedom of the shoulders or has limited overstep.

I'll talk about how to overcome these challenges later in this chapter (see p. 74), but first let's discuss the variations of walk you will be asked to perform in your dressage tests as you move up the levels.

How to Ride and Train

Free Walk
Let's start with the free walk. This is required in Training, First, and Second Levels. Review how the USEF rule book defines it (see sidebar, p. 71).

Rider's Aids

It is important here to again reiterate the walk aids. As a rider, you will feel how the horse, by nature, puts you on alternating seat bones. You need to feel his belly move sideways into your leg; this is the time for you to use your calf to energize the walk.

So the aids are: alternating legs, alternating seat bones. The horse must know this is the walk aid. It will help with the horse's anticipation for transitions; prevent him from jogging during the walk work; and keep him from anticipating the next upward transition.

Remember, the walk has no suspension so it has no impulsion. You must not try to "drive" the horse forward with your seat at walk, because this can cause rhythm problems.

Start on a Circle

Start your walk on a long rein on a circle, and wait until the horse relaxes. Then, to help him stretch more over the back, use this exercise. Take the inside rein, bend, release, bend, release. Create a reason for the horse to "let go." The horse should release the topline as you use these aids. When you shorten the reins to medium walk, also start with submission to the inside bending rein and a little leg-yield from the inside leg. Shorten the inside rein first, and then the outside. Think of this exercise as the "stretchy chewy" circle (see p. 43), but at walk.

In every dressage test, the free walk finishes with a change of direction. Too many riders pick up both reins at the same time, which causes the horse to stiffen in the transition. Work your transitions from free walk to medium walk on a circle

until the horse will stay supple and relaxed. You want your free walk to feel like the "going home" walk when your horse knows he is headed back to the barn after a workout or a trail ride.

JUDGING TIP

The judge will have two scores in mind when judging the free walk. The first has to do with the rhythm and what the legs are doing. Is there *reach?* Is there *freedom of the shoulders?* Does the horse demonstrate *overtracking* and *ground cover?* Is the horse in a relaxed state of mind?

The second score will be the topline. The horse should be walking "through" his back. Think of a chicken in the barnyard: The horse should move or undulate the topline with every stride. Eric Lette once said that a good walk should look like Marilyn Monroe from behind. Another visual is to think about a "panther-like" walk and body movement.

When the rider holds the horse's neck down, the topline will become still and not move. I think both judges and riders need to be cautious of the comment "needs more stretch." This comment tells the rider to try and make the neck lower, sometimes by holding it down, and this just lowers her score even more.

If the poll is at the same height or slightly lower than the withers, for me, this is low enough. Some judges like the nose to be level with the elbow. What is more important to me is how well the horse uses the topline and back in the walk.

I say, *give the reins;* riders, just stop pulling so hard. You must ask for a reaction and then be able to give and reward the horse. Following a supple topline is the most important aspect of the free

USEF Rule Book

FREE WALK

The free walk is a pace of relaxation in which the horse is allowed complete freedom to lower and stretch out his head and neck. The degree of ground cover and length of strides, with hind feet stepping clearly in front of the footprints of the front feet, are essential to the quality of the free walk.

MEDIUM WALK

A clear, regular and unconstrained walk of moderate lengthening. The horse, remaining "on the bit," walks energetically but relaxed with even and determined steps, the hind feet touching the ground in front of the hoof prints of the forefeet. The rider maintains a light, soft and steady contact with the mouth, allowing the natural movement of the head and neck.

COLLECTED WALK

The horse, remains "on the bit," moves resolutely forward, with its neck raised and arched and showing a clear self-carriage. The head approaches the vertical position and a light contact is maintained with the mouth. The hind legs are engaged with good hock action. The gait should remain marching and vigorous, the feet being placed in regular sequence. The steps cover less ground and are higher than at the medium walk, because all the joints bend more markedly. The collected walk is shorter than the medium walk, although showing greater activity.

EXTENDED WALK

The horse covers as much ground as possible, without haste and without losing the regularity of the steps. The hind feet touch the ground clearly in front of the hoof prints of the forefeet. The rider allows the horse to stretch out the head and neck (forward and downward) without losing contact with the mouth and control of the poll. The nose must be clearly in front of the vertical.

STRETCHING ON A LONG REIN

This exercise gives a clear impression of the "throughness" of the horse and proves its balance, suppleness, obedience, and relaxation. In order to execute the exercise "stretching on a long rein" correctly, the rider must lengthen the reins as the horse stretches gradually forward and downward. As the neck stretches forward and downward, the mouth should reach more or less to the horizontal line corresponding with the point of the shoulder. An elastic and consistent contact with the rider's hands must be maintained. The gait must maintain its rhythm, and the horse should remain light in the shoulders with the hind legs well engaged. During the retake of the reins the horse must accept the contact without resistance in the mouth or poll.

and extended walk. Do not block the topline with the contact. Do not try to "hold" the horse's head down as this only decreases the groundcover.

You should free walk several times in your workouts. The horse must relax. Keep walking until the horse *does* relax. Then he will learn what to do when you release the reins.

If your horse tends to wander, put a couple of ground poles along the diagonal line making a path where he must walk either between two poles or along one pole like when he is on the rail. This will help him understand that he must still stay between your leg aids, even if you have little or no contact.

Medium Walk

Again, let's turn to the USEF Rule Book to understand the definition of *medium walk* (see sidebar). Medium walk is required in Training, First, Second, and Third Levels.

The medium walk used to be called the "working" walk: it is the same walk but with a different name. The medium walk is the first walk you ask for that requires contact. If you are not elastic with the reins, the horse will stiffen against the contact and problems begin.

Some phrases that come to mind that *do not* reflect a correct medium walk are:

1 The funeral-procession walk.
2 The horse-leaves-a-"slime"-trail walk.
3 The walking saunter.

How does the horse walk? Does he walk with march? With purpose? Often the horse's free walk is quite good, but when the rider takes the contact, the horse slows down.

The best exercise to work on the medium walk is to go back to your 20-meter circle (see p. 70). Do a lot of transitions from free walk to medium walk. Use your bending to help the suppleness. Take up the inside rein first and push the horse a bit sideways as you do this. If the horse slows down, make your point with your leg, and then leave him alone.

Ground poles are also very helpful. You can shorten or lengthen the distance between the poles. Use longer distances for horses that shorten their stride too much and shorter distances for horses that refuse to become more compact in their stride. The poles also ask the horse to look down and this should help his topline start to loosen and move.

The key to any of the walk exercises is that if you feel rhythm issues or stiffness in the topline, stop. Go back and reestablish these two important aspects of the walk.

Collected Walk

The *collected walk* is difficult and requires a lot of suppleness. It really shows the judge whether the training has been correct up to this point. For this reason, collected walk is not required until Fourth Level. In the FEI levels, collected walk often has a double co-efficient—the USEF Rule Book offers guidance for the collected walk (see sidebar, p. 71).

This walk needs to have the neck up and raised and arched, with the walk steps becoming more active and elevated. Remember, earlier I said collection is not just a shorter stride, but also a *more active* stride. Think of the horse looking "proud" through the topline. When the walk is active enough, you should be able to make quick and uphill transitions to trot and canter.

JUDGING TIP

This walk is interesting for me as a judge. I do not think judges use the scale enough here. The usual score seems to be "6" or "7" or perhaps a "5" with rhythm issues or a "4" for a completely lateral walk. I rarely see "8" and above given for the collected walk. I think perhaps riders are not sure what this walk should look like. Usually my comments are that it "looks like medium walk," "needs higher, more active steps," or "the frame is too long and low."

Extended Walk

Finally, *extended walk* is required in Third Level and above. The USEF Rule Book provides this definition of the extended walk (see sidebar, p. 71).

Extended walk should be ridden like free walk with contact. The difference is that in free walk the reins can be loose or long. In extended walk you need contact and the poll should be controlled. The poll is again about the same height or a bit lower than the withers. The topline must move and the horse must walk through the back. Overstep is required.

JUDGING TIP

Again, the score for this movement is an average of the topline and the legs, just as in free walk. A horse with a good topline ("8") and average leg movement ("6") can still score a "7" for the movement. If your horse is limited in the areas of groundcover or freedom of reach, it is imperative that you work on a correct topline.

Stretching on a Long Rein

The USEF Rule Book offers one final movement in walk, that of stretching on a long rein. This movement is not required per se at any level in the walk, as free walk allows the rider to perform the exercise without any contact. However, the free walk also allows the contact to be maintained, in which case this is a good movement to practice if your horse gets too "touristy" in the free walk with no contact.

This exercise is shown at the trot in the "stretch circle" in both Training and First Levels.

Working on this movement will also improve your extended walk as this movement requires the contact to be maintained. (See the sidebar on p. 71 for the USEF description of this useful exercise.)

This exercise is the proof of correct riding. When your horse is willing to "chew the reins" forward and downward, you can be fairly certain that you have achieved the desirable "throughness" over the topline that accompanies proper relaxation, rhythm, and contact. Think of the "stretchy-chewy" circle in trot (see p. 45). This is the same exercise but in walk.

I would use stretching on a long rein (which will also improve the free walk and the extended walk) many times during your training sessions: first, to encourage the horse to relax and also as a reward for a job well done. You don't want to keep your horse "up" in a collected frame for long periods of time. This frame requires a lot of strength from a horse, and he can easily get tired, which usually causes resistance and loss of suppleness. Even a Grand Prix test only lasts seven minutes. Allowing the horse to stretch and relax his topline muscles after collected work is a necessary part of your training. Remember, you need to *train* the walk!

Cures and Solutions

| **Problem: My horse has rhythm problems, from minor to severe.**

If there is some tension, you may have a few jog steps. Your horse may show a few unclear strides. There may be only a few lateral—or tending to lateral—strides. The worse case is that the rhythm becomes lateral 100 percent of the time.

If you have rhythm issues in medium walk, first check the suppleness of the topline. If the horse is stiff or tense, you have a problem. Work on many transitions from free walk to medium walk until the horse relaxes. Be sure to use your curved lines and the leg-yielding exercise (see p. 51). Also, walking in a bit of shoulder-in position will be helpful especially with the lateral tendency (see p. 78).

Walking over poles on the ground several times in your training session also helps as the horse will look down at the poles and hopefully relax and stretch his topline. Using ground poles can also help sort out rhythm problems: the horse must take the same size steps each time. It helps to improve shoulder freedom, too. If rhythm problems are caused by tension in the topline, the poles on the ground will require the horse to lower the neck, relax the back, and look down.

Remember that a long, ground-covering walk takes time—the tempo may seem slow to you. If you try to hurry a good walk, you will ruin it. When a rider tries to "push" the big walk and make it quicker, the shoulder of the horse does not have time to elevate and then step forward. So the front leg is hurried stiffly through the stride. This will cause the rhythm to be unclear, or in the worst case scenario, lateral. Try to count the tempo of the walk slowly…1-2-3-4. Riders who have had a horse with a short quick walk or riders with less experience will be more apt to make the mistake of hurrying.

However, if your horse is showing rhythm issues only with a true collected walk frame, but his rhythm is better with a lower, more medium walk-like frame, then by all means go for the *correct rhythm*. Correct rhythm is the main ingredient of dressage. The rider needs to maintain a correct rhythm—in the same tempo—to obtain the highest score. (Note: *Rhythm* refers to the "beats," and the walk must have a clear four-beat rhythm. *Tempo* refers to the repetition of those beats, so a four-beat rhythm can be faster or slower.)

The half-steps (see p. 61) will help with the activity of the hind legs. Most horses with a score of "9" or above in the *free* walk can have trouble with the walk on *contact*. You must be careful not to block the topline or to collect the walk too soon. When you have a problem with the walk, work on it in a shoulder-in position (see p. 78). Push the horse a bit sideways as you work. Make sure you are not making the walk too quick. You will get a better score with the comment "needs more march" than with a walk that has lost the correct rhythm.

JUDGING TIP

Novice judges often tell the rider with a "9" free walk that the walk is too slow. They see a correct rhythm, but think the tempo is too slow. Don't listen to this advice. A "9" walk covers a lot of ground and this takes time. It may seem slow to you as a rider as well, but you must realize that you are not feeling the correct thing. Don't hurry a big walk; you will only ruin it.

Putting some ground poles (three or five or another uneven number so it doesn't look like a jump) somewhere in your arena and walking over them several times during your workout can solve rhythm problems, too. Ground poles are also good for horses that need to lengthen the walk stride or to lower and relax the topline more.

2 Problem: My horse is stiff through the topline.

This can be addressed with lots of walk breaks and patience. You must keep walking until the horse relaxes; don't let him think this break is just a short segue into the next training session. Try lots of circle work, going from medium to free and back, over and over. Work with ground poles (see p. 74). Trail rides are also a good option, if possible.

Personal Story

I bought a three-year-old Hanoverian stallion in Canada named Ali Baba. One of the reasons I loved him was his huge walk. I had never owned a horse with a walk like his! I envisioned all the "9s" I would receive on my dressage tests for the free walk.

Ali came home to Colorado, and I began the process of getting him started under saddle. The first time I rode him for Robert Dover, he asked, "Why did you buy this walk?"

I thought, Hmmmm, I need to tell him? "Robert," I said, "So I could get lots of high scores!"

Robert explained the problems I would have in collecting this kind of walk. Chalk it up to another learning experience for Janet. I was very glad I had Robert's experience on my side as we moved forward with training, however, as it saved me from making mistakes with Ali.

8.1 Ali Baba—I loved his huge walk, but didn't realize it would be a real challenge to collect.

3 **Problem: My horse curls up.**

This is related to being stiff through the topline (see p. 75). Using curved lines, you will be able to lengthen one side of the horse with the bend. This should help. Also ground poles encourage the horse to look down and stretch the neck (see p. 74). Start the distance between the ground poles where it is comfortable for the horse to walk. Then gradually lengthen the distance between the poles so the horse has to make an effort not to hit them.

4 **Problem: My horse jogs or exhibits tension.**

Check yourself to see that you are not carrying tension in your own body or inadvertently squeezing your horse forward. Are you using alternating aids? Is your horse fresh from his stall? If so, you may need to longe him briefly or warm up at the trot and canter before introducing walk. Assuming that your horse is not overly fresh and your aids are correct and you are breathing (*don't hold your breath!*), you may try more walk breaks. Patience is necessary! Take as long as you need to get the horse to relax.

5 **Problem: My horse is a "tourist"—he lacks attention when walking.**

This horse is one that may need more exercises incorporated into his walk work. Vary the flex-ion from inside to outside to inside again in a smooth movement. Practice walking on circles or doing leg-yield—or other lateral exercises if he is already working on these movements. Such exercises will help you gain his attention and can, in fact, be especially useful for the horse that is inattentive because he is nervous or spooky. Make yourself and the work more interesting than what is happening around you.

6 **Problem: My horse lacks suppleness in the transitions to and from the walk.**

Go back and revisit chapter 4 where I discussed up and down transitions (see p. 35). Be sure you are using your half-halts to prepare and balance your horse in preparation for the transitions. Check that your horse can flex easily from inside to outside so that he is listening to each of your aids before you ask for a transition. For a downward transition from trot or canter to walk, think shoulder-fore (see p. 9).

7 **Problem: My horse lacks freedom of the shoulders or has limited overstep.**

"Goose-stepping" or tight shoulders—particularly in collected walk—is due to tension in the topline. Work to supple and change the frame; relaxation is important. If the medium walk is clear, don't collect the walk so much for a while until the horse can relax and stays supple.

Shoulder-In

*If you take care of the basics, the movements
will take care of themselves.*

The shoulder-in is the first lateral movement involving collection that you encounter as you move up the levels. Introduced at Second Level, it is one of the most important movements for you and your horse to master.

Imperfections and Evasions

Your horse:

1 Has too much angle.

2 Has too much bend in his neck.

3 Tilts his head.

4 Has haunches falling out.

5 Tends to let his balance fall to his outside shoulder.

6 Loses cadence and regularity.

7 Loses impulsion.

8 Has haunches falling in off the track.

9 Lacks control and thus the angle of the movement varies.

Before I discuss these problems and their resolution (see p. 80), let's talk a bit about this movement and how to perform it.

History and Benefits

History tells us that the first horseman to use shoulder-in was Antoine de Pluvinel in the seventeenth century. In the eighteenth century, the Duke of Newcastle adapted the movement independently, while François Robichon de la Guérinière first practiced it on a straight line. It is still one of the most useful training movements available to us in dressage today.

First, it allows you to move the horse's shoulders. This is necessary for more advanced collection that requires, among other abilities, the mobility and elevation of the shoulders. If you have ridden at Fourth Level or above, think about the canter zig-zags (see p. 157). This movement requires the mobility of the shoulders. It also allows the rider to displace the shoulders without the horse thinking that he must move in the direction the shoulders are pointed.

Moving the shoulders to the inside is also necessary for the horse to bend correctly (see chapter 2, p. 16). For the official definition, read what the USEF Rule Book has to say (see sidebar).

How to Ride and Train

Rider's Aids

1 Inside leg at the girth: This leg keeps the horse's rib cage to the outside, as well as keeping the horse's inside hind leg active. In harmony with the outside rein, it will keep the line of travel. This leg is the *active* leg for this movement.

2 Outside leg behind the girth: This is a *holding* or *passive* leg. It acts as a barrier to keep the horse's haunches from falling out.

3 Inside rein: This is the *direction* rein or the *positioning* rein. It will lead the shoulders and head and neck to the inside track. It is in charge of lateral suppleness or bending.

4 Outside rein: This rein, in concert with the inside leg, is in charge of the line of travel. This rein also controls the shape and length of the neck, as well as the horse's speed. The outside rein controls the amount of bend. You can have too much "neck bend" or you can also restrict the bend.

5 Seat: There are two schools of thought about the use of the seat bones in the shoulder-in. One is to sit to the inside (on the engaged hind leg). I like to sit in the middle, as I find it helpful to make a clear difference to my horses between the half-pass and shoulder-in aids (see p. 121 for more

about the half-pass). So, if I want to easily move from shoulder-in to half-pass, I only have to sit to the inside and activate my outside leg, and the horse will move into half-pass.

The easiest way to teach the horse the shoulder-in is to start with a leg-yield. While I move the horse away from my left leg to the right, I actually start to bend him and move the shoulders a bit to the left. So I am bending the horse left and moving to the right. Once I hit the rail, I keep the shoulders to the inside for about 12 meters. I find that if I just start a young horse in shoulder-in by trying to move the shoulders to the inside directly out of a corner, he thinks that we are turning and going on the diagonal. The horse is then confused when you give him a big correction with the inside leg and outside rein.

Putting the two movements—leg-yield and shoulder-in—together seems to help the horse's understanding. The leg-yield improves the submission to the inside lateral moving leg. The wall helps the horse understand the change in the line of travel.

Once the horse is more confirmed in the movement, then begin the exercise out of the corner. You can make a 10-meter circle first to establish the bend. I like to push my horse out a bit on the second half of the circle, just to have him think more about my inside leg. Then you can think of your shoulder-in as another quarter circle, but going down the track.

For a young or green horse, do not ask for too much angle or bend at the beginning, or you will make the movement too difficult. Expect the horse to lose some impulsion when first schooling this movement.

With all of the collecting movements, you have to think about them as a process. If I were a figure skater, I would first learn a waltz jump, which only entails coming up on one leg and landing on the other—no full rotation. The next jump would have one full rotation, then two, and then three—if I were good enough. Don't expect your horse to perform a triple axel the first time out! Be realistic.

9.2 Melody Miller on the Swedish Warmblood gelding, Passage, riding shoulder-in.

Remember that shoulder-in is a collecting movement. This means it will also slow your horse down, especially at the beginning. Don't do a shoulder-in for the entire long side of the arena. That would be foolish. Even tests only require the movement down half the long side. Get a good response and leave the exercise while you can still reward the horse.

Cures and Solutions

1 Problem: My horse has too much angle.

This is a control and line-of-travel issue. The horse is working hard to avoid collection by changing the angle. Think of riding your outside hand to the corner of the arena with your inside leg. I find it helpful to look where I am going rather than looking over the horse's ears. If you are doing shoulder-in on the centerline, then ride your outside hand to C. Often, you can help the horse understand that the inside leg and outside rein control the angle by only doing a few steps of shoulder-in, straightening a few strides, and then repeating the shoulder-in.

Using the leg-yield-to-shoulder-in exercise discussed earlier may also be helpful (see p. 79).

2 Problem: My horse has too much bend in his neck.

As a rider, you need to pay more attention to the relationship between your upper body and the horse's shoulders, neck, and head. I have a visual I use called "the gunslinger": imagine you are on Main Street ready to draw your guns in a gunfight with your shoulders square and facing your opponent. It's the same when you are riding a straight line: your horse's shoulders, neck, and ears line up with yours. If you were to draw your guns on a straight line, you should be able to shoot exactly over each of your horse's ears.

In shoulder-in, the rider must turn her shoulders and the horse's shoulders, neck, and ears toward the opposite corner of the arena. Here the gunslinger analogy remains true. You should have a direct line from your shoulder, elbow, and hand to the horses shoulder and ear on each side. If you have too much neck bend, the horse's outside ear will be in the middle of your chest, not in front of your outside shoulder and hand. You either have too much inside rein or are allowing too much neck bend with the outside rein.

3 Problem: My horse tilts his head.

This imperfection is due to a lack of suppleness in the horse's poll. The poll is usually the last piece that becomes supple in a horse. This being said, it is impossible to supple the poll with the neck up in the beginning. Work on poll-suppling exercises (see p. 24) during the warm-up phase of your training session. Sometimes head tilting can be addressed by simply changing the flexion for a few strides and then returning to the correct position.

4 Problem: My horse's haunches fall out.

Again, this is a line-of-travel issue and an "escape" for the horse. It can usually be solved with a reminder from the outside leg in the preparation for the movement. I also find it helpful to do a little head-to-wall leg-yielding (see p. 53) on one long side and then a shoulder-in on the next long side.

You may need to have a bit less displacement of the shoulders for a while until the horse becomes more supple and obedient to the exercise.

5 Problem: My horse falls to his outside shoulder.

This can happen when the horse resists taking the weight on his inside hind leg and uses the outside shoulder to maintain balance, instead. Check this first: Do you have too much neck bend? This will usually result in the balance going to the outside shoulder (see Problem 2, p. 80).

The best exercise I know for correcting this issue is to change from shoulder-in to haunches-out (renvers) for a few strides. When you return to the shoulder-in, you should have the correct balance.

Another way to improve the correctness of the exercise is to reverse direction and ride shoulder-out. This places the front legs on the wall and the hind legs on the inner track. For some reason, horses tend to respond well to this movement and do not seem to want to fall onto the outside shoulder. You can use the shoulder-out to strengthen him and gain more submission before going back in the other direction and riding shoulder-in.

6 Problem: My horse loses cadence and regularity.

This is a simple issue of lack of lateral suppleness. When the judge sees a loss of regularity (purity of gait) in a lateral movement, it does not influence the gait score, but does influence the submission score. You will need to go back and work on bending exercises such as circles, serpentines, and figure eights before adding bending with collection to your training plan.

7 Problem: My horse loses impulsion.

This is normal. Most green or young horses need to slow down a bit to learn something new. Try to go forward first out of the corner and then do a few strides of shoulder-in, straighten, and go forward again. Using a bit of a more-forward working or collected trot will help the horse "think" forward first.

I would not practice movements found in certain tests that ask for several collected exercises in a row. When you are training either a lazy horse or a horse that loses impulsion due to greenness, avoid doing a lot of collected exercises one after the other. Instead, use short diagonals or straight lines with short bursts of lengthening or mediums to help keep the horse active and sharp. Be creative, not boring. Work on reactions. Don't drill.

8 Problem: My horse's haunches fall in off the track.

This horse is really sneaky. He allows you to begin the movement is a good way, happily bringing his forehand off the track. However, he then "cheats" simply by moving his hindquarters slightly in, and is soon just going straight down the second track. Be sure your outside leg is not sending the wrong message. If this is not the issue, then you need to work again to emphasize the inside leg to the outside rein. Go back to the leg-yield with some bending into the shoulder-in (see p. 79).

I am not big on pushing the haunches back

9.3 Gwen Blake on Gabriel 2, owned by Christine and Richard Mills, riding shoulder-in.

onto the track when this mistake occurs. I believe the horse should always be straightened by placing the shoulders in front of the hind legs. So when this problem crops up, you can just bring the shoulders more to the inside until you have a three-track movement. You might end up on the centerline but you will have made your point!

6 Problem: The angle of my horse's shoulder-in varies.

This is yet again another line-of-travel issue. The horse is getting out of the work by changing the angle of the movement. The control of this exercise is important (see Problem 1, p. 80).

In addition, sometimes having a visual line to follow helps. When you don't have one, you may be asking the horse to perform the movement for too long a time. Work for shorter periods and see if you can build more strength and suppleness into the horse. Perhaps you are bending too much. You may need to go back to your leg-yield or turn-on-the-forehand and reestablish the inside-leg-to-outside-rein connection.

10

Travers and Renvers

*Don't take your horse's mistakes personally.
Don't train via emotion. Feel with your
heart and ride with your mind.*

Both travers (haunches-in) and renvers (haunches-out) ask the horse to move in the direction of the bend. These are the first exercises that do so, and therefore, they are more difficult than leg-yield or shoulder-in. These two movements are required in the USEF Second Level tests.

In travers, the forehand is on the line of travel and the haunches are displaced to the inside track. In renvers, the haunches are on the line of travel, and the forehand is moved to the inside track. Before I discuss these exercises, let's review the USEF definitions (see sidebar, p. 84).

Imperfections and Evasions

Your horse:

1 Allows his shoulders to leave the line of travel in travers.

2 Allows his haunches to leave the line of travel in renvers.

3 Has difficulty in the movements because his rider sits incorrectly.

4 Lacks angle.

5 Loses impulsion.

6 Lacks bend.

I discuss solutions to these imperfections, beginning on p. 86.

Travers is one of my least favorite movements. I think it can put the horse on the forehand quite easily. It is also one movement where very few riders can really sit in the correct position. I have never given a "10" for a travers.

Renvers on the other hand is very useful for many evasions. It can help put the horse more on the outside rein from the inside leg. It can help teach the horse not to push through the outside shoulder.

How to Ride and Train

Travers

This is a movement on four tracks. In it, the shoulders must stay on the line of travel, which means that the forehand goes straight down the long side, and if you were to paint a white line slightly off the wall or rail and running parallel to it, one of the horse's front legs will be on either side of this line.

So will one of the horse's ears. This means that one of your shoulders should also be on either side of the line, and one of your hands.

The usual mistakes here are that the rider is in the incorrect position or the horse is not supple enough. The rider tends to focus on moving the hindquarters off the rail, and she forgets about the front legs. So, the travers ends up with the correct angle (four tracks) and displacement of the hindquarters—but with an incorrect

---

USEF Rule Book

TRAVERS

This exercise can be performed in collected trot or collected canter. The horse is slightly bent round the inside leg of the rider but with a greater degree of bend than in shoulder-in. A constant angle of approximately 35 degrees should be shown, from the front and from behind one sees four tracks. The forehand remains on the track and the quarters are moved inward. The horse's outside legs pass and cross in front of the inside legs. The horse is bent in the direction in which it is moving. To start the travers, the quarters must leave the track or, after a corner or circle, are not brought back onto the track.

At the end of the travers, the quarters are brought back on the track without any counter-flexion of the poll/neck as one would finish a circle (fig. 10.1 A).

RENVERS

This is the inverse movement in relation to travers. The hindquarters remain on the track while the forehand is moved inward. To finish the renvers the forehand is aligned with the quarters on the track. Otherwise, the same principles and conditions that apply to the travers are applicable to the renvers. The horse is slightly bent around the inside leg of the rider. The horse's outside legs pass and cross in front of

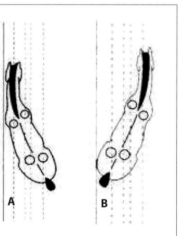

10.1 A & B The travers (A) and the renvers (B).

the inside legs.

The horse is bent in the direction in which it is moving. Aims of renvers: to show a fluent collected trot movement on a straight line with a greater degree of bend than in shoulder-in. Fore and hind legs cross, balance and cadence are maintained (fig. 10.1 B).

bend. The rider will lose the bend in front of the saddle.

Think about the choo-choo train again for a moment (see p. 16). You want your inside leg to act as a post for the train (horse) to bend around. Remember, you have a "hinge" in front of the saddle and a "hinge" behind it. You need to have the same amount of angle in each of these hinges. When the horse moves his shoulders in the wrong direction, the rider will have more displacement from the rear hinge than the front. They should be equal like the letter C.

Rider's Aids
When riding travers to the right:

1 Inside rein: Bending rein: It keeps horse's neck and shoulders positioned to the right, and the front legs positioned straight on the track, so the front legs do not cross.

2 Outside rein: Controls speed and regulates the amount of bend in the neck. Note: too much outside rein can restrict the bend.

3 Inside leg at the girth: This is the active leg, which keeps the impulsion going as well as supporting the bend by keeping the horse's rib cage to the outside. It is the "post" the horse will bend around.

4 Outside leg behind the girth: This is the active leg in the half-halt, and it tells the horse to position the hindquarters to the inside. Once the angle is correct, this outside leg holds the hindquarters to the inside, with our inside leg becoming active (see above).

5 Seat: Sit in the direction of the bend and the movement or to the inside or right (in this direction).

Renvers

Renvers is also now performed on four tracks, just like travers. The FEI changed this angle a few years ago. I am always amazed at how many riders (and trainers, too) do not know about this change and are still training and showing a three-track travers and renvers.

This change means that the movement from USEF Second Level Test 3 in which the rider must perform shoulder-in to renvers is now a bit more complicated. I will explain how to train this later in this chapter (see p. 87).

Rider's Aids
When riding renvers to the left (when tracking right):

1 Inside rein: The inside rein (to remind you, this is the left rein here because we always call the *inside* the direction toward which the horse is bent, regardless of the direction of the movement) positions the head, neck, and shoulders to the left.

2 Outside rein: Maintains the speed. Helps the inside leg keep the shoulders off the track.

3 Inside leg at the girth: This is the active leg to maintain the impulsion. Supports the bend by helping the outside rein keep the shoulders off the track.

4 Outside leg behind the girth: Keeps the hindquarters on the line of travel or on the rail. May

need to be active at the beginning of the movement.

5 Seat bones: Sit to the left, or in the direction of the bend.

Training Exercises and Solutions

Exercise One: Testing the Outside Leg

This exercise helps solve Problems 1, 3, 4, and 5 for the travers—see p. 83).

Start with the horse's shoulders going straight down the long side. You do not want as much neck bend as in a shoulder-in. Make sure your weight is to the inside and your inside leg is at the girth. Use your outside leg behind the girth actively for a few strides and move the haunches to the inside. You need your horse to give you a quick reaction to this aid. If not, go back and review the head-to-wall leg-yield (see p. 53).

Before the horse loses impulsion or tries to move the shoulders to the outside, ask him to go straight again and also use your inside leg to reinforce the "go-forward" aid. Do this three or four times down the long side.

For the rider, it is important that you keep *your shoulders* and *the horse's shoulders* perpendicular to the long side. It will

10.2 Chris Lewman and Valentino in renvers. You can clearly see the four tracks.

feel a bit as if you are ready for a *Cirque du Soleil* contortionist act. Your shoulders stay perpendicular, while your outside hip goes back, and your weight goes to the inside. You will feel quite a lot of stretch through the outside of your rib cage. You have to be aware that one direction will be very uncomfortable, and you will sit crookedly and incorrectly if you do not pay attention to this. We all know that the horse should be equally supple laterally, but for some reason, riders do not think about their own body being stiffer on one side.

Exercise Two:
Controlling the Line of Travel
This exercise helps Problems 2, 3, 4, and 5 for the renvers—see p. 83.

Start by going straight down the second track. Then counterflex the horse toward the wall. Make sure your weight moves toward the wall. Your leg next to the wall is now going to move to the girth. Use your new outside leg (the one to the inside of the arena) to push the horse's haunches to the wall. Your inside leg and outside rein should keep the forehand moving straight on the second track. Do not let the shoulders move to the wall, only the haunches.

Before the horse loses impulsion or tries to fall with the shoulders to the wall, straighten, change the bend, and move forward again. Do this two or three times down the long side. If your horse seems confused, go back, and review the tail-to-wall leg-yield (see p. 53).

Exercise Three:
Maintaining the Line of Travel while Changing the Bend
This exercise helps with the transition from shoulder-in to renvers which helps with Problem 2 (p. 83).

The main issue in riding the shoulder-in to renvers (as is required in the 2011 USEF Second Level 3), is maintaining the hindquarters on the rail while changing the bend.

I suggest you do this exercise at the walk first, until you can control the angles. Start out of the corner with a three-track shoulder-in. Do about 12 meters. Then take away the bending as you increase the angle to a four-track movement. You are really now in a tail-to-wall leg-yield position (see p. 53). Keep this for about 6 meters. During this time, move your weight and change your leg position. It is important that you secure the haunches on the rail first, before changing the bend.

Once you are in the correct position with your seat and legs, very slowly ask the horse to bend in the direction of travel or into a renvers. Remember, the shoulder-in is a three-track movement and the renvers is a four-track movement. That difference must be kept in mind when riding the changeover.

Exercise Four:
Improve the Bend to Improve Impulsion
This exercise will help solve Problems 5 and 6—see p. 83.

Bending and impulsion are closely related. If the horse is not submissive to the bend, he will lose impulsion and cadence. You cannot expect the horse to stay in a fabulous trot if he won't bend. So, take care of lateral suppleness first.

This "exercise" is all about review. You will need to go back and review the head-to-wall and tail-to-wall leg-yields (see p. 53). You may also need to work a bit with increasing and decreasing the circle. This will change the bend and also change which leg you are going to move the horse laterally away from.

Make sure your shoulder-in is of good quality. Remember that travers and renvers are the first movements where we ask the horse to move in the *direction of the bend*. This is "upping the degree of difficulty" quite a bit.

Work on smaller pieces. Only do a movement for 6 meters and then go forward again. Gradually increase the length of the movement. Remember that dressage tests do not require the horse to stay in either travers or renvers for more than 24 meters. So, demanding that the horse do the movement the entire way down the long side makes no sense to me, nor does it likely make sense to your horse, either.

11

The Halt and the Rein Back

There must be an aid, an answer, and a reward.

The halt and rein back movement is a necessary part of dressage tests from Second Level through Grand Prix. The USEF Rule Book provides information on both a good halt and a good rein back (see sidebar).

The rein back is a useful training movement for strengthening the horse's muscles behind the saddle by encouraging him to lower his hindquarters. The rein back also improves submission, yet this seemingly simple movement often causes riders difficulty.

Imperfections and Evasions

Your horse:

1 Resists stepping backward.

2 Does not step back in diagonal pairs.

3 Does not come to a complete halt or anticipates the rein back.

4 Drags his feet backward.

5 Is crooked.

6 Drops his neck and falls on his forehand.

7 Runs backward without your aids.

For solutions to these common problems, turn to p. 91.

How to Ride and Train

The rein back is a wonderful tool to help put the horse more naturally on the hindquarters and should never be used as punishment. The rein back should always be "thinking" forward.

USEF Rule Book

THE HALT

1 At the halt the horse should stand attentive, engaged, motionless, straight, and square with the weight evenly distributed over all four legs. The neck should be raised with the poll as the highest point and the head slightly in front of the vertical. While remaining "on the bit" and maintaining a light and soft contact with the rider's hand, the horse may quietly chew the bit and should be ready to move off at the slightest indication of the rider.

2 The halt is obtained by the displacement of the horse's weight to the hindquarters by a properly increased action of the seat and legs of the rider, driving the horse toward a softly closed hand, causing an almost instantaneous but not abrupt halt at a previously fixed place. The halt is prepared by a series of half-halts.

3 The quality of the gaits before and after the halt is an integral part of the assessment.

REIN BACK

1 The rein back is a rearward diagonal movement with a two-beat rhythm but without a moment of suspension. Each diagonal pair of legs is raised and returned to the ground alternatively, with the forelegs aligned on the same track as the hind legs.

2 During the entire exercise, the horse should remain "on the bit," maintaining its desire to move forward.

3 Anticipation or precipitation of the movement, resistance to or evasion of the contact, deviation of the hindquarters from the straight line, spreading or inactive hind legs and dragging forefeet are serious faults.

4 The steps are counted as each foreleg moves back. After completing the required number of steps backward, the horse should show a square halt or move forward in the required gait immediately.

Rider's Aids

To start my horses, I teach them the aids from the ground first. You can stand at the horse's shoulder with a whip and apply some pressure to the chest with the butt of the whip. At the same time, gently apply some pressure to both reins and say, "Back." With any small step, reward the horse by releasing the pressure and praising him. The release of pressure from the whip and reins when the horse steps back is essential for the horse to understand and comply with the aids.

After about a week, the horse will understand the voice aid and associate it with the give-and-take pressure from both reins. At this point, it is time to have the rider mount and begin the association of the aids the horse understands so far with the rider's aids given from the saddle.

I tell my riders to sit a bit lighter in the saddle ("open the back door," so to speak) and move both legs back behind the girth. Then the rider gives a squeeze with both legs and closes both reins for a moment. From the ground, I say "Back" and use the butt of the whip on the horse's chest, if needed. As soon as one step is taken backward, immediately reward the horse with a pat and relaxation of the rein and leg aids.

The finished rein back will have you pushing the energy to the reins, and then softly "closing the front door." Once the horse steps back you should release the rein aid. Each step must be ridden forward into the hand and followed by the reward. Otherwise, the horse will "run" backward, and you won't be able to control the number of steps back.

Training Exercises and Solutions

Exercise One:
Secure the Halt

This exercise will solve Problems 2, 3, 5, 6, and 7—see p. 89.

Always establish a good halt. Remember that without a square halt it will be difficult to start the rein back in diagonal pairs. I always halt and then relax the reins a bit. The horse needs to learn to "hang out" in the halt.

The horse should also learn how to halt on the bit. If the rider is so busy trying to get the head down at halt, the rein back will also be a disaster. Make sure you are keeping the horse supple in the bend or flexion. Don't use so much outside rein that you counterbend or counterflex the horse.

Prior to the halt aid, try to use your seat and

Personal Story

I was judging in Arizona in the 1990s. I had just received my FEI "C" and was very excited to be asked to judge the Pantano CDI (FEI dressage competition). The CDI classes had not started yet, and I was judging a few USEF (then called AHSA) open classes.

Debbie McDonald was entered with her horse Beaurivage in the CDI Grand Prix. She also had brought along a young chestnut mare named Brentina, who was showing Third Level.

Brentina and Debbie entered my ring and when they halted at A and did their rein back, I gave them a 10. I knew I was looking at something special. Parry Thomas, Brentina's owner, was tickled because he had been the ground-person for Debbie and Brentina in the warm-up.

After all of these years of judging, I must admit that I have yet to give another 10 to a halt and rein back. This one still sticks in my mind as to how a 10 should be performed! Great memories of a great team.

11.1 Debbie McDonald on Brentina, winning one of many championships as the pair moved up the levels and on to represent the United States in international competition.

upper leg to start a half-halt and only use the reins if you need to reinforce the "Whoa" aid. Use your voice as well if you need to help the horse understand. Then be sure to reward the horse for a good effort by releasing the reins. The horse should stand still without any contact. This is the "self-carriage" part of the half-halt, as well as of the halt. A horse that won't stand still without contact will also run through your release of the half-halt at the other gaits.

The halt should also be straight. By this, I mean slightly shoulder-fore. If you are on the left rein, prepare by making sure the horse has the hind legs on the track and the shoulders are slightly to the inside track. I like to do three half-halts, thinking "little," then "more," and finally "most" for the halt. These half-halts should shorten the stride when at trot or canter. It will be easier for the horse to halt in balance from a shorter, more compact and engaged stride.

When adding the rein back to the halt, make sure you do not rein back after every halt or your horse will think he knows what is coming and not wait for your aids. Judges don't give extra credit if the horse does the movement on his own!

By halting in a shoulder-fore position your horse should also stay more uphill in the halt. If your horse still wants to lean onto the forehand, then do your halts from shoulder-in to help the engagement. You will need to establish a good halt from both directions. Work on halts on the quarterline as well. I rarely practice the halt on the centerline as the horse has a way of anticipating it and taking over, usually at the wrong time!

Exercise Two:
Getting the Horse to "Think Forward"
This exercise will solve Problems 1, 4, and 7—see p. 89.

Once your horse is balanced and calm in the halt, proceed to the rein back. Go back only one or two steps and then move forward quickly into trot. With repetition of this exercise, the horse will anticipate the move off and begin to "think forward" on his own. This is a great exercise for all those lazy horses!

Exercise Three:
Improve Confidence
This exercise will help with Problem 1—see p. 89.

This horse needs to be reschooled and rewarded from the ground. Work daily with verbal commands and the groundwork described earlier prior to mounting (see p. 90). I find some very tall horses have difficulty becoming coordinated with their long, spider-like legs. Sometimes the resistance is only a lack of confidence, not a show of temper. Be content with willingness and don't expect perfection. Willingly backing a few small steps will be fine for early training. The number and length of steps can then be improved as the horse gains confidence.

Exercise Four:
Shoulder-In, Halt, Move Off
This exercise helps Problems 4, 5, and 6—see p. 89.

Use your shoulder-in to keep the horse more engaged and uphill prior to the halt. Bad halts are usually a result of a crooked horse. You will be able to feel which aid the horse wants to resist if you do the halts in this exercise off the rail. Did the shoulders fall out? Did the "caboose" of your choo-choo train fall out? Did the horse push his rib cage against your inside leg? Move off again following your halt.

Exercise Five:
Using the Indirect Rein of Opposition
This exercise will solve Problem 5—see p. 89.

This rein aid takes your inside hand toward your outside hip, across the neck, and is sometimes used by hunter-jumper riders. Generally this is not a good aid for dressage because the rider's hands should stay directly above the horse's shoulders. However, this aid will help in a rein back to keep the horse straight and not allow him to move his haunches to the inside.

With a horse that likes to be crooked in the rein back, be sure to halt in a shoulder-fore position. Experiment with how much outside leg you really need if the rein back is along a rail. Perhaps you will only need a bit of inside leg behind the girth and less outside leg. The outside leg should not be taken off, however, as the horse will find the "open door" and "escape" by pushing the haunches to the outside.

Note: it is embarrassing when the horse kicks over the dressage ring in a rein back!

Exercise Six:
It Must Be Your Idea
This exercise helps to improve Problems 3 and 7— see p. 89.

This is really a philosophy for all your exercises. It is nice to have a horse that wants to "volunteer," but the exercises must be on your aids. Was it your idea to go faster? Or slower? Whose idea was it to make the circle smaller or larger? I think you get the idea!

The horse that "runs" back is not waiting for the rider's aids. The mistake might have been taught by the rider not rewarding the horse for each step and taking the aids off or releasing the contact. You will have to go back and work slowly on this. First the horse must halt without anticipating a rein back. This may take some time.

Then, once you put the rein back with the halt, be sure to do one step, then say, "Whoa," and relax your aids. This is much like the turn-on-the-forehand exercise from many chapters ago (see p. 50). There must be an aid, an answer, and a reward.

PART 2

Achieving Success
at Medium Level
(Third and Fourth Levels)

CHAPTER

12

Turn-on-the-Haunches and Walk Pirouette

The wonderful thing about these two movements is they are "non-brilliance" movements. In other words, your horse doesn't need to be a "fancy mover" to score well!

I am always asked the same question regarding these two movements. Riders want to know what is the difference between them? *Turn-on-the-haunches* is done in *medium* walk, while the *walk pirouette* is done in *collected* walk. The other difference is the movement's size. The turn-on-the-haunches is allowed to cover about 3 meters. The *walk pirouette* should be small, with the horse stepping around his inside hind leg.

JUDGING TIP

There is another question I always get about the turn-on-the-haunches, and that is concerning the score. Riders seem to think that they must make the turn-on-the-haunches very small in order to receive a good mark. This is not true. If you take a risk and make it small you can get a "10." If you make it a larger size but do it well, you can also receive a "10."

The wonderful thing about these two movements is they are "non-brilliance" movements. In other words, your horse doesn't need to be a "fancy mover" to score well! Before reading further, review the two definitions from the USEF Rule Book (see sidebar, p. 98). Note that we are focusing on the walk pirouette, although the pirouette is performed in canter at the upper levels and sometimes in piaffe in freestyle competition.

Imperfections and Evasions

Your horse:

1 Steps backward.

2 Has hind legs that "stick" or loses the walk rhythm.

3   Has a walk that becomes lateral in the turn or the preparation.

4   Lacks bending or lateral position.

5   Allows his haunches to fall out against your outside leg.

6   Ignores the turning aid.

You can find solutions to these issues beginning on p. 100.

You can find solutions to these issues beginning on p. 100.

USEF Rule Book
TURN-ON-THE-HAUNCHES

For younger horses that are still not able to show collected walk, the "turn-on-the-haunches" is an exercise to prepare the horse for collection. The "turn-on-the-haunches" is executed out of medium walk prepared by half-halts to shorten the steps a little and to improve the ability to bend the joints of the hindquarters. The "turn-on-the-haunches" can be executed on a larger diameter (approximately one meter) than the pirouette in walk, but the demands of the training scale concerning rhythm, contact, activity, and straightness are the same. A turn-on-the-haunches is to be judged like a regular half-pirouette except that full credit must be given for a well performed, but larger (one meter) turn-on-the-haunches. Full credit should also be given for a well performed, regular sized half-pirouette. A significant deduction should be made if a rider attempts but performs poorly a regular half-pirouette.

How to Ride and Train

Rider's Aids
When riding a turn-on-the-haunches or walk pirouette to the right:

1 Inside rein: Bends the horse's head and neck and slightly positions the shoulders in the direction of the turn.

2 Outside rein: Supports the collection and helps to maintain the size of the pirouette.

3 Inside leg at the girth: Is the active leg and keeps the horse actively walking. It also helps support the bend.

4 Outside leg behind the girth: Keeps the horse on the inside hind and helps create the turning aid along with the rider's weight aid.

5 Seat: Sit in the direction of the turn or to the inside.

JUDGING TIP

The correct walk rhythm must be maintained in the turn. In the show ring, I am seeing more and more horses that are becoming lateral in their turns. You will lose points for every step that loses rhythm. In addition, the horse must be positioned in the direction of the turn. In other words, think of the bend you have on a 20-meter circle and maintain that bend in the turn for your turn-on-the-haunches. Since the walk-pirouette will be smaller, you will need as much bend as in a 10-meter circle. This is important, as many riders

USEF Rule Book

PIROUETTE

- The pirouette (half-pirouette) is a circle (half-circle) executed on two tracks with a radius equal to the length of the horse, the forehand moving round the haunches.

- At the pirouette (half-pirouette) the forefeet and the outside hind foot move round the inside hind foot, which forms the pivot and should return to the same spot, or slightly in front of it, each time it leaves the ground.

- At whatever gait the pirouette (half-pirouette) is executed, the horse, slightly bent in the direction in which he is turning, should remain on the bit with light contact, turn smoothly and maintain the cadence of that gait. The poll stays the highest point during the entire movement.

- During the pirouettes (half-pirouettes) the horse should not move backward or deviate sideways. In the pirouette or half-pirouette in canter, the judges should be able to recognize a real canter stride although the footfalls of the diagonal— inside hind leg, outside front leg—do not occur simultaneously.

- The quality of the pirouette (half-pirouette) is judged according to the suppleness, lightness, cadence, and regularity, and to the precision and smoothness of the transitions; pirouettes (half-pirouettes) at canter are judged also according to the balance, the elevation and the number of strides (at pirouettes six to eight, at half-pirouettes three to four are desirable). When the turn is too large and the hind steps come off the prescribed line of travel, the correction is to take a straight line back to the track. Correction by use of half-pass or leg-yielding may result in a deduction of points.

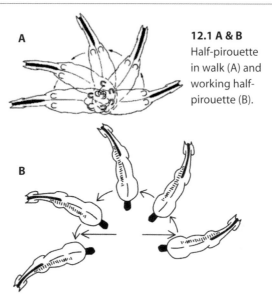

12.1 A & B
Half-pirouette in walk (A) and working half-pirouette (B).

- The quarter-pirouette. As a preparatory exercise, the quarter-pirouette is usually executed on the track at a given letter, the horse being highly collected for one or two strides before and then through the execution of a 90-degree turn around the haunches in two to three strides, maintaining a correct canter footfall.

- The working pirouette and working half-pirouette. The pirouette (half-pirouette) is a turn of 360 degrees (180 degrees) executed on two tracks, with the forehand moving around the haunches. The size of the working pirouette should be approximately 3 meters. The requirements for a working half-pirouette are identical to those of a regular half-pirouette, except that the allowable diameter is increased to approximately 3 meters. A working half-pirouette is to be judged like a regular half-pirouette except that full credit must be given for a well-performed, but larger (3-meter) half-pirouette. Full credit should also be given for a well-performed, regular-sized half-pirouette. A significant deduction should be made if a rider attempts but performs poorly a regular half-pirouette (figs. 12.1 A & B).

have the horse too straight or even counterflexed, which take your marks down. The horse also must accept the turning aid and turn the shoulders around the hind legs.

Here are some tips to help you develop the turn-on-the haunches and walk pirouette correctly.

Maintain the Line of Travel

Do turn-on-the-haunches and walk pirouettes up and down the centerline or the quarterlines so you have a lot of room to prepare.

If you start your right turn in shoulder-in, you will need to walk a few strides of shoulder-in right on the centerline. Turn. You will finish a bit in a renvers right position. The haunches will stay on the centerline. Walk forward a few steps in this renvers right position to show that you have finished the exercise and still have control. Then change the bend to shoulder-in left. The legs should still be on the same line of travel. Prepare for the next turn and finish in the same manner.

The key with the walk pirouette is to keep the horse's hind legs on the line of travel and move his shoulders from one direction to the other.

How to Finish a Turn-on-the-Haunches

This is a problem all of its own. How do you finish these turns when you can move 3 meters from the line of travel? First, be sure you finish the turn, maintaining your bend, and walk a few steps straight ahead to show you still have control. If you have performed the movement from the rail, you will now be walking down the second track. Do not half-pass back to the rail. Once you have

finished and walk a few steps straight ahead, make a diagonal line back to the rail. If you are performing these between the long sides, then you would finish the same way.

Don't Be in a Hurry

Take all the time you need to perform this movement. If the test says the movement can be between G and H, then go to near H, and use the rail to help you collect the horse. Too many riders try to make these turns too close to G. Rushing will not improve this movement!

Training Exercises and Solutions

Exercise One: Ride a Square

This exercise solves Problems 1, 2, and 6—see p. 97.

This exercise will teach the horse about the turning aids. Most young horses fall out through the outside shoulder in one direction. So this is an important aid early on.

Ride the horse on a square. At each corner, ride a half-halt, and then use your turning aids for a one-quarter turn. The aids should be in this order: First, use the outside rein to slow the horse down. Second, use the inside rein as a turning aid, like a turn signal "on/off." This is an open leading rein, opening in the direction of the turn. Then you need to shift your weight to the direction of the turn. Last, move your outside leg a bit forward toward the shoulder and tap lightly. Your inside leg will be used at the end of the turn to send the horse forward again.

You may need to take your whip or bat and tap on the horse's shoulder as you use the aids above. Soon the horse will understand the turning aid. You will feel him lift his outside shoulder and step over and across the inside front leg. As I am working on this aid, I am not really too concerned with the hind legs. I want the horse to understand each piece that makes up this movement.

You will usually find that your horse turns more easily one direction than the other. This is normal—even for the *perfect* horse!

When your horse's inside hind leg "sticks" or he "thinks backward" during this movement, ride the Ride a Square exercise, then turn a few steps and use your inside leg to send the horse forward. Repeat. Working with half-steps will also help (see p. 000). If you can train a medium or collected walk with more activity and higher, quicker steps, you will have less chance of the hind legs "sticking."

If your horse still thinks backward, be sure you are not holding on the reins. Remember, you must half-halt, give the aid, and then you must relax the contact to allow the horse to step forward and sideways.

Exercise Two:
Quarter-Turns
This exercise solves Problems 4 and 5—see p. 98.

Once the horse understands the turning aid (see Riding a Square, p. 100), I try to put more pieces together for the horse. Your horse should understand leg-yield well by now. Turn onto the centerline and begin a leg-yield. Gradually start to flex the horse more in the direction of travel. This will

be a "baby" half-pass. It gets the horse stepping in the direction of the turn. This will also help create some lateral suppleness. When you feel you have control, ask the horse to do a quarter-turn. Once you can do this successfully 90 percent of the time, increase the difficulty and do a half-turn and go directly back into the half-pass.

The issue riders seem to have with this movement is that they allow the horse to lose the bend and fall onto the inside leg at the end of the movement. This is a mistake at the walk, but in the canter pirouette it will cost you your canter lead, so don't create this problem now.

Exercise Three:
Determine the Set-Up
This exercise solves Problems 5 and 6—see p. 98.

You may find that in one direction the horse will not turn easily. I would start your turn with shoulder-in this direction. Get the bend and move the shoulders in front of the hind legs to start.

In the other direction your horse will want to push his haunches out against your outside leg. Start your preparation with travers this direction. Work your horse so that you can start the turn either in shoulder-in or in travers.

Exercise Four:
Supple and Release
This exercise helps solve Problem 3—see p. 97.

A lateral rhythm can come because of tension in the horse's topline. Check your aids and make sure you are not holding too much contact in the reins. Then, consciously supple and release as the horse steps around forward and sideways.

It is common that in the preparation for these movements there can be some change of the rhythm until the horse is confirmed in them. If your horse has a huge walk with lots of overstep, he may be more prone to this rhythm problem. In such cases, lateral suppleness and stepping sideways will sometimes help clear up rhythm issues.

Note that this problem, if it persists, should be addressed by a professional as it can quickly become a habit that will be almost impossible to cure.

CHAPTER

13

Strengthen the Pendulum—
Third Level and Above

There is a fine line between brilliance and resistance.

Does your horse have the ability to move on to Third Level and above? Can your horse maintain the correct balance and carriage? Please review chapter 7 (see p. 57). I am now going to be talking about the transitions required for Third Level through Intermediate I.

In this chapter, I'll talk about some of the more sophisticated transitions and paces you and your horse must accomplish to advance up the levels. While not all horses can achieve success at Intermediate II and Grand Prix, with the right training and instruction, you and your horse may indeed find success at Third Level and above.

Here are some challenges you may encounter with your horse as you advance beyond Second Level.

Imperfections and Evasions

Your horse:

1 Changes leads behind, either at the beginning or end of medium or extended canter.

2 Has transitions that judges say are "vague" or "gradual."

3 Lacks groundcover.

4 Loses his clear, three-beat canter rhythm.

5 Gets crooked.

6 Falls downhill.

7 Gets stiff in his back, neck, and/or topline.

USEF Rule Book

MEDIUM TROT

This is a pace of moderate lengthening compared to the extended trot, but "rounder" than the latter. Without hurrying, the horse goes forward with clearly lengthened steps and with impulsion from the hindquarters. The rider allows the horse to carry the head a little more in front of the vertical than at the collected and the working trot, and to lower the head and neck slightly. The steps should be even, and the whole movement balanced and unconstrained.

EXTENDED TROT

The horse covers as much ground as possible. Without hurrying, the steps are lengthened to the utmost as a result of great impulsion from the hindquarters. The rider allows the horse to lengthen the frame and to gain ground while controlling the poll. The forefeet should touch the ground on the spot towards which they are pointing.

The movement of the fore and hind legs should reach equally forward in the moment of extension. The whole movement should be well-balanced and the transition to collected trot should be smoothly executed by taking more weight on the hindquarters.

MEDIUM CANTER

This is a pace between the working and the extended canter. Without hurrying, the horse goes forward with clearly lengthened strides and impulsion from the hindquarters. The rider allows the horse to carry the head a little more in front of the vertical than in the collected and working canter, and at the same time allows the horse to lower the head and neck slightly. The strides should be balanced and unconstrained.

EXTENDED CANTER

The horse covers as much ground as possible. Without hurrying, the strides are lengthened to the utmost. The horse remains calm, light, and straight as a result of great impulsion from the hindquarters. The rider allows the horse to lengthen the frame with a controlled poll and to gain ground. The whole movement should be well-balanced and the transition to collected canter should be smoothly executed by taking more weight on the hindquarters.

VERY COLLECTED CANTER

In executing the pirouette or the half-pirouette in canter, the rider should maintain perfect lightness of the horse while accentuating the collection. The quarters are well-engaged and lowered and show a good flexion of the joints. An integral part of the movement is the canter strides before and after the pirouette. These should be characterized by an increased activity and collection before the pirouette and, the movement having been completed, by the balance being maintained as the horse proceeds.

13.1 Gwen Blake and Sancette in medium trot at Third Level.

8   Won't lengthen his frame.

9   Gets "earthbound."

10 Shows no clear difference between the medium and extended paces.

I'll give you exercises to correct these deficiencies later (see p. 108), but first let's turn again to the USEF Rule Book for definitions of the new paces: *medium and extended trot and canter* and *"very collected" canter,* also known as the *pirouette canter* (see sidebar, p. 104).

New Transitions and Paces

Review the diagram of the Pendulum of Elasticity on p. 58. We are now ready to move the Pendulum more to the left and more to the right in order to introduce the following transitions:

1 Medium trot and canter to and from collected trot and canter.

2 Extended trot and canter to and from collected trot and canter.

When Linda Ohlson first brought Moshne to me for a lesson, I thought, "Hmmm, very 'earthbound' and flat." Linda wanted to move her horse up the levels. He was a Thoroughbred/Akhal Teke cross, seven years old at the time, and schooling about First Level. His favorite trick to escape when the work got hard was to bolt off across the arena, usually through the left shoulder. Linda weighed about 100 pounds and was really taken for a ride.

The first thing I suggested was that Linda start Moshne on Legend® and perhaps an oral supplement, such as Cosequin®, as well. I have always felt that once horses start collection, we as their riders, should help them out a bit with something to help "lube up" the joints. (Now that I am approaching 60, I admit liking my own morning dose of Aleve®!) Correct work will also help the muscling of the topline, which takes away a lot of stress from the knees and hocks down. Good riding reinforces the saying, "Motion is lotion," for the joints.

Due to Moshne's natural lack of suspension, it became clear that if Moshne were going to progress and be able to learn movements such as passage and extended trot, he could only do so if he was strengthened via the Pendulum of Elasticity (see p. 58).

Individual movements were quite easy to teach—except the flying changes, which was a problem because his canter lacked suspension. Over two years, Linda gymnasticized Moshne's body through the use of the Pendulum, he developed more suspension in the trot, and he became able to do some passage. The canter became much more elastic and suspended, and now he can also do a few one-tempi changes.

I love the photo here of Moshne, showing his great muscles and new body. He did quite well for Linda through Prix St. Georges, enabling her to win her Silver Medal from USDF.

13.3 Linda Ohlson Gross on Moshne showing off his well-muscled and gymnasticized physique.

3 Collected walk to extended walk to collected walk (see chapter 8, p. 69).

4 Collected canter to very collected canter back to collected canter.

I like to think of the medium paces as the ones that come the most off the ground. A good medium trot makes me think that training this horse in passage will be easy.

The extended paces lose some of the airtime because they are the paces that go the most over the ground. There must be more overtracking in them. The frame should also lengthen. The horse should be strong enough now so that he can stay uphill and lengthen his frame without losing balance.

JUDGING TIP

You must be careful not to ride the same trot and canter for both medium and extended paces. Years ago, I was at an FEI dressage judge's forum with Eric Lette. He was explaining to the judges that we must be clear with our marks, and ensure that riders ride the correct trots and canters. Kyra Kyrklund raised her hand and said, "Well, Eric, that is good, but if I ride the same I will get an '8' for my medium and a '7' for my extended." I agreed with her, as at that time it was how I had been coached to ride them, as well. Now, judges and trainers agree that they should be different.

13.2 Here I
demonstrate
extended trot
on Halloh.

How to Ride and Train

Don't Bore the Horse

It is very important that the horse is kept happy and involved with his training. I see many riders who just ride around in the same trot, in the same direction, doing the occasional movement. The horse "falls asleep" in these situations. Creative riding is important for the dull horse because you can keep him "awake" with your requests for reactions from him. In the case of the very smart horse, you keep his brain engaged with your requests, rather than letting *him* get creative—and possibly take over!

Try to make the work session interesting. Use your corners to collect and make smaller, more active steps. Then go forward out of the corner and ride a movement. Change direction and gait frequently. Do a lot of transitions within the gaits. Give the horse short breaks and rewards. Try not to keep him working for more than three or four minutes before a break or a stretch. This is so much more beneficial than riding around for 45 minutes doing nothing interesting.

Muscles and Strength-Building

FEI dressage is all about building quick and correct reactions in the horse, and about building muscle strength. The next time you are at a show, look at the Training Level horse's physique compared to a top Grand Prix horse. A horse without the correct muscling will not be able to perform the movements required in the correct balance.

This muscle building and strength building takes time. Also, teaching and confirming some of the more difficult movements takes time. You cannot just decide that next year you are going to ride Grand Prix and try to teach your horse one-tempi changes, the piaffe, and the passage in 12 months. Your work for these upper level movements should have started when the horse was doing First Level work. Consider the learning process of the horse—he needs at least a year to learn and confirm each movement.

Have a Checklist

Every time you ride you need to think of a pilot completing his checklist prior to takeoff. Is the horse quick off my leg? Check. Is the horse supple to the bend? Check. Is the horse straight? Check.

Think of the Classical Training Pyramid as your checklist (see p. 11).

I hope that my pilot never takes off without completing the checklist successfully. Too many riders never have a checklist. They just start right into the movements and wonder why they fail. If you take care of the basics and the correct reactions, the movements will take care of themselves.

Training Exercises and Solution

Exercise One:
Use Cavalletti
This exercise will help to deal with Problems 3, 4, 7, 8, and 9—see p. 103.

I love cavalletti. If you don't have Reiner and Ingrid Klimke's book *Cavalletti: The Schooling of Horse and Rider over Ground Poles* (Trafalgar Square Books, 2008), buy it. Horses love to do something different. These exercises will really improve your horse's trot!

If you have a horse that is a bit "earthbound," use your cavalletti and place them close together at to the lowest level off the ground—the distance is determined by the length of your horse's stride. Usually about 3 to 4 feet apart will work. Ride through them once and if the horse is having difficulty, either move them closer together when the horse is having to reach out too much, or spread them out a bit if he is stumbling over them.

Trot the horse through several times during your workout. This teaches the horse to articulate his joints more and gain a bit more "air." Think of the "Flying Tomato"—what makes champion snowboarder Shaun White great is his airtime.

13.4 Kelly Boyd on Nikko of Noble, owned by Michelle Guest, in medium canter.

One of the thrills of watching the Winter Olympic Games in 2010 was to see Shaun fly through the air with multiple gymnastic movements all flowing together in a way that made it look easy!

If your horse gets a bit tense in the back, cavalletti are a great way to encourage him to look down and stay stretched over his back into the contact. This also helps the horse learn to lengthen the neck a bit.

You can put the cavalletti closer together and a bit higher to encourage more suspension and more articulation in the joints. Also, lengthen the distance between them to encourage more groundcover.

If you are a bit nervous about riding your horse through the cavalletti the first few times, then set them up on a circle and longe the horse over them in the beginning until you both have some confidence. Remember, always use an odd number of cavalletti, otherwise the horse will visualize an "in-and-out" jump!

For the canter, some free jumping or jumping over a small pole on the ground or raised cavalletti, will encourage the horse to "snap" his back and bascule. This will lift his loins and belly muscles, which are the muscles he needs to use to improve the quality of the canter.

Exercise Two:
Make Sure the Horse Is Listening to the Seat and Outside Leg

This exercise will help with Problems 1, 2, and 8—see p. 103.

Once the horse has an idea about flying changes, he can use them against us in the medium canter on the long side or diagonal. At either the begin-ning or the end of the medium canter movement, the horse will sometimes change his lead to the outside lead; he may only change behind and end up cross-cantering. Usually this is because the horse misunderstands the rider's aid. The rider goes on the long side or the diagonal and rides the horse forward off the inside leg. The horse thinks, "Aha! Here comes a flying change!" And so, trying to be a good boy, he makes a change. The judge may be amused by the antics, but can only score the mistake with a "4." So, what to do?

Simply ride the horse forward with the *outside* leg when doing a medium or extended canter on the diagonal. Then, be sure to collect with the outside leg being active, or the horse will change on his own accord.

The other reason a horse will change leads behind is stiffness in the back. If the horse is tense, or changes, first check your weight and your seat aids. Make sure *you* are not the problem. If you are correct, push the haunches in the direction of the lead first and then collect.

At Training Level, the horse is 90 percent on the leg and hand. By Third Level, the horse should be at least 50/50. At Grand Prix we like it to be 10 percent hand and leg, and 90 percent seat. The horse should have been educated to understand that the seat says "go" by allowing the energy to cover more ground. This is not a heavy, driving seat. That type of riding will make your sensitive Arabian or Thoroughbred hollow and stiff in the back. It is an "allowing" seat. Then if the horse doesn't listen, the leg can reinforce the seat.

I always start my down transitions by closing my upper leg first. By my securing my upper leg a bit, my horse knows (by repetition) that a transition or a half-halt is coming. It also gives my seat

13.5 Gwen Blake riding Talisman in extended canter.

and back and overall position more security and strength in case the horse tries to lean into the reins at this moment. Then I restrict the motion of my seat. The lower leg should be saying, "Horse, take smaller higher steps." You need to make sure the hind legs are active in all downward transitions. If the horse needs a reinforcement to the "Whoa" aid, then the outside rein should be used.

Think of a car. In neutral, the driver revs the engine. Then he shifts into first gear. The horse should have the same rpms throughout the work. Your lower leg is the gas pedal or rhythm stick, and your seat is the gear shift. Reins are there to keep the shape and suppleness of the horse's topline and the position of the bend in the neck.

If you feel as a rider you need to create more energy prior to a medium or extended pace, then you will not succeed. You should already have the energy packaged like a coiled spring in a supple horse so you can just *allow* the energy to cover more ground.

Exercise Three:
Working on Circles in Canter

This exercise will help with Problems 1, 2, 3, 4, and 6—see p. 103.

Horses have more balance on a curved line. If you try to start working on your mediums on the straight line, often the horse will get crooked and fall on the forehand. Often with this loss of straightness comes a loss of rhythm.

Remember that your horse will not have enough strength at the beginning of schooling this exercise to stay in an uphill balance on the entire long side. So, you need to think of your Pendulum to strengthen your horse and give him confidence. Ride a lot of transitions through the paces, work on the reactions, make sure the Pendulum and your transitions from collection to extension flow smoothly—and with suppleness and balance.

Start on the 20-meter circle with a little haunches-in. This keeps the horse submissive to the outside leg and should help him lower his hindquarters a bit and load his inside hind leg. Think of beginning to work now on the *very collected canter* you will need for Fourth Level and the start of your working canter pirouettes (see p. 147).

When the horse does lower his hindquarters and takes more weight on his inner hind leg, usually you will feel the tempo of the canter get slower. This is because the horse is "sitting," or taking weight on the hindquarters, and staying for a longer period of time on the hind leg, which is what you want. Riders who do not have experience with this movement often panic and "chase" the horse with their legs and seat, immediately unloading the hind leg. If the horse trots by mistake, quietly walk, push the haunches in a bit, and return to canter. Try to use this mistake to teach him something. Kicking and whipping him back into canter will only make him fearful.

Once the horse understands what you want and can hold the increased engagement for four or so strides, you can ask for more activity. First, however, comes "sitting" and lowering of the hindquarters. This lowering of the hindquarters requires the horse to bend the joints of the hind leg more. When the horse first learns to carry more weight, or "sit," often the tempo of the canter will slow down. This is okay for a while as the horse gets stronger. Once he understands the half-halt and the "sitting," you can ask him to increase the activity without fear that he will misunderstand and "unload" the hind leg.

This very collected canter is now how you want to start your mediums. Collect, straighten the horse, and allow him to take three to four larger strides. Remember, he won't go from very collected canter directly to medium. Think of how the Pendulum swings. It is a smooth swing without abruptness. In the same way your transitions between the paces should be smooth and not abrupt. It will take two or so strides to get into the medium. Then, ride the medium canter for three or four more strides and begin with your half-halt to gradually bring him back to the very collected canter. Remember to begin the transitions with your seat. Then reinforce with the leg or hand, if needed.

Once you are succeeding 90 percent of the time, raise your standards and try to get into the medium canter in one or two strides and come back into collection in one or two strides.

One lead will be easier than the other. If your horse stiffens at the end, push the haunches in a bit prior to the collection. Try to keep the suppleness of the topline throughout the exercise. Many riders concentrate so hard on the "go" part that they stop communicating with the reins.

Once your horse is succeeding 90 percent of the time on the circle, move the exercise to the long side. Use the corner for the very collected canter. Make sure the horse is straight (that is, shoulder-fore) prior to allowing him to move forward into the medium. Check the straightness again prior to the collection at the end. Don't school the entire long side in the beginning. Perhaps go half way, collect, and then go again. If your horse is changing leads in the transitions, check your weight, use your outside leg to start and end the movement, and perhaps try pushing the haunches in a bit at the beginning and the end.

Exercise Four:
Use 10-Meter Circles as a Collecting Tool

This exercise will help Problems 1, 2, 6, and 7—see p. 103.

Many horses love to go but are difficult to bring back. Arabians, Trakehners, and Thoroughbreds all have a great "go" button. They also can get stiff in the topline as they "go." I found that, with horses like these, I had more success with training the downward transitions from medium and extended canter by always adding a 10-meter circle in the corner at the end. The horse would be smart enough not to try to run through this circle, and soon after many repetitions, he would anticipate the small circle in the corner and start to come back himself. This saved a lot of half-halting. And with a "goer" type of horse, when he runs through the half-halt he also shortens his neck.

With a horse that likes to get stiff and braced in the topline the 10-meter circle helps the suppleness prior to the medium or extended canter.

Exercise Five:
Shoulder-In to Medium Trot to Shoulder-In

This exercise will help Problems 2, 3, 6, 7, and 8—see p. 103.

Shoulder-in is an awesome collecting tool. You can use this movement to help engage your horse prior to the medium trot. Ride a three-track shoulder-in on the rail for about 12 meters. Then you must straighten the horse or he will fall on the outside shoulder when you move him forward. Ride a medium trot across the short diagonal to the far quarterline and then, rather than collecting at the end, ride a shoulder-in the other direction to help him understand these transitions must be uphill and energetic.

So you would start on the left rein. Shoulder-in left for 12 meters on the rail. Straighten, medium trot to far quarterline, and immediately into shoulder-in right.

Exercise Six:
Executing the Beginning and the End

This exercise will help solve Problems 2, 5, and 6—see p. 103.

Don't be sloppy! My main criticism of my clinic students and my show-ring customers is that they are careless. They do not use the corners of the arena. (Remember the corner is your friend!) They do not set the horse up properly for each movement, and they don't finish the movement correctly either.

You will never ride a wonderful dressage test if you do not practice accurate figures at home. Each movement must have correct preparation. If your horse is stiff, he must be suppled. If your horse is lazy, he needs to have a wakeup call.

An example is the Prix St. Georges trot work. The shoulder-in is a three-track movement. The volte has the least amount of bending, so the rider should straighten the horse a bit prior to starting the circle. The more the rider bends the horse on the small circle the more the horse's shoulders go down. Think of the small circle as turning the horse's shoulders around the hind legs. The hind legs must stay on the line of travel, not fall out, which happens when there is too much bend. Then the rider must be sure to *finish* the circle!

Too many riders are in too big a hurry to get to the half-pass. If you start your half-pass when the horse's front legs hit the rail, the haunches will be leading. Finish the volte with a stride of shoulder-fore, and then start sideways. The half-pass is on four tracks and is the movement that has the most bend.

By *riding from half-halt to half-halt* instead of *running from movement to movement,* your entire test will improve and will not be as hectic. You must work on this at home, so when you go to the show and your nerves hit you, your good training and reactions at home take over. Remember you have eight to 10 minutes reserved just for you in the show ring.

Exercise Seven:
Count Your Strides
This exercise will help solve Problems 3 and 10—see p. 103.

If you work alone a lot, you need a technique to help you discover if you are headed in the right direction. I love this exercise.

Using the letters R and P, you can do this exercise in trot or canter. First count your strides in your working trot between the two letters. Let's say you have 16 strides. Count when the inside front leg comes up and your body is at the letter. Then try a trot lengthening. You might have 14 strides, which would show you that you are increasing the groundcover. Now collect your

trot. You should have more strides, perhaps 18. They should be shorter but more active. I often have students who say to me, "You must love this trot because I can't sit it." To repeat what I said earlier in the book, I always tell them that if the trot feels divine and easy to sit, it must be wrong!

Now on to the extended and medium trot: The extended trot should have the fewest strides, perhaps 11 or 12. Then the medium would be about 13 strides, in between the extended and lengthening.

Count the canter as the inside shoulder is coming up.

Now, work on your collection prior to the other trots and canters. Think very collected canter first and at the end. Give yourself a few strides to develop the new pace and to collect at the end. For the trot, think about your half-steps prior to starting and then go back to them at the end.

13.6 Kathy Simard riding a 10-year-old Lipizzan, Maestoso II Odetta II, owned by Deborah Bennett, in "very collected canter." Kathy is improving the engagement by riding a little haunches-in on the circle.

Exercise Eight: Dealing with Rhythm Problems

The canter exercises that follow help solve Problem 4—see p. 103. In fact, all of the exercises I've mentioned in this chapter help with rhythm issues in the trot and canter—and here are a few more.

At the Trot

Most rhythm issues in *trot* are due to some basic training faults. Be sure you ask yourself a couple of questions:

1 First, is my horse straight? A crooked horse will not carry weight equally and will usually show irregularities.

2 Second, am I, the rider, the problem? I see many wild and banging lower legs from riders. This only encourages the horse to take faster, shorter strides. Think about the rpms in your *collected trot*. When you improve the cadence and strength in the collected trot, the mediums and extensions will also improve. Don't try to train your mediums and extensions by running across the entire diagonal. You will only fail.

Correct use of the Pendulum will strengthen your horse. Only when you can coil the spring of the hind leg (collection) will you be able to uncoil the spring and send the horse up in the air (elasticity) and more over the ground (medium/extended). *Do not* kick every stride. On the diagonal, I like to think about using a "go" aid at the beginning, at the first quarterline, at X, and at the last quarterline.

At the Canter

Rhythm problems in the canter can be caused by:

1 Tension. If your horse is very tense in the back, he will perhaps show some rhythm problems in the medium or extended canter.

2 Lack of straightness. Again, if you are allowing the haunches to fall in and the shoulders to fall out, you run the risk of having rhythm problems. Make sure you check the straightness out of your corner, prior to beginning the more forward canters.

3 Lack of strength. Go back to your circle and work more slowly within the steps of the Pendulum to build strength.

4 Lack of balance. Using counter-canter (see p. 115) will improve your horse's balance, suppleness, straightness, and quality of canter. Ride a few strides of medium canter on the long side while in counter-canter. This will often improve the rhythm.

Practice the exercises in this section faithfully and creatively, be patient as your horse develops strength and confidence, and you will be surprised at the progress you can make as you work the Pendulum of Elasticity. Mastering the ability to smoothly, and with an uphill balance, "shift" your horse's gears from collection to extension (the goal of the Pendulum of Elasticity) should be the focus of every rider aspiring to the FEI levels.

Counter-Canter

*Counter-canter is not just cantering
around on the "wrong" lead.*

Counter-canter is used as a strengthening, balancing, and straightening exercise. Remember, this is not just cantering on the "wrong" lead!

When you work on counter-canter exercises with your horse, you may be prone to the following problems:

Imperfections and Evasions

Your horse:

1 Won't pick up the correct counter-canter lead.

2 Breaks into trot.

3 Loses his lead in front.

4 Loses his lead behind.

5 Leans in like a motorcycle going around a turn.

6 Does a flying change over and over (won't "hold" the counter-canter).

First, take a look at the USEF Rule Book definition for counter-canter (see sidebar, p. 116).

The easiest test pattern is in USEF First Level Test 3. This simple loop allows the horse to maintain the same direction and lead with a small loop of counter-canter in the middle. The most difficult comes in the FEI Prix St. Georges where the horse must maintain the counter-canter through a corner, staying on the aids and in balance until the flying change is asked for at C.

How to Ride and Train

Rider's Aids

In order to correctly ride a counter-canter the horse must have a well-balanced and collected true canter. The horse must also have a good understanding of your outside leg behind the girth. Most horses will lean into the arena in the counter-canter. Your outside leg acts as a barrier to help keep the horse upright and engaged on the leading hind leg. For example, if you are in the right lead counter-canter, the horse should be engaged on the right hind. This hind leg will be on the track or on the line of travel. Your outside leg behind the girth (*outside* is the arena side)—here, your left leg—will be important to keep the horse from leaning left.

Most riders bend their horse's neck too much in the counter-canter. This happens when the rider feels the horse starting to lose his balance and lean to the outside. The rider feels this and uses more inside rein as a result. More neck bend causes the horse to lean more in the wrong direction. The rider needs to react to this loss of balance by increasing the submission to the outside leg behind the girth, literally *pushing* the horse back onto the leading hind leg. Straightening the neck a bit with the outside rein also helps.

Riders need to also be aware that they may sit in the wrong direction if the horse leans that way. Again, this will only increase the problems for the horse. Be sure you are sitting over the hind leg that needs to be engaged or carrying weight.

Introducing Counter-Canter

When first schooling the counter-canter, I often just canter out of the corner onto the quarterline, and canter straight down the quarterline. The horse needs to learn to not be insecure when you leave the rail. The second half of the lesson is to canter down the quarterline, but this time return to the track at the end of the long side and go into the corner. When the horse is confident with both halves of the lesson, ride it as one loop.

In First Level Test 3, the loop is: first corner to X to second corner. You can make it easier at first by only going from the first corner to the quarterline and back to the track rather than to X. If your horse tries to lean in the new direction, then actually push him a bit sideways in the direction of the lead with your outside leg before you return to the track to help him understand he doesn't need to lean.

Do not try to go all the way around the arena in the beginning. Use shorter, easier lines so the horse can gain confidence. Master the First Level Test 3 loop. Then begin easy patterns such as a half 10-meter circle onto centerline from A or C, returning to the track at E or B. Counter-canter down the long side and prior to the corner, make a transition.

USEF Rule Book
COUNTER-CANTER

The counter-canter is a balancing and straightening movement that must be executed in collection. The horse canters in correct sequence with the outside foreleg leading with positioning to the side of the leading leg. The foreleg should be aligned to the same track as the hind leg.

Securing the Line of Travel and Engagement

Once the horse can easily do the exercise explained on p. 116, I then like to reinforce the submission to my outside leg. I ride counter-canter down the long side and then walk. In the walk transition, I push him into a renvers (haunches-out) and stay in renvers through the corners. This will reinforce that he cannot lean into my outside leg in the turns. He needs to stay a bit positioned in the direction of the lead, but with more submission to the bend behind the saddle than in the neck. Too much neck bend will cause problems with balance.

Personal Story

My riding student and co-writer Nancy Jones had a 21-year-old bay Thoroughbred gelding who taught her about keeping her weight on the inside seat bone during the counter-canter. Chance Commander, given to her by Barbara Long, dearly loved the flying changes and waited for every opportunity to offer them.

When he and Nancy began working on counter-canter, they progressed from gentle curved lines to an exercise in which they rode a figure eight consisting of a 10-meter circle in true canter into a 20-meter circle in counter-canter. This was Nancy's first venture into counter-canter circles, and sometimes her weight slipped to the outside seat bone. Voilà! As soon as she shifted her weight, Commander offered a perfect flying change, never losing balance or rhythm.

Nancy soon learned to keep her weight anchored correctly if she wanted him to remain in counter-canter!

Commander, incidentally, was a "schoolmaster" in the best sense of the word, and he taught Nancy the tempi changes and canter zig-zag as well—performing the flying changes just as calmly when she asked for them as when she didn't!

14.1 Nancy Jones and Chance Commander, a Thoroughbred and Bold Ruler grandson, with her Cardian Welsh Corgi, Caley, after a trail ride.

Try to ride the counter-canter with the haunches on the rail and the forehand going down the second track, or in a renvers position with less angle. Once the horse understands, and I can feel he is no longer trying to lean, I will continue through the corners in the counter-canter. Your outside leg may need to stay active in these exercises for a while.

Increase the Submission and Suppleness

This is a more advanced counter-canter exercise and the horse should have the counter-canter fairly well established before working on it.

I like to be able to counter-canter and supple my horse in either direction. The horse should understand the aids well enough so he will canter in the direction of your aids, not the direction of the bend. This is important later when you begin flying changes (see p. 131).

Using the medium canter in counter-canter is a great way to help teach a horse the medium, especially when the horse wants to be crooked in the true canter. This is also a good opportunity to help a horse with a long stride learn to collect and shorten his stride a bit without the rider doing so many half-halts.

Remember to work in short periods of counter-canter at first until you build up the strength of the horse. Don't be greedy and keep going until the horse makes a mistake. Find a place to end where the horse has succeeded and can be rewarded.

Training Exercises and Solutuions

Exercise One:
Understanding the Aids for Counter-Canter

This exercise will help with Problems 1, 3, 4, 5, and 6—see p. 115.

First make sure your horse is quickly answering your canter aids from the walk in the direction of the true lead. Also make sure you can do these departs on the quarterline with absolute straightness.

If your horse seems confused about picking up the counter-canter, then try turning on the quarterline, establish your bending and walk a few steps in a half-pass bending toward the rail and ask for the canter. You can also work on a short diagonal line toward the rail. Don't make the horse nervous about this exercise, however. Have patience. If he makes a mistake, quietly make a transition to walk and begin the process again. Check your aids and your weight.

Exercise Two:
Clarifying the Gait for Horse and Rider

This exercise will help Problems 2 and 5—see p. 115.

When the horse breaks gait or drops the canter, usually the horse has lost his balance or the rider has shifted her weight to the wrong seat bone. Quietly go back to walk. If you allow the horse to keep trotting, he will think that is what you asked of him in the first place. Reestablish the submis-

sion to your outside leg and check your seat position before beginning again.

Exercise Three:
Keep the Shoulders under Control
This exercise will help Problems 3 and 5—see p. 115.

When the horse has started to lean on the outside shoulder and into the rider's outside leg, the rider feels this leaning and tends to correct it in the wrong way by bending the neck more in the direction of the lead. Use a more active outside leg, and try to ride a bit off the track so you can push the horse more toward the track and onto the inside engaged hind leg when you feel this evasion.

I tell my students this is like walking down the street and tripping and losing balance. Your first reaction is to throw out your arm to catch your balance. The horse does this as well with his front leg. This disrupts the footfalls of the canter and the horse must trot.

Exercise Four:
Keep the Haunches under Control
This exercise will help Problems 4, 5, and 6—see p. 115.

When you have let the horse put his front legs on the rail during the counter-canter, resulting in the haunches falling to the inside track, walk quietly. Reestablish submission to the outside leg, and watch your line of travel. Sometimes trouble with the haunches can also be due to tension in the horse's back. If the horse is tense, you must stop this exercise and go back and reestablish the topline suppleness and

mental relaxation required in the Classical Training Pyramid.

Exercise Five:
Keep the Horse Upright and Engaged
This exercise will help with Problems 5 and 6—see p. 115.

When the horse stays in the counter-canter lead but does not stay in balance, counter-canter becomes simply "cantering on the wrong lead" as there is no balance, suppleness, or collection. Again, do shorter periods of counter-canter and go back to the straight lines you started with (see p. 116). Ride a bit off the track so you can push the horse a bit sideways toward the rail onto the leading hind leg rather than let him lean into the outside shoulder. Reestablish submission to the outside leg behind the girth.

Exercise Six:
Eliminate Confusion between Counter-Canter and Flying Changes
This exercise will help Problems 3, 4, 5, and 6—see p. 115.

There are many stages to learning counter-canter and flying changes. At some point in the horse's learning process, the counter-canter will lack submission. Don't worry, once the horse is more established in flying changes, usually this problem resolves itself.

Do not punish the horse for the flying change when he offers it. Remember, you never want to punish the horse for something you want later in training. The horse needs to understand the direction of travel and that perhaps the direction of bend or lateral suppleness have nothing to do with the aid for the flying change.

If you horse does a change without your help (remember, everything we teach him he will "use against us" eventually!), quietly go to walk. Emphasize your outside leg with a little bump or tap with the whip and pick up the counter-canter again. Be sure to check that your weight is correct as moving your weight slightly as part of the aid. You may need to use your outside leg as the active (or the "keep-cantering" aid) for a while, as the use of the inside leg may confuse the horse. Eventually he will understand that as long as the outside leg maintains the barrier, he must stay in the counter-canter.

Half-Pass

The horse must move away from the leg,
under your weight. When you put the lateral
moving leg on, the horse had better scoot.

The half-pass is the final lateral move-ment your horse needs to learn. This movement is at the top of the Pyramid of Lateral Movements (see p. 50). Most imperfections in the half-pass are issues having to do with correct reactions from requirements lower down on this Pyramid.

Imperfections and Evasions

Your horse:

1 Leads with or trails his haunches.

2 Loses cadence or impulsion.

3 Performs with his forehand not on the line-of-travel.

4 Tilts his head.

5 Lacks submission to the bend.

6 Has limited lateral reach.

7 Won't go sideways enough.

8 Experiences confusion regarding the aids.

9 Goes too much sideways and lacks engagement.

I'll provide solutions to these common prob-lems beginning on p. 126. First, read the definition of the half-pass from the USEF Rule Book (see sidebar, p. 122).

How to Ride and Train

Rider's Aids
When riding half-pass to the right:
I Inside (right) rein: Positions the head, neck, and shoulders to the right, onto the line of travel.

2 Outside rein: Controls the speed. Helps the inside leg maintain the front legs on the line of travel.

3 Inside leg: This is the active leg, which maintains the impulsion. Also supports the bend by keeping the rib cage to the outside and helps keep the inside shoulder up and mobile.

4 Outside leg behind the girth: Maintains the position and angle of the hindquarters. Can be active in the half-halt.

5 Seat: Sit in the direction of the bend and the movement or to the inside.

Half-pass is the second movement in dressage where the forehand is on the line of travel. The first is travers (haunches-in)—see p. 84. Half-pass has the line of travel on a diagonal line rather than a straight line. In half-pass you must think that the position of the shoulders and neck is a shoulder-in going sideways. Read the chapter on shoulder-in and review "the gunslinger" image (see p. 77). You should have the same image in mind for the half-pass.

USEF Rule Book
HALF-PASS

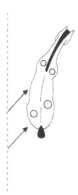

This movement is a variation of travers, executed on a diagonal line instead of along the wall. It can be performed in collected trot (and in passage in a freestyle) or collected canter. The horse should be slightly bent around the inside leg of the rider and in the direction in which it is moving. The horse should maintain the same cadence and balance throughout the whole movement. In order to give more freedom and mobility to the shoulders, it is of great importance that the impulsion be maintained, especially the engagement of the inside hind leg. The horse's body is nearly parallel to the long side of the arena with the forehand slightly in advance of the hindquarters. The bend in the half-pass should increase with the steepness of the diagonal. In the trot, the outside legs pass and cross in front of the inside legs. In the canter, the movement is performed in a series of forward/sideways strides.

15.1 The half-pass.

  Aims of half-pass in trot: to show a fluent collected trot movement on a diagonal line with a greater degree of bend than in shoulder-in. Fore and hind legs cross, balance and cadence are maintained. Aims of the half-pass in canter: to both demonstrate and develop the collection and suppleness of the canter by moving fluently forward and sideways without any loss of rhythm, balance, or softness and submission to the bend.

15.2 Gwen Blake on Sancette riding a Third Level half-pass. Sancette is showing good lateral reach and bend, but his poll could be a bit higher.

I find when riders think travers, they tend to push the haunches ahead and move the shoulders in the wrong direction. Then the exercise never really supples the horse laterally or engages the hind legs. Think about placing the outside shoulder between the hind legs. The beauty of a wonderful half-pass is the lift and crossing of the outside shoulder. This outside front leg should be pointing to the letter where the exercise will finish.

JUDGE'S TIP

The amount of lateral reach is a consideration for a very high score in the half-pass. Many horses can get from Point A to Point B, but one horse will take ten strides while another only seven. The ability to have this huge amount of lateral reach, plus the elevation of the horse's shoulders, is what makes a "9" or "10."

Many riders teach their horses the wrong response by not thinking about how to start and end each half-pass.

The Start

From the Centerline

When you start your half-pass on the centerline, be sure you put the haunches on the line of travel (that is, the centerline) first. You should actually think shoulder-fore on the centerline prior to going sideways. If you don't do this, you will have the haunches leading every time. Remember that the haunches come around the corner last! This will also give you time to point the shoulders to the letter that is your destination or to put them on the line of travel. Don't forget that half-pass is one of the exercises that have the shoulders on the line of travel, not the haunches.

From the Rail

This is a bit harder and needs to be approached differently. First you need to move the horse's shoulders, head, and neck toward the letter that is your endpoint. The horse should not move sideways yet. If he does, then just do an exercise where you bend the neck in a few strides and send the horse forward with your inside leg until he understands. Once the forehand is displaced, push the haunches around your inside leg, and then move your weight.

Because the half-pass from the rail is more difficult, usually the haunches will trail in this exercise. Make sure you have "captured" the haunches with your outside leg before you shift your weight and ask the horse to move sideways.

The Finish

With the half-pass from the centerline, you will end up on the rail. Think about a few steps of renvers but with only a slight angle. Place the haunches on the wall and keep the horse's shoulders slightly to the second track. Engage the new inside hind leg with your outside leg, then change the bend or position to shoulder-fore in the new direction.

This is also important prior to your flying change in the canter half-pass. If you are able to control the finish and ride your horse a bit more forward, your flying change should be straight and uphill with good expression. If you are sloppy and the horse usually puts the shoulders on the rail and pushes the haunches to the inside of the arena, the change will be downhill and crooked.

With the half-pass that ends on the centerline, think of the exercise from half-pass to shoulder-in described on p. 127. This is the way to finish, but with shoulder-fore, not shoulder-in. In this way you will be able to keep the horse's haunches on the centerline and won't lose your engagement.

To turn in the opposite direction, you need to move the horse's shoulders in that direction while keeping the hind legs on the centerline. You should be able to do this prior to the turn. You must be careful not to teach your horse that he can fall sideways or always turn in the direction of the bend because such a habit could ruin your counter change of hand and zig-zags later (see p. 157).

JUDGING TIP

Often riders have too much bend and they lose the cadence. Of course, for the highest score for this movement you need to have both. If you

Personal Story

I do have a caution for everyone getting ready for Third Level. Do not put the flying changes and the half-pass together too soon. I made this mistake and paid for it dearly!

Once the horse is truly confirmed in the changes and no longer thinking they are a great movement to "use against you," you are ready to combine the two. Until then, work your half-passes to the wall, continue to counter-canter through the short end of the ring, and make the change on the opposite long side. Another way to school the half-pass at the canter is to come from the rail to the centerline and then continue on the same lead and turn the same direction.

I had a wonderfully talented Trakeh-ner stallion named Maroon. He felt he was much smarter than me. And in this case he was, because I put the changes and half-pass together too soon.

I still clearly remember the show. Mike Mathews was judging. My test was going super. I started the canter work and things went south. The canter half-pass left from the centerline to the rail consisted of out-of-control

15.3 I'm on the Trakehner stallion, Maroon, who I owned with Dr. Jane Rutledge.

tempi changes. Maroon did not lose any bend and the canter did not change at all. He stayed nicely on the bit, but not on the aids. I received a generous "2" for the half-pass and also a "2" for the flying change. The comment about the movement was, "Very difficult and would have scored highly if this was a freestyle."

15.4 Hibernian Breeze and me, showing at Fourth Level. It was my first outing at this level, and you can see that I have not learned to sit in the direction of the half-pass! It was hard, but with work and longe lessons, I eventually could sit on the left side of the horse as well as the right!

have cadence and some bend, you will score about a "7" with the comment, "Good cadence, needs more bend." With too much bend your horse may lose the cadence. This will result in a "6" with a remark like, "Fairly good bend, but needs more cadence."

Losing the regularity or cadence in a lateral movement won't affect the gait score, but it will influence the submission score.

Training Exercises and Solutions

Exercise One:
Leg-Yield to Half-Pass

This exercise will help solve Problems 5, 6, and 7— see p. 121.

This exercise is a great way to introduce a few

half-pass steps into the training. Start leg-yielding across the diagonal. Be sure the horse is quick off your lateral moving leg. Then, slowly bend the horse in the direction of travel for a few strides (into half-pass). When you lose impulsion or the sideways inclination, turn the exercise back into leg-yield and reinforce the lateral-moving leg again. In other words, start with the easier exercise, add a few steps of the more difficult exercise, then go back to the easier exercise.

Exercise Two:
Change the Angle of the Haunches
This exercise will help solve Problems 1, 3, and 5—see p. 121.

This is a great exercise because it gives the rider control over the horse's "caboose" in your three-car choo-choo train (see p. 16). If you can master this exercise, you will have total control in the show ring to either add more angle or take some angle away.

Start on the diagonal line, just as if you were going across the diagonal. The key to this exercise is that the forehand must stay on the line of travel. If you draw a line across the diagonal, the horse should have one front leg, one shoulder, and one ear on either side of the diagonal line. The rider should have one shoulder and one hand on either side of the line.

At about the quarterline, displace the haunches into a three-track travers (haunches-in). Near X, displace the haunches more into a four-track travers for a few strides. Then return to your three-track angle and make the horse straight on the diagonal line prior to the corner.

If you have a horse that won't displace the haunches enough or the comment on your test is "haunches trailing," it is okay to even push the haunches ahead for a few strides to make your point.

Exercise Three:
Head-to-Wall Leg-Yield
This exercise will help solve Problems 1, 5, 6, and 7—see p. 121.

A good half-pass cannot be accomplished without a quick reaction to the outside (or "go-sideways" leg). The horse must really scoot when you use this aid. The rider cannot worry about impulsion or cadence without this reaction first. I see many riders struggling with this, to the point they move the outside leg farther and farther back, which only puts the leg in a weaker position. Riders who sit to the outside usually receive a less-than-stellar reaction to the outside leg and then try to "shove" the horse over. Remember the horse must move away from the leg, under the rider's weight. This is the aid you taught your horses in leg-yield. The only difference now is that you are adding bending.

Go back and review the chapter on leg-yielding (see p. 49). Work on the head-to-wall leg-yield until your horse can easily, and with impulsion, do a four-track leg-yield in trot.

Exercise Four:
Half-pass to Shoulder-In
This exercise solves Problems 1, 2, 3, 8, and 9—see p. 121.

This exercise will help the rider and the horse better understand the role of the inside leg. You will go to the right. Start your half-pass. Half-pass right for 5 meters. Then use your inside leg actively at the girth and move your weight back to the center. The horse should change the line-of-travel and now be moving straight toward the short end in shoulder-in right. Once the horse accepts the inside leg, move your weight to the right and activate your outside leg behind the girth to move into half-pass again. Keep making transitions until your horse understands.

In the beginning, when teaching half-pass, you will need to use the outside leg as the active leg most of the way through the movement. Once the horse gets more supple, however, he will quickly start to go too much sideways. Then it is time to teach him about the inside leg. This exercise will help him understand both legs.

A warning to riders: You will use your reins first when you feel the horse going too much sideways. You will either pull your hands in the wrong direction or you will use the inside rein as an indirect rein of opposition or toward the outside hip. This should not be a rein correction; it must be a leg correction. Half-pass has the shoulders leading. The inside front leg will be the first leg to touch the track at the end of your half-pass. By using the reins incorrectly you are actually using conflicting aids and pulling the shoulders to the outside.

Exercise Five:
Half-Pass to Travers
This exercise will help solve Problems 5, 7, and 8—see p. 121.

This exercise helps the submission to the outside leg. When your horse has his haunches trail-ing, then just pushing harder with your outside leg usually won't help. It will probably cause the whole horse to fall sideways more quickly.

Start on the rail in travers right. Once you are happy with the submission to the outside leg, swing the horse's shoulders over to the right, and do about 5 meters of half-pass right. Then stop the forehand and ride the "dining car" of your choo-choo train and your horse's shoulders straight ahead toward the short end of the ring with your inside leg and outside rein. Then activate your outside leg again and ask for more angle from the "caboose." You should now be in travers right. In both the half-pass to shoulder-in, and half-pass to travers, the bend won't change, just the line-of-travel.

Exercise Six:
Half-Pass to "Bendy" Leg-Yield
This exercise helps solve Problems 2, 5, 8, and 9—see p. 121.

This is a great exercise for the trot. If you do this exercise at canter, do not change your weight when you go back the other direction because your horse might think you are giving him a fly-ing change aid.

Start with your half-pass right out of the corner. Only ride four or five strides and then, keeping the bending to the right, send the horse back to the wall with your inside leg. Then change your weight and use your outside leg and develop your half-pass for a few strides. Once again, use your inside leg and change your weight and send the horse back to the wall.

Exercise Seven:
Poll Suppleness
This exercise solves Problems 4 and 5—see p. 121.

When the horse tilts his head it is a sign that the poll is not supple. Go back to the warm-up chapter and read the poll suppling exercises (p. 24). Work with your stretchy, chewy circle to loosen the poll and then bring the frame back up and try the half-pass again. You may need to overbend the neck to the inside or allow the neck to get a bit lower for a while to allow the poll to get supple and make it easier for the horse. You can also work with some counterflexing as well.

Exercise One will also help as it will decrease the difficulty of the movement for the horse (see p. 126).

Exercise Eight:
Bending Exercises
This exercise helps solve Problems 2, 4, and 5— see p. 121.

If your horse is truly not laterally supple to both sides, you will struggle with half-pass. Review the Pyramid of the Lateral Movements and slowly work your way back up, from the very bottom to the very top (see p. 50).

Exercise Nine:
The Archery Bow
This is helpful for Problems 1 and 3—see p. 121.

If you think of your horse as an archery bow that is strung, you will have a bow that has a curve. You want your horse to mimic the bow with his body, showing an equal curve from poll to tail. This bow should be wrapped around your inside leg. There should not be more bend in front of the saddle or behind it. The connection between the cars of your choo-choo train should be in the same position.

When you are riding your half-pass, you can look at the horse's inside ear and then look just over your inside shoulder. You should see the inside hip of the horse. If you don't see the "caboose," then you have lost the haunches and need to develop more submission to the outside leg. If you see the top of the croup, then your haunches are leading or your shoulders are perhaps slipping in the wrong direction.

Exercise Ten:
Challenge the Bend, then Relax
This exercise will address Problems 2, 3, and 5— see p. 121.

Start your half-pass on the diagonal line. Every four strides increase your inside rein and outside leg behind the girth. Think bend more! Hold for two strides and relax those aids. Do this several times across the diagonal.

16

Flying Changes

*Everything we teach the horse
he can "use against us."*

How many horses and riders find their dressage career stalling out at Second Level because they can't manage the flying changes? I've worked with many *difficult* horses over the years—it is very seldom a horse easily learns flying changes without encountering problems due to conformation, temperament, or both. And, conformation and temperament challenges result in any manner of imperfections in performance.

First, it's important to understand just what the flying change is, so read the definition from the USEF Rule Book (see sidebar, p. 132).

Imperfections and Evasions

Your horse:

1 Runs away.

2 Throws his head up.

3 Is late behind.

4 Is late in front.

5 Has a canter that isn't forward enough.

6 Has a long stride with little suspension (an "earthbound canter").

7 Performs changes that are unequal.

You can find solutions to these common imperfections beginning on p. 142. In addition, on the pages ahead I'll not only provide you with a sensible and logical system that will work for teaching the flying changes to all horses, I'll also give you tips for working with the "challenged" horse.

But before we begin, I do need to be clear on one point: if you have never ridden a flying change to get the "feeling" and timing of the movement, you should stop reading here and send your horse to a good professional who will teach him the change while you ride a school-master a few times to work on your timing. Then, learn how to correctly ride the preparatory work for the changes, which I'll explain next. Once the horse understands what you want and you have an idea of how to correctly influence him, you can ride and train him yourself (improving his changes or teaching your next horse from the beginning).

Be honest about your abilities. It is usually a total disaster when novices try to teach the changes to their own horse. Once a horse learns to be late behind, or in front, it is very difficult for him to "unlearn" this fault.

The other issue is the horse's mental and physical tension. Training a horse up the levels will result in some tension. The horse usually gets a bit nervous when you teach him something new or ask him to work harder. The most important aspect to know now is that horses almost *always* get tense when being introduced to the flying change.

You must be calm and patient and *never* punish the horse for a volunteered change at this early stage. There is time later on when the changes are confirmed to have training sessions that will entail teaching the horse to change only on the rider's aids. But in the beginning, never punish for what you want later: if the horse is tense and nervous and makes a mistake, and you then punish him, the tension will escalate and sometimes the changes will *never* be performed without tension. If during this process you feel there is a mounting tension in the horse, again, get professional help.

How to Ride and Train

Let's say you are ready to take on the flying change challenge, with competent instruction and good eyes on the ground.

The Correct, Three-Beat Canter
Before you think about teaching the horse the actual flying change, you need to understand the basics of the canter as a gait. Let's review the steps in a correct, three-beat canter stride that we discussed in chapter 2 (fig. 16.1):

1 The horse strikes off with his outside hind leg.

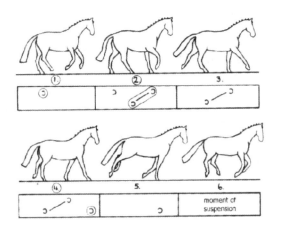

16.1 The three-beat canter stride.

2 The inside hind leg and outside foreleg strike the ground together.

3 The inside foreleg (the leading leg) is the last leg to strike the ground.

4 This is followed by a moment of suspension in which all four legs are in the air.

That moment of suspension is when the horse has the opportunity to change leads. Perhaps you have felt the change when your horse

Ways Your Horse Might Be Not-So-Perfect for the Changes

Physical and Conformation Challenges

Your horse:

- Is croup high and/or has physical attributes that make it difficult for him to lower his hindquarters to elevate the forehand.

- Is long-backed and has trouble collecting at the canter or reaching well under his center of gravity.

- Has breed-specific characteristics such as those of Morgans, Friesians, and Spanish horses that result in a highly elevated move-

ment of the forelegs and less elevation of the hind legs. The actual biomechanics of the gait are different.

- Has flat, earthbound canter strides that make it difficult for him to bend his joints and carry more weight on the hindquarters effectively.

Temperament Challenges

Your horse:

- Is easily excitable and tends to "grab the bit" and try to run with you when you ask for more collection or difficult movements.

- Becomes stubborn and cantankerous when you try to move him beyond his comfort zone.

- Gets tense in his learning process and becomes upset when he doesn't understand what you are asking him to do.

- Is a solid performer once he knows what is expected of him but takes a long time to process new information.

- Is a bit dull to the aids and can be lazy.

16.3 Junior rider Audrey Jones and her horse Rhondo show an uphill canter with lots of expression. This type of canter makes flying changes easy.

As I've said, it is very seldom that a horse easily learns the flying changes and never looks back. In my career, I've had only one such horse, Halloh, who had a wonderful canter, very uphill and balanced. He was the first very expensive horse that I had bought myself that did not belong to a sponsor.

Halloh did the flying changes calmly on the first attempt…and on every subsequent attempt. No excitement, nothing. Of course, he was not fond of the idea of tempi changes, and I had to enlist Robert Dover's help for these. (So maybe even Halloh had some "issues" with the changes.) Poor Robert. Halloh left the arena on the side of a hill (Robert was in Malibu then) and off they went—crash bang through the scrub oak. But bless Robert! The next day he mounted up again, this time with a helmet and success! So as you can see, even I am not above seeking help from a professional when I feel I need it.

offered one on his own because you shifted your weight and aids unintentionally, or he lost his balance. Or possibly you are a rider who has had success getting changes in Western riding or the hunter/jumper ring. Still, you may sense something is missing from your understanding of flying changes as we teach them in dressage. You are not alone, believe me!

The Flying Change Pyramid

So what do you need to know and feel in order to reliably ask for—and get—a flying change from your horse? Again, both of you need a good foundation in the basics before you attempt to train the movement.

In my opinion, every movement should have its own "Training Pyramid," and in particular, the flying change. All movements would start with the quality and regularity of the gait. Then the horse must be supple and truly using his muscles in a correct way. This is enhanced by the horse's reaction to the rider's aids (also by the other movements that are required to build the more advanced movements).

Think of your training like building a house, using the flying change as an example. You would never put the roof on the house first. So, logically, you cannot ask for a correct flying change when there is no foundation or first floor. For the flying change, the different requirements, from the most important foundation at the base of the pyramid (the house) to the goal at the pinnacle are as follows.

Quality of Canter

Some horses will have an easy time with the changes due to their wonderful balance and elas-

Personal Story

My first experience with flying changes was actually when I was riding Western as a teen. I took lessons on my Appaloosa Popeyed Chief ("Pepper") from a well-known Colorado reining rider, Murphy Bryant. Pepper was a speed horse and loved to run barrels and poles. However, he would not walk or calm down at all afterward. So Murph and I decided perhaps he would enjoy the mental challenge of reining and Western riding. Both classes required flying changes, although Murph called them "swapping leads."

The change technique was not difficult. You ran really fast on one lead and then turned the horse sharply in the other direction. The horse either fell down or "swapped leads." Pepper became quite good at this type of change with the barrel racing and pole bending. He could also "sit" and spin, so rollbacks were very easy for him. We won a lot of youth reining classes at the local gymkhanas and Appaloosa shows.

Pepper also became my rodeo queen horse. In 1971 I was chosen "Girl of the West" for the Pikes Peak or Bust Rodeo. So before anyone tells me I am prejudiced about reining, let me tell you many of those riders know a lot! The best—just like the best dressage riders—are quite sophisticated and subtle in their aiding. I have worked with several Colorado reining riders on the flying changes exercise so they can actually do tempi changes on a straight line in their reining freestyles. It's as breathtaking as watching a Grand Prix dres-

16.2 Here I am with Popeyed Chief during my reign as "Girl of the West."

sage freestyle! I loved watching the reining at the 2010 Alltech World Equestrian Games in Kentucky. I don't blame Anky Van Grunsven a bit for getting hooked!

Still, sophistication and subtlety weren't my style back in those days. I loved my outfit, though. Royal purple chaps with white buck stitching and a purple hat. I didn't have all the bling today's riders wear, but it was very smart for the time! I still have those chaps and lots of memories. (Too bad I can't zip them up anymore!)

ticity in the canter. However, as mentioned in the sidebar on p. 133, for many horses, their conformation makes them less-than-perfect candidates for the changes. Horses with long, flat strides and marginal suspension will find them more difficult. As said, Friesians or Morgans with very high and expressive front legs, but hind legs that are low off the ground are, in my opinion, the most difficult to teach. I'll give you techniques on how to work with your "imperfect" horse shortly. But, first, let's look at the rest of the Flying Change Pyramid.

Counter-Canter

I was always taught through the years that the counter-canter must be in place *prior* to the changes. I have begun to rethink this a bit as I now feel that if you make the horse too submissive to the counter-canter, it makes the idea of the change more difficult. I am discovering if the horse has a difficult canter, then counter-canter is very helpful. For a horse with a high quality canter, I now teach the changes first and *then* establish the counter-canter. And I am careful not to take away a young horse's "will" to change on his own.

When you have a horse that needs to work in counter-canter first, remember the counter-canter must be upright— no leaning onto the outside shoulder or outside leg!

Simple Changes

Okay, the simple changes are important for this

16.4 The Flying Change Pyramid.

reason: your horse must be willing and collected enough to come from the canter directly into a relaxed walk. Then walk him a few steps and return promptly into canter on the other lead. Your horse must remain on the aids and be straight for these transitions. If he cannot go directly to walk without stiffening the topline, or with a few trot steps, you are *not* ready for the flying changes.

This transition becomes the half-halt for the change itself and is thus *part of* the half-halt. The horse must easily go from one lead to another in balance, be straight, and be supple through the topline.

When the horse *drifts left or right* in the simple changes, it creates difficulties with the flying changes later. *Hollowing or stiffening the topline* also causes problems later on, such as bolting and changes that are late behind. *Lack of straightness* causes changes that are out of balance or late in front or behind.

A simple canter depart on the quarterline must be established prior to trying the changes. Without the promptness to the canter aid, the horse may ignore the flying-change aid.

"New" Half-Halt

I think it is important to have a slightly different half-halt for the counter-canter than for the flying change. This way my horses are not confused as to which movement I am asking for at the time.

For the counter-canter half-halt, think *inside* leg

Flying Changes

New Half Halt

Simple Changes

Counter Canter

Quality of Canter

active to the outside rein. The inside rein keeps the horse positioned in the direction of the lead, not the direction of travel.

For the flying change half-halt, you must put the horse with the *new* inside leg up into the *new* outside rein and increase the suppleness in the new direction. So, if you are riding the right lead canter, your left leg behind the girth would become the active leg and your right rein would become the new outside rein. Your left rein would help supple and horse in the new direction. I discuss this in detail next, as we reach the top of the Flying Change Pyramid.

The Flying Change

With most horses the aids for the change should be given as their shoulders are coming up in the moment of suspension (see fig. 16.1 and the description of the canter on p. 133). To prepare for and perform the flying change:

1 Check your horse's adjustability by riding from medium canter to collected canter and back a few times.

2 Round the short side and leave the rail on a short diagonal.

3 As you approach the rail, flex your horse to the new "inside" direction and slide your outside leg back, letting it rest quietly. Your "old" outside leg is still in position, keeping your horse on his current lead.

4 When you are ready for the change, when the horse's shoulders are coming up, move your new inside leg forward and press your horse's

side with your new outside leg. (I'll explain a few exceptions to this later.)

5 Note: I do not do much with my seat; I just move my new inside leg forward and press the horse's side with the new outside leg. I am very short, and if I tried to swing my legs a lot I would move too much out of the saddle. It is imperative that the rider sit quietly so as not to cause a balance problem with the horse. The old style of aid was lots of lower leg swinging with the rider almost standing up out of the saddle and moving side to side. I believe this was due to the calm and somewhat dull nature of the old-style Warmblood. Trying this technique on a hotter, more modern Warmblood or a Thoroughbred would result in quite a lot of hysteria!

Riding the Flying Change
Rider's Aids

Be sure to read and understand the preparation for the new half-halt for the flying change (see p. 136) and then the steps to performing one (at left). Without the correct reaction to the half-halt, your aids for the flying change won't work. A summary of the aids for a change from right to left are as follows:

1 Inside rein: You are on the right lead, so this is the right rein. This rein is the half-halting rein in the aid for the flying change.

2 Outside rein: This is the left rein. It will cease to be the half-halting rein and becomes the suppling rein. It must remain elastic to allow the horse to change the inside foreleg.

In addition to Western riding, in my youth I also became involved in Pony Club, where I was first exposed to dressage. Then, during a stint in England, I took group dressage lessons with the Oxford Riding Club. When I returned from England, I wanted more and began to work with trainer Bodo Hangen. He would come every month to Table Mountain Ranch in Golden, Colorado. (You can read more about my time with Bodo on p. 24.)

I had a Thoroughbred mare in training named Hibernian Breeze. Her nickname around the barn was "Breeze Bomb." Breeze had come to me from the mountains of Colorado, and she was very thin and lacked muscle when I put her in my trailer and made my way down an icy I-70 back to Golden. She was a doll for about 30 days, then as we fattened her up we found out she had quite a personality. When she was in heat, she was very sensitive to the leg. She squealed; she kicked. She could also throw her head up and run away. Hence the nickname "Breeze Bomb."

In any case, Bodo eventually declared the time had

come to teach Breeze flying changes. So one month he gave me all the preparatory work to do before his next visit. I did it diligently every day. I could not resist, however, just *trying* the new movement out a week before Bodo came to Golden. Then, in my lesson the following week, I proudly showed him the changes.

"Ja," he said, "that is good. Now I will ride her."

He could not get one change. He asked me what aids I had used. Hmmmm. Good question. I told him I really did not know, but I think I just turned her in the other direction.

"Now we teach her the classical way," he said.

I tell this story to many of my students who moan over the time it takes to correctly and calmly teach a horse the flying change. I tell them that when

16.5 I am showing Breeze Bomb at Second Level. Who knew what excitement was waiting?

they get to Horse Heaven and Ahlerich, the late Reiner Klimke's 1984 Olympic Gold Medal mount, is offered to them to ride, they will have mastered the classical way and will actually be able to produce tempi changes!

Incidentally, Breeze was also the first horse I ever trained "up the levels." She ended up at Prix St. George and won the AHSA Regional Finals at that level in 1982. Then she was given to Sandra Hotz (now a USEF S Dressage Judge) as a Young Rider Prospect. Sandy had the best seat around and was one of the few Young Riders who could handle the Breeze Bomb.

3 Inside leg: This is your right leg. It will be the active leg in the aid for the flying change and moves behind the girth. The outside rein and leg (right) "close the door" for the change. When the right door is closed, the left door will open so the legs can change position in the air.

4 Outside leg: This is the left leg. In the aid, it moves forward to the girth to allow the left hind leg to change. Once the new lead is established, this leg will activate the left lead canter.

5 Seat: You will need to move your left hip slightly forward. If you keep your weight to the right you will block the change. Do not think of "leaning" in the new direction, however, as this will cause the horse to lose balance.

In the preparation for the flying change, I like to use my outside leg to help activate the new inside hind. This is also an aid to tell the horse this "outside door is closed." This leg keeps the horse from leaning into the direction of the new lead. I also ask my horse to become supple to the direction of the new lead. I like to think of being able to push the rib cage a bit to the outside as I make sure the shoulders are slightly inside of the new hind leg. When the horse takes the half-halt from the new inside leg to the new outside rein, you are ready to use the aids for the change.

Of course, simply knowing and correctly applying the aids in their correct sequence is only part of the story here. To regularly produce simple, quiet changes requires much more work.

My System

After being able to take the horse up and down the Flying Change Pyramid I've just described, I then work with what I quite simply call "My System." Other trainers may have slightly different versions of this system. The most important aspect of training flying changes, however, is to maintain *one system* for the entire process so you do not confuse the horse. Confusion leads to tension and mistakes. This is one movement that if learned incorrectly—say the horse is always late behind or in front and he becomes used to this mistake—he will continue to make it for his entire lifetime.

1 First I have the horse counter-canter on the rail. Remember that in counter-canter, the hind legs should be on the line of travel—that is, on the rail—which makes it necessary for the shoulders to be slightly on the second track in a mini renvers. I then use my outside leg as the active leg to hold the horse against the wall and tell him that "this door is closed."

2 Once the horse understands the counter-canter and will stay there with no problem, I start to supple him to the other direction, toward the inside of the arena, riding short periods with slight position or bending to the inside. For example, if you are in the left-lead counter-canter, the left hind leg of the horse is on the rail and is the engaged, leading hind leg. I now start to supple him to the inside of the arena, or to the right. I only do this on the long sides of the arena, and then position him back in the direction of his lead on the short ends.

3 When the horse finds it easy to do this exercise going both ways, I go back to the simple changes.

My first Friesian was a mare named Mighty Aphrodite ridden by USEF S Judge William Solyntjes in Minnesota. She had placed very high in the USDF Horse of the Year awards at Training, First, and Second Levels. However, she was one of those horses for whom the flying change stood in the way of Third Level and beyond.

We used the same technique I had used previously with then student Amy Fowler (later Larson) and her Morgan mare, The Colonel's Lady, nicknamed "Kimmie," that she ultimately showed at Grand Prix. Amy received her USDF Gold Medal with Kimmie and also did great freestyle exhibitions at the Morgan Nationals for years. She is a perfect example of achieving success with an "imperfect" horse.

Kimmie and Aphrodite were similar in their conformation challenges, but quite different in temperament and response. Bill and I worked at putting Aphrodite's front end more on the ground and got the hind end bouncing in the air. A good buck would have

been wonderful, but Aphrodite was not that sensitive. We had to do with the bouncing! Kimmie, on the other hand, was quite sensitive and as she did a change, she also liked to kick out a bit. The kickboards in the arena took a beating!

Mares sometimes kick toward the whip, in which case I carry the whip in the inside hand. Dr. Jane Rutledge's mare Easter was one of these. She was 17.2 hands of "German woman." One direction was always late behind. I used all the techniques I had in my bag of tricks, but nothing was working with her. So, knowing how

16.6 Amy Fowler and her Morgan mare, The Colonel's Lady ("Kimmie"), eventually earned their USDF Gold Medal.

she loved to kick at the whip instead of move away from it, I moved the whip to my inside hand, and as I aided with my outside leg, I also tapped her with the whip on her inside hip. Mission accomplished! Easter kicked at the whip and the change was clean! Eventually she figured it out and I no longer needed the whip. If the horse is not sensitive to the aid, then I use the whip in the outside hand to reinforce the aid.

4 I now start to ride the simple change with a "new" half-halt (see p. 136). I begin in counter-canter, supple the horse in the new direction, and with my new inside leg, which is still behind the girth, I put the horse up against the new outside rein and walk. I then quickly go to the new lead by changing my leg aids.

5 As I've said, I really do not like changing a lot with the seat. I want the horse to move quickly but in a straight line into the new lead. I don't want him to think that the lead change or the new bend has anything to do with the direction or the aid.

6 Once the horse understands the new half-halt and is quickly taking the new lead, I remove the walk steps and ask for the change in the air.

Most horses learn this quickly. Some need to have this exercise taken onto a 20-meter circle where the rider pushes the horse away from the new inside leg. This is helpful for the horse that wants to fall into the new lead.

Remember, the key is to have the weight on the horse's outside legs so the new inside legs can "fly."

Every Different Breed Does the Changes Its Own Way

I have tweaked my system over the years as I have worked with more and more different types and breeds of horses in my clinics. They do not all fit neatly into the same system.

As I've mentioned, Friesians, Morgans, Luisi-tanos, Andalusians, and sometimes draft crosses usually have very high and expressive front legs while their hind legs work quite close to the ground. The challenge is getting them to change *behind* first. The front is no problem. With some of the Baroque breeds, consequently, at the beginning, it is better to give the aid, still quietly, as the horse's shoulders are coming down (see fig. 16.1, Phase 5, p. 133). This allows the hind legs a bit more time up in the air, which should make the change easier. Once the horse understands the change, the aids should revert back to the classical system and be given as the horse's shoulders are coming up.

Thoroughbreds, Quarter Horses, and some other breeds have flatter strides than many Warmbloods. Horses that are croup-high or long-backed have a harder time lowering the hindquarters and stepping more deeply under the center of gravity. These conformational challenges can be helped with the exercises I list, beginning on p. 142.

FCH ("Flying Change Hell"!)

Even without conformational and temperamental challenges (see sidebar on p. 133), most horses get very excited when learning the flying changes. The first day they usually perform the changes very nicely. Then they think about it overnight, and voilà. You are about to experience FCH! This is one reason I *never* teach flying changes in a clinic when the rider only has one lesson. I would look like a star on that day; however, the rider would pay for it the next time she attempted the changes on her own.

How long does FCH last? At least a month; sometimes three. First, the rider must be committed to working on the changes every day. You as the rider may be tempted to say, "He was so wild;

I'll back off so he will be better." I have news for you. The horse needs to get *bored* with the idea. Flying changes need to be part of his daily work. Period.

I usually start the flying changes right after the last show of the season so I have time to work through this stretch of time. You need to accept that daily work will be only canter exercises for a while. Trot work can be used in the warm-up, but the schooling focus is on canter.

Remember that you must address the mental and physical tension this exercise will create. You need to recognize if your horse is no longer learning but rather becoming afraid of the exercise. At this point, you need to find professional help. Some tension is normal. You must deal with it in a calm and logical way.

Exercises to Help Your Horse Understand So You Avoid FCH

1 If your horse is getting nervous or running, go back to the simple changes. You can place the simple changes on the spot where you would normally want the flying change in the test. Even doing three simple changes on the diagonal helps tempis later on. Once the horse is again accepting the half-halt, try adding one flying change.

2 Horses with less suspension and more earth-bound strides can benefit from putting a pole on the ground and cantering over the pole. Once the horse is calmly cantering over the pole, you can ask for the flying change in the air.

3 I also like the idea of increasing and decreasing the circle. This is helpful for a horse who will not accept the counter-canter exercises. Supple the horse to the outside and push him into a smaller circle with your outside leg. Then supple inside and push him back out with your inside leg. Once the horse accepts this exercise you can do your preparatory work by suppling to the outside and moving him slightly to the inside and then asking for a flying change onto another 20-meter circle.

4 Know that your counter-canter is going to be lost for a while. There will be plenty of time later to go back and reestablish the submission to the counter-canter. You must be very creative as your horse will start to anticipate the changes. Again, remember the tension and don't punish your horse for anticipating the change until you feel you are 90 percent successful with a clean and calm flying change.

Cures and Solutions

Finally, here are solutions to the common imperfections and evasions listed on p. 131.

1 **Problem: My horse runs away.**

This evasion could be due to temperament or conformation problems (see sidebar, p. 133). When the horse is running away, he is likely out of balance. *Go back* in the Flying Change Pyramid! Reestablish the basics and work on the simple changes again.

2 **Problem: My horse throws his head up.**

This is usually due to temperament and balance issues. A professional may choose to use draw reins here if the horse is very hot and out of control. I question, however, if draw reins are needed. Perhaps the horse is not really well enough established in the basics, and the balance is not correct—in which case, again, you need to go back and solidify the foundation skills of the movement.

3 **Problem: My horse is late behind.**

This can be due to conformation problems with a slow hind leg or lack of suspension, or it can be an alignment issue. Go back and make sure the horse is really on your aids in the canter depart and is straight. I sometimes find that doing some work in-hand with the piaffe to activate the hind legs can be very helpful (see p. 62).

In addition, I often work with a little pirouette canter (a very collected canter almost on the spot), to get the horse in a shorter, higher stride (see p. 111). This often makes the horse a bit more mobile and able to make the change easily. Remember, like the mare I described in the sidebar on p. 140, if your horse kicks at the whip, then you can help the horse get a clean change by putting the whip in the inside hand and tapping the horse's inside hip as you apply the outside leg.

4 **Problem: My horse is late in front.**

This is mostly due to straightness issues: usually the horse's shoulders are falling to the wrong direction (outside) instead of the rider keeping them positioned in front of the new inside hind. Go back to suppling exercises and simple changes on the quarterline. Work on exercises that move

the shoulders around (see chapter 9, p. 77). Work on the quarterline, keeping the haunches on this line while doing a few strides of shoulder-in one direction, straightening, and then moving the shoulders to the outside in shoulder-out (or toward the wall).

5 **Problem: My horse's canter is not forward enough.**

Here is a problem for the horse that is a little bit dull or not sensitive to the driving aids. Try a few strides of medium canter prior to the change and then again a few strides after. The horse will start to anticipate the medium and go more forward on his own.

6 **Problem: My horse has a long stride and little suspension.**

This type of canter, which is breed-specific, requires a lot of work with counter-canter and suppleness. I also find using the pirouette canter helpful (see p. 111).

7 **Problem: My horse's changes are unequal.**

One side shorter behind can be the result of the individual strength and/or weakness of one of the horse's hind legs. To address this issue, do the flying change on the side that is short behind by cantering a circle and changing to counter-canter on the circle through the flying change.

Good luck! Now, I'll see you and your horse competing at Third Level!

PART 3

The Pinnacle
of Dressage

The Pendulum in Full Swing—
Fourth Level Through Grand Prix

*Riding the Pendulum of Elasticity every day is the
best way to strengthen your horse. Only when your horse
is strong enough can you add more bend and
more impulsion and therefore more brilliance.*

To ride the Pendulum of Elasticity in full swing, you must be able to smoothly accomplish the earlier phases of the Pendulum. Please review chapter 7 (p. 57) and chapter 13 (p. 103) before you begin working on the advanced transitions described on the following pages. Note that I am organizing this chapter a bit differently because it's important that I talk about your horse's strength, conditioning, and natural abilities. We have also begun Part III of this book: this entire section deals with the FEI movements and the amount of strength and balance it takes to perform them with ease.

Your horse should now be fairly well-muscled and strong. He should understand the half-steps in trot and the very collected canter (see p. 104).

These two exercises help to move the Pendulum to the left. He should also be able to stay in balance and move forward with more groundcover in the medium trot and medium canter. Regarding strength, your horse should now be able to accomplish the working canter pirouettes from Fourth Level.

The collected trot and canter should be confirmed within the balance necessary to perform a USEF Fourth Level Test. The extensions in trot and canter might still be a bit green due to balance or strength issues. This chapter should help you develop more strength and increase the amount of swing to the left and right in your Pendulum of Elasticity.

When your Pendulum is in full swing and

your horse is very strong, you can now add as much bend as you want and he should be able to maintain the balance and cadence in the gaits. Remember, however, that the strength comes first, and the amount of bend you can have comes second.

Evaluation of Your Horse's Potential

You need to look at your partner with a critical eye and decide if he is really able to move up into the FEI ranks, or if he is really a bit limited in his athletic ability. If the latter is the case, it is better to keep him at Fourth Level rather than trying to show him at the FEI levels. And here I would like to make a particular point about the not-so-perfect horse.

I have had many students who have come to this crossroad, and we've kept on training the movements and working on strengthening the horse. Every so often a horse surprises me and makes a huge leap in training that I don't expect. Usually, the horse is able to learn some of the new FEI movements, and this is useful to the rider so she can learn the aids. However, without the correct balance it is unfair to the horse to put him in the show ring at the FEI levels. There is a big difference between schooling the movements individually at home and demonstrating them in a complex test when each movement comes up very quickly and must be performed with the utmost correctness and ease.

If you have your heart set on showing at the FEI levels, then this may be the decision point where you have to perhaps sell or lease your horse to someone who is looking for a school-master to help her move up the national levels.

If you have done your homework and trained well with your current horse, you should be able to find a horse with more athletic ability that is better poised to take you where you want to go. Once you have trained one horse correctly, training a more athletic mount to the FEI levels will progress more quickly.

Roadblocks That Prevent You from "Going All the Way"

Here I am going to mention some of the issues that may help you make the decision about whether or not to move your horse up into the FEI ranks.

1 Your horse exhibits explosiveness or major resistance. I have judged many horses who know that piaffe is coming and are ready to employ the escape button before the rider ever puts the aid on. Rearing, stopping, running sideways or backward are all signs of tension. Sometimes, the rider has put the horse into the ring a bit too soon and the piaffe has not really been confirmed. In any event, when the horse learns to avoid the piaffe in this manner, it is very hard to overcome it. I have seen a few horses overcome this fear and resistance, but it can take a few years, and often the rider has to remove the horse from the show ring for a time.

2 Your horse lacks ability in one movement for Grand Prix. Some horses just don't want to "play." It can be heartbreaking for the rider to have come this far and have an issue with *one* of the Grand Prix movements. Personally, before I decided to show a horse at Grand Prix, I would make sure he would do piaffe, passage, and the one-tempis at home. This is not to say that they were all "perfect." I expected some mistakes and some resistance as the horse learned the test and gained confidence.

My horse Gaspadin never learned the passage but had wonderful one-tempis and piaffe. I never showed him at Grand Prix. Raubritter could do all three movements, but only with a high or swinging croup. I did not show him at Grand Prix, either.

If you can buy or lease a schoolmaster, do it! Such horses can be a wonderful asset to your learning process. You may need to make a decision at this point, however. A schoolmaster, possibly with some age on him, might know the movements but not have the necessary strength to perform them in the correct balance needed for the FEI level. He could have difficulty staying regular in the extensions.

JUDGING TIP

You should not show at FEI level until the horse you are riding is strengthened sufficiently. Why? First, the judge must judge from an international standard, and you might be eliminated for lack of regularity. If the balance is not correct and the horse is struggling with the demands of the test, you will receive low marks. This is not a good experience for you, the horse, or the judge. You should consider showing below the FEI levels.

Before you enter the show ring, where you must do the movements exactly as written in the test, make sure your horse has enough strength to do the entire test. Work with your instructor, as well, in how to lay out and prepare for your test. Too often, the rider is in a panic and "runs"

the horse from movement to movement. In the Grand Prix, you must ride from half-halt to half-halt, always checking your basics (especially the suppleness) and your engagement.

3 In the show ring it becomes apparent you have a "hole" in your training. If, in every test you ride, you always receive a "4" for the same movement, then you have a "hole" in your training. I am never too worried when I see a student's tests with a "4" in one and then a "7" in the next for the same movement. Mistakes can happen. However, if there is a pattern and you are always marginal or insufficient in the same movement, you must go back and do more homework.

4 You are receiving a "4" in the "Submission" score. This tells me that there are too many mistakes and that you certainly do have a hole in your training (see above). When your horse cannot do either line of tempi changes; he cannot perform either canter pirouette; or he doesn't have the piaffe or perhaps passage, you will receive a "4." The "Submission" score reflects the performance of the movements in the test and problems with the horse's neck and/or mouth. In other words, can the horse *do* the movements?

JUDGING TIP

Judges tend to get a bit stricter at the FEI levels than they are at the lower levels of dressage. Try to raise your standards and make sure you have done everything you can to prepare your horse for this challenge.

5 You are receiving a "5" or lower on your "Rider Marks." This is a pointed directive from the judge that you are not correctly influencing or preparing your horse for the requirements and movements in the test. Take this to heart and work on your seat and your aids. Remember, the FEI score sheets only have one score worth 20 points for the rider's performance.

6 Your lowest score in the "Collective Marks" is the "Engagement" score. When this is the case, the judge is telling you that you are performing the movements but without the correct balance or elasticity. In other words, your Pendulum is not well established. The "Engagement" score

reflects the performance of the horse's hind legs and back, and the correct balance. Has the horse enough support from the hind legs? Can he do the movements required in the test in the correct balance or not?

The Extended Paces

Let's turn first to the USEF Rule Book to review the definitions of extended trot and canter (see sidebar, p. 151).

Imperfections and Evasions

In the extended trot, your horse:

1 Trails his hind legs.

2 Pushes with his hind legs instead of "carrying."

3 Is crooked.

4 Is wide behind.

5 Shows a loss of rhythm.

6 Falls downhill.

7 Falls out with his haunches in the corners.

8 Is short in the neck.

9 Breaks to canter.

10 Lacks energy.

11 Shows improved freedom but lacks groundcover.

In the extended canter, your horse:

1   Falls in with his haunches.

2   Falls downhill or gets croup-high.

3   Loses correct rhythm.

4   Gets short in the neck.

5   Changes lead (either entirely or just behind).

6   Falls out with his haunches in the corners.

How to Ride and Train

Rider's Aids

The aids for riding the extended trot and canter are as follows:

1 Inside rein: In trot, the horse will be straight with no bending or shoulder-fore position. In canter, it keeps the horse slightly positioned in the direction of the lead.

2 Outside rein: Keeps the horse round through the topline in both the trot and canter extensions.

3 Inside leg: In trot both legs move into the same position near the girth so you don't push the haunches sideways. In canter this is the leg in the direction of the lead. This leg keeps the activity.

4 Outside leg: In trot, both legs move into the same position near the girth. In canter this leg keeps the horse "trapped" on the inside hind, and it can be used at the beginning and end of the extension as an *active* leg to remind the horse not to lose the lead behind.

5 Seat: In trot you sit equally on both seat bones or your horse might think of cantering, or he might become irregular. In canter, sit on the seat bone in the direction of the lead.

USEF Rule Book

EXTENDED TROT

The horse covers as much ground as possible. Without hurrying, the steps are lengthened to the utmost as a result of great impulsion from the hindquarters. The rider allows the horse to lengthen the frame and to gain ground while controlling the poll. The fore feet should touch the ground on the spot toward which they are pointing.

The movement of the fore and hind legs should reach equally forward in the moment of extension. The whole movement should be well-balanced and the transition to collected trot should be smoothly executed by taking more weight on the hindquarters.

EXTENDED CANTER

The horse covers as much ground as possible. Without hurrying, the strides are lengthened to the utmost. The horse remains calm, light and straight as a result of great impulsion from the hindquarters. The rider allows the horse to lengthen the frame with a controlled poll and to gain ground. The whole movement should be well-balanced and the transition to collected canter should be smoothly executed by taking more weight on the hindquarters.

17.1 Nicole Glusenkamp riding Eeltsje F, owned by Paula Marsh and Wyning Edge Friesians LLC, in a powerful extended trot.

Lengthened Stride, Lengthened Frame

The extended paces take the most strength from the horse and go the most *over* the ground. To accomplish this, the horse will lose a bit of suspension. The horse must *carry weight;* in other words, the hind legs must engage, or increase the bend and flexion of the joints, as the hindquarters lower over the hind leg that is on the ground. This hind leg must then propel the horse uphill and forward.

The horse lands on the opposite hind leg, which should immediately engage and allow the horse to again lower the hindquarters over this hind leg.

When the horse gets crooked, one hind leg does not engage as much as the other. This can cause regularity issues, or even one front leg becoming "unlevel." This means one front leg will come higher in the air than the other—that is, as the horse moves in trot in diagonal pairs, when one hind leg is "cheating," the opposite shoulder will fall down a bit. This impedes the freedom of the front leg.

In the extended paces it is of utmost importance to be able to allow more freedom of the neck in order to earn the highest mark. The frame must show some lengthening as well as the steps. If the horse is not strong enough, the rider will be unable to do this and will have to use her own strength to help support the horse.

Remember you will never be able to train the extended paces by just going faster and faster across the diagonal. The horse will need to gain strength and confidence with your transitions within the Pendulum of Elasticity.

JUDGING TIP

In the freestyle, show your extensions on a straight line for maximum impact. A medium pace can be shown on a curved line, but I would warn you not to confuse the judges. If there are no mediums required at your level of freestyle, then don't do one on a curved line. If you must, then show the required extension first, and show your medium, perhaps as a way of interpreting the music.

Cures and Solutions: Extended Trot

| Problem: My horse's hind legs are trailing.

In this case, you have allowed the horse to push his hind legs out behind his tail. This is usually a strength issue but can also be a conformation problem. Go back and strengthen the horse. Work with short periods of the extended paces, followed by moving back into your half-steps

quickly, which will put the hind legs back under the body.

If your horse, by nature, does not have very flexible hind legs, you can try working with some raised cavalletti to help strengthen the correct muscles.

JUDGING TIP

This is one area you may need to be happy with a "6" as it may be the best your horse can do. If you try for a "10," you will only create more problems and make the score even lower.

Remember not every horse has the talent for a huge extended trot. This evasion is seen often with Friesians and Spanish horses. Even with an uphill balance and overtrack, the score cannot be a "10," because the hind legs need to stay under the body for a "10." However, if you can keep the horse in a correct balance, the score can still go up to an "8."

2 Problem: My horse's hind legs are pushing, not carrying.

This means the horse is really doing more of a *lengthening,* in that there is additional ground-cover, but he is lacking the correct uphill balance and power required in a true *extended* trot. The hind legs must carry weight in order for the horse to stay uphill. Again, go back, and make the horse stronger!

3 Problem: My horse is crooked.

This is usually fairly easy to fix if you are diligent. Watch the corners. Take a bit more time once you come out of one to make sure you have the horse straight and are in control of both hind legs. Again, the horse only is crooked because both hind legs are not equally strengthened. The horse will generally push into the stiff side. If your horse likes to bend right, and you approach the diagonal on the right rein, you run the risk of the horse falling left after the corner. If you do not fix this, he may canter. Try working with a little counterflexing in the corner and make sure the horse is not leaning into your outside rein and leg. Go back and do more homework.

4 **Problem: My horse is wide behind.**

This can be a conformation issue or an "escape" issue. This escape is usually seen in stallions. It is also seen in horses that are shorter or squarer in their body, as well as Arabians. You will need a ground person to tell you at which point your horse starts to go wide behind. In the show ring, don't exceed this limit. At home, go just to this point and then take the Pendulum of Elasticity back toward collection again. Keep strengthening. If the horse learns this evasion it is a very difficult one to solve.

5 **Problem: My horse loses rhythm.**

There are many reasons for this imperfection. Unfortunately, this will result in a low score. Make sure he is straight, and you are not running him out of balance, that is, asking him for more than he can do. Make sure there are no vet issues. (See Problem 3 above.)

6 **Problem: My horse falls downhill.**

This is, again, usually a strength issue. Work to strengthen your horse, but also know his limita-tions. Do not ask for more than he can do in the correct balance (see Problem 3, above).

7 **Problem: My horse's haunches fall out in corners.**

This is a rider issue. The horse is using the corners to escape the engagement. You need to capture the hind legs in the corner to make sure they will carry weight through the extension. Think about working with your half-steps in the corner, making sure the horse doesn't push the hind legs out. Think of your corner more as two straight lines connected by a turning aid—a quarter-pirouette, if you will. The horse must keep the outside of his body "framed-in" in order to keep the engagement on the inside hind in the corner. In trot, don't bend too much in the corner; this can also encourage the hind legs to escape.

8 **Problem: My horse is short in the neck.**

This can be due to mental tension in the horse or a rider who has too much contact. It also can be a strength issue in the horse, and the rider is there offering too much support. Deal with the negative tension in your horse and address your riding position.

9 **Problem: My horse breaks to canter.**

This imperfection is usually a crookedness issue. The horse starts to drift over a shoulder at the beginning, loses balance, and canters. It can also be a rider issue if you override the horse and run him out of balance.

10 Problem: My horse lacks energy.

This is usually due to the collected trot being too lazy. The hind legs need to have a wakeup call! Use lots of quick transitions out and back, keeping those hind legs active and awake.

11 Problem: My horse shows improved freedom but lacks groundcover.

This can still score a "7" from most judges. Many different breeds of horses will receive this comment. If there is a lack of natural elasticity, this will also occur. Again, know your horse. If this is the best he can do, then take your "7" and move on!

Cures and Solutions: Extended Canter

1 Problem: My horse's haunches fall in.

Horses will be straight one direction and crooked the other. Again, this is just an evasion to carrying weight on one hind leg or another. Make sure on the crooked side you take more time to straighten the horse with a little shoulder-fore out of the corner prior to starting the extended canter.

2 Problem: My horse falls downhill or gets croup-high.

Again, this is an engagement issue. If the horse starts well, then the croup gets high, you don't have enough strength for an extension the entire diagonal or long side. Work again on your Pendulum of Elasticity and work on strengthening the horse.

JUDGING TIP

When the test has the pattern that shows the extension *toward* the judge, it usually scores one mark higher than the one *away* from the judge. The front end of the horse and the lifting of the shoulders are much more obvious when the horse comes *toward* C.

3 Problem: My horse loses rhythm.

When the canter has been a clear three-beat rhythm prior to the extension, you first need to check the horse's straightness and the balance. As soon as the shoulders fall down, the rhythm is at risk. Often working in counter-canter and doing your Pendulum of Elasticity forward and back on the long side will help with strengthening and also straightness, which, in turn, helps improve the rhythm.

4 Problem: My horse's neck gets short.

The neck will be short in the extended canter for the same reasons it was in the trot extension. The same exercises and corrections apply (see Problem 8, p. 154).

5 Problem: My horse changes lead (either entirely or just behind).

This imperfection could be due to tension in the back or a lack of straightness. If the horse is leaning into your outside leg, or if there is tension in the back, he will be more prone to changing his lead behind to avoid taking the weight on the leading hind leg.

Working with some travers on a circle to

supple the horse a bit in the loins, and making him a bit more submissive to the outside leg should help this issue. Also, think about sending the horse more forward at the beginning of the movement with your outside leg, and think about using the outside leg a bit more actively prior to your collecting half-halt at the end.

6 Problem: My horse's haunches fall out in corners.

First, review Problem 7 on p. 154. In working with the corners as a quarter-canter pirouette as prescribed in the extended trot, you will increase the engagement of the inside hind leg and in doing so, help avoid evasions.

Where the Pendulum Swings Next

You have now read about how to deal with imperfections in the extended trot and canter and swing your Pendulum completely to the right. To help your horse turn the half-steps into piaffe and develop your passage, move to chapter 20 and chapter 21 (pp. 173 and 183). I discuss developing working canter pirouettes into half and full pirouettes in Chapter 22 (p. 189). These are the movements that will swing your Pendulum all the way to the left. The piaffe, passage, and full canter pirouettes are some of the most demanding movements in the FEI tests. They take incredible strength, suppleness, and submission from the horse! It is my hope that the chapters ahead will help you achieve the best chance of success!

CHAPTER

18

The Zig-Zag

Personally, I think the Grand Prix zig-zag is the hardest movement in dressage to execute for a "10."

In Third Level dressage, one half-pass is introduced. And in Fourth Level, there are two consecutive half-passes to perform. These two half-passes are called a *"counterchange of hand."*

In Intermediate I, a series of three half-passes are required. When there are three or more half-passes ridden in a series, they are called zig-zags. In the beginning the zig-zags are ridden from location to location. In other words, the test directives say: *"The first half-pass to the left for 5 meters, the second half-pass to the right for 10 meters, the third half-pass to the left for 5 meters."*

This type of zig-zig can be ridden in trot or canter. Take a look at what the USEF Rule Book and FEI Dressage Handbook: Guidelines for Judging say about the zig-zag (see sidebars, this page and 158).

Imperfections and Evasions

Your horse:

1 Leads with his haunches when you change direction (the "changeover").

2 Goes more sideways in one direction than the other.

3 Anticipates the movement.

4 Changes late (in the changeover).

USEF Rule Book
ZIG-ZAG

A movement containing more than two half-passes with changes of direction. The horse should be straight for a moment before changing direction.

5   Rides a figure that is incorrect.

6   Falls from one direction to the other.

7   Goes the incorrect number of strides due to a rider counting problem.

You can find solutions to these issues beginning on p. 161.

How to Ride and Train

Before you begin, be sure to review chapter 15 on the half-pass (see p. 121).

To ride the zig-zags, first, you must control the haunches in the change of direction (the "changeover"). Start this exercise at walk. You need to be able to identify any evasions.

This exercise has different degrees of diffi-

FEI Dressage Handbook
THE ZIG-ZAG

In the zig-zag half-pass movement the horse should bend equally to both sides of the centerline and maintain balance and cadence. Zig-zag half-passes are judged as one exercise.

The zig-zag must have the correct number of meters/strides and be performed symmetrically to the centerline.

The change of bend in a zig-zag starts when a horse has finished the half-pass to one side. In the flying change the horse has to be straight.

---

culty. I will start with the easiest version and then finish with the more difficult one. This is how you should ride other exercises as well—starting easy and increasing the difficulty. It is easier if you do these variations without impulsion first, or at the walk.

Easiest

This is the first and easiest exercise to gain control of the haunches in the changeover. Remember that you and the horse both will need to put this exercise into your brains slowly at first before trying it at trot and canter. So always start in the *walk*.

Start from the rail on the right rein. Begin with shoulder-fore, change your weight and use your outside leg behind the girth, and ride a half-pass right to the quarterline. When the front legs hit the quarterline, send them straight ahead with your inside leg and outside rein. At the same time, push the haunches to the right of the quarterline with your outside leg. You will be now walking in travers-right position. This will be travers because the forehand will be on the quarterline, the line of travel. Once you have control, you should still be using your outside leg as the active leg, change the bend into a shoulder-in-left position and then change your leg position and move your seat back into a neutral position. Be sure your upper body is now correctly in shoulder-in left position. You should still be moving straight ahead.

The horse must accept that your left inside leg is sending him forward. This is the engagement portion of the half-pass. He should not anticipate moving in the direction of the new bend. This is of utmost importance for the success of the zig-zag. If you have control of the line of travel, then move your weight to the left and

activate your outside right leg behind the girth, and move the horse into half-pass left. Once you approach the rail, repeat the same process, thinking renvers left on the rail (as the haunches will be on the rail), shoulder-in right, then half-pass right.

Once the horse is submissive at walk, go to trot. Make sure the horse is waiting for the new "go sideways" aid. If he anticipates and starts without you, stay in shoulder-in for a few more strides, and emphasize your inside leg until the horse waits for your "go sideways" aid.

Once you have mastered the exercise at the trot, then move on to *canter*. In the canter, the changeover is also the preparation for the flying change. Again, if your horse starts to run sideways in the direction of the flying change, don't go sideways, ride the horse forward in the new direction for a few strides prior to starting the next half-pass.

Note that this *Easiest* method of training actually addresses the Imperfections and Evasions Problems 1, 3, and 6 (see p. 157). *The More Difficult* exercise (which I explain next), can help you with Problems 2, 5, and 7. Also, there are more solutions on p. 161.

More Difficult

Once you have success and control with the most basic changeover (see p. 158), here is what you need to do for the highest zig-zag score: You have *to change the bend and direction in one stride.*

As mentioned, I suggest you practice this

Personal Story

Back in the old days, when I rode Grand Prix, the test called for six half-passes in canter, starting on the centerline. The first half-pass was three strides, then the next four half-passes were of six strides, and the last half-pass was again three strides, landing you back on centerline. The movement then required a flying change at G.

Finally, when the FEI asked if any judge had ever given a "10" for this movement, it was decided it was too hard. So, the FEI removed one half-pass of six strides, and now the movement flows much better. I still have not given a "10" in competition, but I did see Edward Gal and Totilas perform the Grand Prix zig-zag during a schooling session at the World Equestrian Games in 2011 that was excellent and would have scored a "10."

Stephen Clarke, the FEI 5* judge from Great Britain, was conducting our FEI judges forum in Europe. We were talking about the Grand Prix zig-zag, and Stephen said, "We have one of the best riders in the world for this movement here in the room." He introduced Jennie Loriston-Clarke, who rode Dutch Courage, and her most famous movement in the freestyle was to put her reins in one hand and ride a zig-zag. Most amazing. Jennie came to the front of the room and told us her secret: "You must make the horse go, go, go away from the outside leg!"

18.1 Lauren Sammis and Sagacious HF, owned by Al Guden, show the lift and reach through the shoulders that allow the horse to make the zig-zags look easy!

your seat and leg position and move into the half-pass left.

As the horse gets more confident, use fewer strides to straighten and change the bend. Here, I will use a zig-zag with eight strides in each half-pass as an example.

For a true zig-zag in canter that counts the strides, you need to learn how to count. Go to canter (there is no counting in trot) and come out of the corner. Start to half-pass right and count the strides, one, two, three, four. Ride straight ahead. Make a flying change and half-pass left back to the rail and count the strides. Hopefully, it will take you four strides to return to the rail. This is the exercise you need to help teach you to control the sideways movement in both directions. When you go right off the rail in four strides and it takes you six strides in the left half-pass to get back to the rail, you have not balanced your half-passes.

In the beginning, try to make your half-passes equal by not going as much sideways to the easier direction. This way you won't be pushing your horse out of balance trying to frantically go more sideways in the less athletic direction.

JUDGING TIP

You can ride your canter zig-zag this way in the show, but you may not score more than a "6."

exercise first in walk—in other words, work on the submission and mechanics of the exercise *without* the impulsion. Once you and the horse understand, move into trot. Once there is understanding in the trot, move on to the canter. Remember, the more impulsion, the more difficulty!

Start your half-pass from the rail to the right. Keep your right bend for about four strides. Then keep pushing the horse sideways, but make the horse straighter for two strides, and then bend the horse in the new direction (he is still moving in the old direction). Then in one stride change

In order to get a higher score you have to keep the bend throughout all the half-passes and only have one stride of straightening prior to the changeover.

To improve your score in competition, start your half-pass right. Count the strides—one, two, three, four. On five and six make the horse straight. On seven and eight change the bend. On the new "one" or nine, you are moving in the new direction.

To earn the highest score you will need to keep the bend of the first half-pass through count seven. On eight you can change the bend. On nine you should be moving into the new direction on the new lead.

Top riders can move the shoulders from one side to the other and change the bend and direction in half a stride. This is the ultimate in the idea of lightness and mobility of the shoulders or forehand. Remember, however, that the key to the zig-zag is balance and the flow of the movement. Also, you should be able to cover the same amount of ground each direction. You will not get "extra credit" for trying to do the changeover in one stride if your horse is unbalanced and frantic.

Training Exercises and Solutions

Exercise One:
Use a Variety of Locations
This exercise helps solve Problems 3 and 5—see p. 157.

Try to avoid using the centerline to school your zig-zags. This is where the movement is always located in the test. Horses learn through repetition, and your horse may very likely "learn" the movement and be quite happy to perform it any time on the centerline—and without any help from you! In dog obedience, they call this becoming "pattern trained" as opposed to truly being attentive to the handler's commands. Remember that attentiveness is an important quality of the horse's submission.

So to mix it up and keep your horse waiting for your aids, ride quarterline to quarterline, or rail to quarterline, and be creative in general. Don't do the movement in the same way more than once. For example, if your goal is to ride a zig-zag of 5 meters, 10 meters, 5 meters (as is required in the current Intermediate I test), you should perhaps ride 10 meters, 5 meters, 10 meters. Change things around. You will need to make sure the horse can move easily over the required amount of ground, but if he goes easily to the right and labors to the left, you need to work to the left. Your goal is to have the horse able to ride a correct zig-zag with the correct number of strides. This is the ultimate in control.

Exercise Two:
Make Your Half-Passes Equal
This exercise helps solve Problems 2 and 5—see p. 157.

Count the number of strides in the trot or canter from the rail to the first quarterline. Then you should be able to return to the rail in the same number of strides. You will discover that your horse will have more lateral reach in one direction than the other. Your goal is to make them *even*. At the horse show, however, you should not try to make the harder side better, but rather restrict a bit the amount of ground covered on the good side. If you don't, you will end up too much on one side of the centerline and will never be able to smoothly come back.

At home and when schooling, however, work on that stiff side and try to increase the lateral reach! You should take away some of the bend first, and make the work a bit easier for the horse. Make him really "scoot" off that outside leg. Once the horse has more freedom and submission to that outside leg, then put the bend back into the work.

Exercise Three:
Learning to Count
This exercise helps solve Problem 5—see p. 158.

Learning to count your canter half-pass strides will help you learn to count your tempi changes when the time comes! However, the most important part of this issue is that you must have a reliable and supple half-pass in both directions. It's just like the tempi changes: when your one single change is a problem, it follows you into the tempis. So if your half-passes are not equal, you must go back and try to solve this more basic issue before facing new challenges.

To repeat: counting is *not* necessary for the *trot*. Only the *canter* zig-zag needs to be counted. Once you have mastered the exercise with the half-passes coming off the rail and going back to the rail, it is time to add the flying change into the count.

Up until now, you have only counted the half-pass strides, ridden straight ahead, made the flying change, and then ridden the next half-pass. Now you need to be able to put these movements closer together. Count one, two, three, four; make a flying change; and immediately go into the next half-pass. The flying change will be *count one* in the next sequence:

One, two, three, four,
Half-pass, half-pass, half-pass, half-pass,
Flying change, half-pass, half-pass, half-pass,
One, two, three, four.

Exercise Four:
Clean Up the Changes
This exercise helps deal with Problem 4—see p. 157.

It is reasonable to expect a few problems with the flying changes as you learn the zig-zags. As I've said, your horse will likely be a bit nervous, as well. The easiest way to make sure your horse will still maintain the correctness of the flying change is to ride your half-pass and then take a bit of time riding straight ahead and prepare for the change.

If your horse goes into the new half-pass on the wrong lead, then go back and teach the horse about his reaction to your flying change aid. These movements now are so many pieces of the puzzle all put together. You need to make sure all the pieces are correct and on the aids.

Believe it or not, sometimes doing a zig-zag actually *improves* the changes, especially if the horse has a tendency to be late in front. Working on your changeovers should help the horse learn to lift and move his shoulders from one side to the other more quickly.

Exercise Five:
Correctly "Place" the Movement
This exercise helps with Problems 2 and 5—see p. 157.

1 Begin by dividing the movement in half. For a counter-change of hand from F to X and X to M

(remember, this is two consecutive half-passes), plan it in this manner. Be sure your half-pass left can get to centerline *before* X. You will need two strides in the beginning to do a changeover. When your horse's front leg hits X it should be the flying change to the right. Then you must half-pass right and end up on the rail *before* M. Again, you need time to ride a bit forward and prepare for the flying change, which should be at M, not in the corner.

Try not to put this movement together all the time. Ride a half-pass left from F to X and make sure you can go sideways enough and have a good flying change. Then turn right at C and ride the same half-pass to the right from M to X, again making sure you are on centerline prior to X. Once you succeed in this exercise 90 percent of the time, put it together. Remember that a counter change of hand or a good zig-zag is really just many well ridden half-passes put together in a row.

2 If you are riding three half-passes in trot or canter on the centerline—and the directives in the test call for a first half-pass of 5 meters, the second of 10 meters, and the third of 5 meters—you will need to think of the placement this way:

Divide the entire movement of the three half-passes in half with the halfway point on the centerline at X. Find how much of the movement will need to be ridden *before* X and how much of the movement would need to be ridden *after* X.

The directives say the movement starts at D and ends at G. So at D you would start your half-pass to just touch or "kiss" the quarterline. Think of billiards, where you bank a ball off the rail. Do *not* go past the quarterline. Then your second half-pass should arrive on centerline at X. If the middle of your second half-pass arrives on the centerline *past* X, you'll need to go more sideways in this half-pass. Or perhaps you went past the quarterline in your first half-pass? Identify your mistake! The second half-pass should the finish by "kissing" the quarterline, and your last half-pass should arrive back on centerline by G.

Now, I'll review this and give you another way to think about this movement; this time the zig-zag will start from the centerline. Make sure you take time to align the horse correctly for the first half-pass, just as you did for Third Level (see p. 124). Then half-pass to the quarterline. Take your time for the changeover. Half-pass over to the other quarterline. The middle of this half-pass should go through X as this is the halfway mark of the movement.

Should you find yourself beyond X, you must try again. Perhaps your changeover took too long? Perhaps your second half-pass did not move sideways enough? Perhaps your first half-pass went past the quarterline and you have too much ground to make up? If your middle half-pass does not pass through X, you will finish too late and not have time to go straight for a few strides on the centerline to prepare for the turn at C.

So that your horse does not get ahead of you, this exercise can be easily ridden by starting on the quarterline, riding to the other quarterline (which would be 10 meters), and then returning to the original quarterline. This takes the movement away from the centerline.

3 Once you have mastered the zig-zag ridden in trot or canter in Step 2, you can move on to something more difficult, which is ridden only in canter.

This zig-zag also asks the rider to count the strides. It is known as the 4-8-8-4 and is required in Intermediate II. The first half-pass and the last half-pass have four strides and the middle two half-passes have eight strides, which means that in the eight-stride half-passes, count four will be back on the centerline. In other words, half of the eight will be on one side of the centerline, while the other half are placed on opposite side of the centerline.

This exercise is also ridden on the centerline. You will once again break it in half to make sure you understand the placement. If the middle of the movement is X, and it starts at D and ends at G, you have one half-pass of four, and one half-pass of eight *before* X; and one half-pass of eight and one half-pass of four strides *after* X.

I like to ride the first half of this exercise, go straight ahead, then ride the second half, and go straight ahead. I will only put it all together a few times so the horse does not get *too* smart!

4 The ultimate zig-zag, which is required at the Grand Prix level, has a count of 3-6-6-6-3. This means that the first half-pass is three strides. A note here: judges do not count the strides in this first half-pass, as we are not sure where you really start. So the count from the judge starts with the first flying change, which is "one" in the second half-pass. Then we have three half-passes of six strides. There should be three strides placed equally on either side of the centerline, with the last half-pass of three ending up on the centerline before G.

Again, if you divide this in half, it means that between D and X there should be the first half-pass of three strides and the second half-pass of

six, with the third stride of the middle half-pass crossing through X.

Do not keep riding the entire exercise with mistakes, as it will never improve. Break it down into pieces and then put the entire package together.

JUDGING TIP

Don't worry about counting the first half-pass; we don't! We are not sure where you are starting, so we begin our counting with the first flying change. As a judge, I find it helps to keep track of errors on my fingers. While I am counting, when I see a flying-change mistake, I use my left hand, and for a counting mistake, I use my right hand. I try to do this is a very inconspicuous fashion as I don't want my scribe to laugh at me!

As judges we are told that it really is not about averaging the half-passes for the score. We are told to give the score for the entire movement that belonged to the lowest scoring half-pass. As a rider, I am not sure this is fair, but at present this is what the FEI is teaching.

So you must be careful, if your changeovers are not in balance and the haunches start to lead in all the half-passes, your scores will go down. I believe you should work on balance and the quality of canter as well as the flow. The amount of bend you have can come later as icing on the cake. You will not get more credit for a lot of lateral suppleness if the uphill balance is lost. Remember, the idea is to make this movement look easy.

Good luck with your zig-zags; this is an awesome movement to do well, and usually there is a double coefficient score for it, so it really helps your score to have a good presentation!

19

Tempi Changes

*If you have to think, you will be
behind the movement.*

Tempi changes are merely a line of single flying changes put together (see p. 131). Mistakes happen in the tempi changes when there are small training issues with the single changes.

When you only have to do one change on the short diagonal, it doesn't matter too much if the horse drifts a bit after the change. It becomes a very important issue now, however, in the tempi changes. The closer the tempi changes get together, the more upright the horse must stay. In the four-tempi and the three-tempi changes, the rider has a small amount of time to straighten and fix any problems. Once the rider attempts the two- or one-tempi changes, any shifting of the horse's balance to the right or left will cause interruptions and mistakes.

When the horse loses the balance, he is losing the carrying power of one of the hind legs. Both hind legs must carry an equal amount of weight in the one- and two-tempi changes. When one hind leg gets a bit lazy, mistakes will occur.

Imperfections and Evasions

Your horse:

1 Takes control or "gets strong," and the rider has no half-halt.

2 Starts throwing changes without any aid from the rider.

3 Changes late in front or behind.

4 Drifts from the line of travel.

5 Swings his hindquarters or becomes croup-high.

6 Gets excited or tense.

7 Changes shorter on one side behind.

8 Has a rider with counting problems.

9 Is late to the aid in one direction.

IO Loses impulsion and the changes get shorter and shorter.

I provide solutions to these problems beginning on p. 169. In the meantime, the USEF Rule Book reminds us not only about the quality of the flying changes in general but also about the quality of the tempi changes in particular (see sidebar, below), and the FEI Dressage Handbook: Guidelines for Judging offers useful guidelines for the tempis (see sidebar, p. 167).

USEF Rule Book
FLYING CHANGE OF LEAD

The flying change is performed in one stride with the front and hind legs changing at the same moment. The change of the leading front and hind leg takes place during the moment of suspension. The aids should be precise and unobtrusive. Flying changes of lead can also be executed in series at every 4th, 3rd, 2nd, or at every stride. The horse, even in the series, remains light, calm, and straight with lively impulsion, maintaining the same rhythm and balance throughout the series concerned. In order not to restrict or restrain the lightness, fluency and groundcover of the flying changes in series, enough impulsion must be maintained. Aims of flying changes: To show the reaction, sensitivity and obedience of the horse to the aids for the change of lead.

How to Ride and Train

Rider's Aids
For each change:

1 Seat: Sit on the inside seat bone.

2 Outside leg: It is slightly more active and behind the girth.

3 Inside rein: Still supples.

4 Outside rein: Maintains the frame and speed.

5 Inside leg: Acts as the post that the horse bends around. It can be active if more energy is needed. Make sure this leg stays *at the girth*. If you move it back, it will confuse the horse in regard to the flying change leg aid.

Start Easy
How do you train these tempi changes? First, review your single flying changes (see p. 131). Make sure you can do them on the quarterline: straight and on the aids. Then, proceed to the diagonal line. Remember the line of travel! Look up and make sure *you* are going where you want to go, *not* where the horse wants to go.

Start with an easy exercise. Think of Fourth Level Test Two, which asks for three changes: one near the first quarterline, one near X, and one near the second quarterline. This is an excellent way to begin. Do three changes when the horse is ready, *not* worrying about accuracy in counting at the beginning.

If the horse accepts this exercise and stays quiet and calm, you can begin to count the strides and work on the tempi changes in a count. Remember, however, it is baby steps at first. Even when you can only do three good changes in the count of four, be sure to reward the horse. Do not keep going until the horse makes a mistake and you have to make a big correction! Build confidence slowly. This idea should be carried through all of your work whether you are working on four-tempis or two-tempis.

If the horse gets nervous on the diagonal or starts to anticipate, then move the exercise to the quarterlines. The quarterlines also help with straightness because you can see how much your horse in drifting in relation to the wall.

One-Tempis

The one-tempi changes are the pinnacle of flying changes. First you must be able to do two-tempis up to a fairly good standard—in other words, nine times out of ten, you succeed.

I like to start on the rail. I use "out/in" or "tick-tock" as a way to describe the first short series of one-tempi changes. You could also think "right/left." In other words, say you are on the left lead canter, you'd then do a change "right/left" in one stride.

The horse must now be absolutely straight and jump from one loaded hind leg to another. When he gets crooked, he will *unload* a hind leg and you will have a mistake. The rider really doesn't have time to think, either. If you think and your brain tells your body what to do, it is too late! You must *just react*—as should the horse.

You will find at the beginning that the horse is better on either the left or the right rein. Don't worry; this is normal. If the horse is better on the left, stay there. You can work the other side

---

FEI Dressage Handbook
FLYING CHANGES IN SEQUENCES

While judging flying changes in sequences, it is important that the sequence is judged as one movement even though multiple flying changes are shown. The flying changes in sequences should be well placed (symmetrical) and should show the required number of strides.

---

once you have the movement confirmed.

Once the horse understands the "out/in" exercises, I add one more change so it is "out/in/out." Then I go to five, then seven, then nine changes. I don't know why, but I have found that I have more success in adding the changes in odd numbers.

Once I can do about seven changes, I start to think about the quality. Do I need to do a few changes and then go into medium canter? Do I need to do a few and think about the straightness? Where am I losing the Classical Training Pyramid? The final number you need in the test will happen when you keep all the basics in mind.

Again, having a schoolmaster to help with this is invaluable. Remember, you cannot think. If you have to think, you will be behind the movement. It must just be a reaction. You must sit still in the middle of the horse. If you start throwing yourself side to side you will create crookedness and balance issues in the horse.

Personal Story

Patty Russell owned a Hanoverian/Thoroughbred mare named Cielo Azul that I trained to Prix St. Georges. Patty then had a great teacher horse on which to learn all the movements. She won a breeding to a Trakehner stallion, Handel, and bred Cielo to him. The result was Hallmark, otherwise known as "Bug." When Bug was three, she brought him to my barn and we started him together. She was the first rider on his back.

He was a wonderful horse, with a great desire to please. Patty did most of the training, with only lessons and an occasional training ride from me. Patty and Bug won their Adult Amateur classes at the USEF/USDF Regional Championships from Training Level through Prix St. Georges.

Eventually, it was time to put the two-tempi changes on Bug. However, Patty would get 2-3-2-3-2. Very strange. I could not see the problem from the ground so I asked to get on Bug. I had not ridden him for quite a while as things had seemed to be going great.

I did a single change left. No problem. Then I did a single change right. Problem! He reacted one stride *after* my aid. In other words, his reaction to my flying change aid was not prompt or correct. He gave me a delayed reaction, which is a disaster in the tempi changes as it causes mistakes in the counting. I had to address this error.

Actually, I was amazed that Patty could be riding the three-tempi changes (and four, for that matter) without any counting mistakes.

19.1 Patty Russell and Hallmark.

Somehow her brain had got used to the horse's late reaction in the one direction, so she was able to compensate for it in her counting. She had somehow trained her body to give the aid in the one (slow) direction a stride earlier than was really correct. On any other horse she would have ridden changes in this count: 3-2-3-2-3 instead of the correct 3-3-3-3-3. However, these two-tempis caught her out.

We had to go back to the single change and work with Bug, reminding him that change now meant *now*—not one stride later!

Only your lower leg moves. In the old days, when horses were not as sensitive, you would see riders, out of the saddle with their lower legs moving far back for the aids. If you try this with your sensitive Trakehner, beware!

Training Exercises and Solutions

Exercise One:
Changes on a 20-Meter Circle

This helps to solve Problems 1, 6, and 7—see p. 165.

This helps to solve Problems 1, 6, and 7—see p. 165.

Go onto a 20-meter circle. When the flying change from left to right is the one that is short, start on the left lead. By asking for the right flying change to the outside, it will tell the horse to take a bigger step with the right outside hind in order to change.

For a horse that is nervous or tense, the circle doesn't run out (it just keeps going) so working on it will sometimes help calm the horse down. Stay on the circle, ask for a flying change, then continue cantering until the horse relaxes again and ask for another flying change. Repeat the exercise.

Many times the horse is just trying to figure out what you want. He gets excited and antici-pates. This is normal. Be sure not to make your horse tenser with abrupt corrections or punish-ment. Try to reassure him.

Tempi changes are a movement where once the horse figures out what you want, he will change his evasion a lot. This is not a bad thing. When he starts changing his evasion, he is actu-ally learning. I used to say that I would only get seriously depressed about training if the horse did the same darn thing to me day after day!

Exercise Two:
Simple Transitions

This exercise helps solve Problems 1, 2, and 9—see p. 165.

This exercise helps solve Problems 1, 2, and 9—see p. 165.

Go back to simple canter departs on a straight line. Work on the quarterline and make sure your horse is quickly answering your canter depart aids. Also notice the straightness. If the horse is pushing the haunches in or out, fix this now.

This exercise will also help horses that want to drift in the tempi changes. Work on your quar-terlines and make simple canter-walk-canter tran-sitions. Pay attention to the horse falling in or out. Take time in between the transitions to make a correction each time the horse tries to lean in one direction or another. Teach him to stay upright in his balance.

For a horse that tries to take over or run through the half-halt, I like to mix up simple changes with flying changes. For example, on one diagonal, do simple changes on the first quarterline, at X, and at the second quarterline. If the horse performs quietly, then on the next diagonal, try three flying changes in the same spots. Sometimes you need to have a goal, but be willing to change things up!

For example, your goal may be three flying changes. The first one is super, and then the horse gets strong. So, at X change your plan and make a simple change. Then, if all goes well, ask for a flying change on the second quarterline. Keep using the more simple exercise to help the horse understand and gain confidence in the more dif-ficult exercise.

You can also use 10-meter circles. If you start on the right lead and change to the left, and the horse is strong, do a 10-meter circle to the left until you have control and then continue. The danger with this exercise is that you may teach the horse to think that he always turns in the direction of the flying change, so use it sparingly!

Exercise Three:
Keep Your Horse Uphill
This exercise helps cure Problems 3, 4, and 5—see p. 165.

When the horse has the haunches swinging, sometimes in both directions, and sometimes only in one direction, the real problem is that the shoulders are down, which allows the haunches to bounce all over!

Here is a great exercise to help this problem. Start slowly at first. Remember it takes a lot of strength for a horse to do the one- and two-tempis.

Start on the diagonal line on the left lead. Ride a very clear shoulder-fore left. Walk. During the few steps of walk, keep the haunches on the diagonal line, and move the shoulders to a shoulder-fore right position. Then canter on the right lead. Try to do three simple changes in this manner on the diagonal. When you can do this smoothly and quickly, take out the walk steps. Try to move the shoulders slightly from the old lead into the direction of the new lead before aiding for the flying change. You may need to exaggerate this a bit in the beginning. Remember, do not accept any crookedness from your horse. Use a walk transition to make your point if you need to. If you ask for the change when the horse is crooked, he will think this is okay.

Straight and uphill changes are only the results of keeping the haunches on the line of travel and the shoulders up!

Exercise Four:
Teach Your Horse to Do Tempis in Both Directions
This exercise deals with Problem 2—see p. 165.

Horses learn by repetition. It is very unwise to only practice your three-tempi changes off the same lead that is in the test. Your horse should be able to do any of the tempis off any direction or even down the centerline. You never know when the FEI will change the direction of the tempis and then you will be stuck!

One student of mine learned this the hard way. She had a bit of a hot horse and felt that if the horse "knew" what was coming, he would relax and perform the movement in a better way. She only schooled the tempis off the lead they were asked for in the test. Then the test changed. Her horse was convinced she was wrong and it took her several months and many low scores on her changes before she was able to correct her bad training.

Exercise Five:
"Listen to My Aids!"
This exercise helps with Problems 2, 4, and 6—see p. 165.

Every horse thinks he is doing a great job volunteering changes all over the place. In the beginning, remember, I said you should never punish a horse for something you want later. Now, however, it is time to explain to the horse that you are thrilled he is willing, but that he must wait for *you!*

Judges do not give extra credit for movements "volunteered" by the horse.

Try this exercise; it is a good one. Start on the quarterline on the right lead. Push the haunches a bit to the right with an active left leg for a few strides so the horse is paying attention to the leg that tells him "door closed." Then, straighten for a few strides and ask for a change to the left. Use your right outside leg now and push the haunches to the left for a few strides, again emphasizing the "door-closed" leg. Continue once around the arena. Then try a diagonal. Don't move the haunches too much unless you have to in order to make a point. Eventually, the horse will understand which leg is the aid for the change and which leg tells him, "No, don't do it." If the horse changes without you asking, do not turn around and start again. This teaches the horse nothing. Use the mistake to teach him something!

Stay on the line on which you are traveling. Make a transition to walk and quickly give him a kick with the outside leg. (In other words, if you were on the left lead, you would use the right outside leg.) Then pick up the lead you started on, and push the haunches a bit over to make your point.

Exercise Six:
"Think Forward"
This exercise helps solve Problem10—see p. 166.

Most horses, when they start the changes, learn them with a "smaller" canter. Once the changes are confirmed, it is time to think about the quality and the uphill balance and expression.

Start the changes on the diagonal. Do perhaps two, four-tempi changes and then ride for-ward in medium canter. If you have room, ask for one more change. Basically, you need to ride forward a bit *before* the horse starts getting behind your leg. You can also work with the single changes thinking a bit of medium canter before and after the change. Remember that flying changes should be ridden in the least collected of collected canters!

It is not important at the beginning of the tempi work to get all the changes in. Think more about the quality. Try to encourage the horse to think forward. As soon as the canter is too small and lacking quality, stop doing the changes and return to improving the basics and the quality of canter. Remember, what you practice is what the horse learns! Practice makes perfect only if the practice *is* perfect!

Exercise Seven:
"If Only I Had Played in the Band!"
This exercise helps solve Problem 8—p. 165.

Okay, now we get to the rider. Counting is not easy to learn if you have not ever played an instrument and learned to count beats and rests. You need to think of your three-tempi changes every fifth stride in this way (italic indicates a lead change, the "and" the "half-beat" you need to add musically to aid at the right time for the change—see p. 166 for the aids): *one*-two-three-and, *two*-two-three-and, *three*-two-three-and, *four*-two-three-and, *five*-two-three.

Start out just cantering on a circle. When the leading inside leg comes up, count one. Count the strides on the circle: one-two-three-and, two-two-three-and, three-two-three-and, four-two-three-and, five-two-three. Repeat. The problem is that the aid must be given on the "and" beat, not the downbeat. So you really need to think: one-two-three-*and*...You must train your brain to give the aid on the "and," and also keep the correct count.

When I was in grade school, we became a "herd" of horses—mares that, during recess, ran wild in the field. We trotted, cantered, and had a great time. Now think back to those good ol' days and in the privacy of your own home, act like a horse. Find a lead and canter. Count your strides. Then count and do flying changes. When you change your "lead" leg, you will actually be changing the aids in the way they need to be given for the tempi changes.

When you have mastered the four-tempis in your living room, get on your horse and try to get the same reaction. When you are learning to count, I am here to tell you, the changes will be a mess. You will have late changes, crooked changes, and more.

If there is a schoolmaster at your barn, try to arrange a lesson to learn how to count. I was lucky in that when it was time for me to learn how to do the one-tempis, I had two wonderful instructors in Dennis Callin and Robert Dover. Both of them let me ride their horses and practice the one-tempis. I am sure I ruined their horses for them, but I still thank them to this day!

If you can, for the three, four-tempi changes, make a change on the first quarterline, at X, and at the second quarterline. Unless your horse has a very long or very short stride, this should give you the correct count.

It is a good idea to watch some videos of top riders and see how they aid their horses. With Brentina or Ravel, you can barely see the aid. This is what you must keep in mind.

Piaffe

Sitting on a good piaffe will feel like the horse is doing nothing. In other words, both hind legs are engaged and carrying weight equally, and there should be no unloading of the hind legs. A good piaffe will have the horse jump from one loaded hind leg to the other. As the rider—sit still! I have seen too many riders with a better piaffe than their horse!

The piaffe is one of the requirements of Intermediate II and Grand Prix. It and the passage are the pinnacle of competitive dressage training. The piaffe has the quickest tempo in the trot rhythm. (Remember the tempo is the *repetition of the rhythm.*) It is quickest because it has little suspension or airtime between the beats. This is because the horse jumps from one loaded hind leg to another without unloading the hind leg. The unloading is what creates the upward thrust. When executed correctly, piaffe is the ultimate in collection and lightness, a treat to watch and to ride.

Imperfections and Evasions

Many riders experience problems with this difficult movement. Here are some of the challenges you may encounter. The horse:

1 Loses rhythm in the piaffe or the transitions. (Here I'm referring to rhythm as the diagonal pairs.)

2 Has uneven steps. ("Uneven" refers to the length of stride the hind legs take.)

3 Moves with unlevel steps. ("Unlevel" refers to the height of the stride the hind legs take.)

USEF Rule Book
PIAFFE

1 The piaffe is a highly collected, cadenced, elevated diagonal movement giving the impression of being in place. The horse's back is supple and elastic. The quarters are slightly lowered, the haunches with active hocks are well engaged giving great freedom, lightness and mobility to the shoulders and forehand. Each diagonal pair of feet is raised and returned to the ground alternately, with an even cadence.

2 In principle the height of the toe of the raised foreleg should be level with the middle of the cannon bone of the other foreleg. The toe of the raised hind leg should reach just above the fetlock joint of the other hind leg.

3 The neck should be raised and arched, the head vertical. The horse should remain light on the bit with a supple poll maintaining a light and soft contact on a taut rein. The body of the horse should move up and down in a supple, cadenced, and harmonious movement.

4 The piaffe must always be animated by a lively impulsion and characterized by a perfect balance. While giving the impression of being in place there may be a visible inclination to advance, this being displayed by the horse's eager acceptance to move forward as soon as he is asked. The horse is permitted to advance up to one meter forward in the Intermediate II test.

5 Moving even slightly backward, irregular or jerky steps with the hind or front legs, no clear diagonal steps, crossing either the fore or hind legs, or swinging either the forehand or the hindquarters from one side to the other, getting wide behind or in front, moving too much forward, or double-beat rhythm are all serious faults.

4 Loses straightness in piaffe or transitions.

5 Moves with grounded front legs and a bouncing croup.

6 Hindquarters don't lower and take enough weight.

7 Says, "No thank you, not today." (This is when the "piaffe button" you are hoping to install is replaced by the "naughty button.")

Some solutions to these issues start on p. 176. But before we go further, take a look, as always, at the USEF Rule Book definition of the movement (see sidebar, p. 176).

How to Ride and Train

Which First, Piaffe or Passage?

I often have riders ask me which to train first, the piaffe or the passage. In my opinion it depends on what type of horse you have. A horse that is very elastic and a bit slow behind will love to passage, and will actually use that "hovering" feeling to avoid the "carrying" in the piaffe. This type of horse definitely needs to learn the piaffe first. His hind legs need to be quicker. If you allow him to passage first, it will be difficult to really teach him a correct piaffe. He will try to passage in place. The horse with less suspension and a quicker hind leg will learn piaffe a bit more easily.

I try to teach the piaffe or the half-steps first and early on in the training. If you need a review go back and read chapter 7 on starting in-hand work (see p. 61).

In the beginning, allow the horse to move a bit forward. The quality is the most important

thing, not how "on the spot" the horse can stay. This movement "closes the front and back door," which can be quite traumatic and claustrophobic for the horse. A good quality piaffe that moves forward will always score better than a poor quality one that stays on the spot.

Rider's Aids

I Inside and outside rein: In this movement as both hind legs are carrying equal weight and the horse is

20.1 I'm on Halloh in piaffe. The horse's legs are working in diagonal pairs; however, there could be more activity in the hind legs. Ideally, the hoof of the front leg should be elevated to the middle of the cannon bone and the hind hoof elevated above the fetlock. It's possible if this piaffe had been photographed in a sequence that the next two photos would have shown better activity and elevation. The tail is also caught "swishing" at this moment, but as there are no other signs of tension (mouth, tongue, ears), judges would not mark this down.

20.2 Caryn Vesperman, an adult amateur, winning her USDF Gold Medal on Salope, a Hanoverian mare. I would like to have Caryn sitting a bit deeper with a longer leg position. This would give her a better influence over the movement. "Sally" is working her legs in diagonal pairs, but they could have more elevation.

totally straight, you do not have an inside or an outside rein. You maintain a soft and supple contact on both reins and if a half-halt is needed, you can use both reins at the same time with a soft release.

2 Inside leg and outside leg: Again the horse is straight so both your legs are equal and move slightly behind the girth used in a soft "brushing" motion in the rhythm of the trot.

3 Seat: Sit equally on both seat bones and maybe lighten the seat just slightly.

Training Exercises and Solutions

Exercise One:
Reaction to the Aids
This exercise helps solve Problems 1 and 7—see p. 173.

This is first because I think this is the most important thing to address via preparation. I see so many riders who ask for the piaffe and the horse does not respond so they keep asking and then start using the whip and pretty soon there is a fight. In the test you do not have 30 seconds to "develop" piaffe. You have to do it "now"!

If you have done your in-hand work well, your horse should understand the aids and not be afraid of this movement. If you have skipped the in-hand work, you need to go back now and take care of this issue.

I always gave my horse a little "heads up" prior to putting on the piaffe aids. I used a little "fluffing" of both reins and then a little cluck. The fluffing is just a slight lifting of both reins—think of a little bouncing in both reins in an upward direction. This should be a very small aid; it is not like throwing pizza dough in the air! The cluck goes back to the aid from the ground in the in-hand work, so the horse should understand. Try not to cluck for any other movement so you won't confuse your horse.

The aids I use are: both legs positioned back slightly behind the girth to just very softly "brush" the horse's sides; I lighten my seat slightly, but keep my upper leg closed; I close both reins for a moment and then relax both reins. Remember

20.3 Tanya Hennes and Romeo in piaffe. This photo shows clearly that the horse is active and working nicely within the rhythm. I really like how the joints in the hind leg are working. It might be the angle of the photo, but it looks like the left front leg could be moving a bit too far back behind the center of gravity. It is also possible the horse could be slightly over at the knee. The horse has a very nice expression and seems very happy to piaffe for his smiling rider!

in piaffe the horse should be carrying weight equally on both hind legs, so you have the horse totally straight —that is, with no bend or flexion. Thus, you really don't have an inside rein or outside rein anymore.

That being said, I am talking about the test and riding for the highest mark. At home, in schooling, I like to use the rail and ride a little shoulder-fore to help keep the horse a bit honest and not let him develop any straightness issues.

Test this reaction a lot through your work. Do a little relaxing walk. Then pick up the reins. "Fluff" and cluck and then put your legs on. If there is no reaction, you must quickly remind the horse with your leg or the whip or spur. As soon as he reacts, quietly walk again and reward him.

In Atlanta at the Olympics, I was watching the schooling the day prior to the Grand Prix team test. Isabell Werth and Dr. Uwe Schulten-Baumer were working at G, the first place the piaffe had to be performed from the walk. Isabell would walk through the short end; near G she would get a reaction, and never do more than five or six steps of piaffe. Then her coach would feed the horse a sugar cube.

Do not hesitate to go back and work in-hand, or ask someone to help you from the ground. Only ask someone who has experience, however, as you do not want to create any fear issues for your horse.

Exercise Two:
Trot to Piaffe

This exercise helps Problems 1, 2, and 3—see p. 173.

For the horse that has difficulty working on the piaffe from the walk, you need to approach it from this angle.

Your horse by this time should have a good idea about collected trot. He should be able to work in-hand with the engaging exercises discussed in chapter 7 (see p. 61). It is best to have someone in the arena on foot near the rail. When you come through your corner, start to shorten the horse's trot. As the horse nears the ground person, he should be able to tap the horse on top the croup for a few strides, while clucking at the same time. When you feel a few correct steps, you should move off into collected trot. Make a circle and come back around near the ground person again.

As with working from the walk, in the beginning, do not overdo the exercise. Be happy with a few good responses from the horse. Praise and reward often.

Sometimes if the horse doesn't understand how small the trot needs to be, the ground per-

son may need to hold a bamboo pole in front of the horse in order to act as a barrier to say, "stay behind this barrier and trot more in place" (see p. 180 for more information on using the bamboo pole).

Exercise Three:
Rein Back to Piaffe

This exercise will help solve Problems 5 and 6— see p. 173.

The rein back is an exercise ridden to encourage the horse to lower the haunches and engage the hind legs. If your horse does not perform the rein back for at least a "7," then you will also have problems with the piaffe. Because the rein back is in diagonal pairs, practicing it will help the horse understand the diagonal pairs for the piaffe.

Your horse must be strong enough to be confident he can keep both hind legs engaged for a few steps. If you have only a "6" on your rein back, I would work on improving this movement. Work on the ground with your horse until he understands that he must engage and stay straight. Review chapter 11 on rein back (see p. 89). Remember, my example for a "10" rein back was Brentina—and she got quite a lot of "9s" and "10s" on her piaffe. The piaffe doesn't just start when the horse is working toward Grand Prix. The basic tools and reactions should have been started at Training and First Level.

I start this exercise with the rider on the horse while I am on the ground with the piaffe whip or the bamboo (see p. 180 for more about this), depending on how the horse reacts to each tool. As the rider starts to rein back, I cluck and give a little tap on top of the croup. We ask for a few steps and then walk forward and reward the horse. Start the rein back in a shoulder-fore on the rail, so you will have better straightness. Without this, the horse will "escape" and not load the hind legs equally.

Exercise Four:
Walk to Piaffe
This exercise can help with Problems 2, 3, and 4—see p. 173.

Some horses are not able to figure out how to move from the four-beat walk into a two-beat piaffe. If you are having trouble with this, train the half-steps from the trot rather than the walk. Or see Exercise Three for rein back to piaffe (p. 178).

For piaffe from the walk, I first ask the rider to halt the horse on the rail. I pat the horse, give him some sugar and stroke him with the whip. I also test and make sure he will react to a slight touch of the whip on the inside hock. I then test the reaction to the outside hock. If the reaction is not a quick one, then I will spend some time here to refocus the horse on this quick reaction.

I try to have the rider do little. The worst problem here could be the rider getting so involved with "giving an aid" that she gives too much of an aid and confuses the horse.

I want the rider to keep the horse in a little shoulder-fore to help keep him straight, and also for my own protection should the horse kick out! I ask the rider to close the reins and release the reins softly, "closing the front door" a bit and walking very slowly forward. I then cluck and touch the horse with the whip. If we get a quick reaction, we halt and reward the horse with praise and sugar.

Try not to overdo this training as the horse will soon get bored and evasive. If you can get three or four good reactions once around the arena, move on to another topic.

As the training progresses, your goal is to have the horse react from the rider's aids. The rider should fluff the reins a bit, cluck, and then softly brush the horse's sides with both legs behind the girth. Again, ask only for a few steps and then praise.

Do not whip train the piaffe. Read the sidebar on p. 180.

Exercise Five:
Helping the Rhythm into Piaffe
This exercise will help with Problems 1 and 7—see p. 173.

Some horses learn the piaffe better out of trot, which is in the same rhythm, and others are better from the walk. You may need to experiment to find the answer for your horse. If he is getting very resistant from the walk, go back and work from the trot. Usually, once the horse is a bit stronger and has more confidence, he will feel more comfortable trying it from the walk again.

Go into collected trot, then use your fluff and cluck aids and ask the horse to shorten the trot stride. If he tries and succeeds for a few strides, go back out to collected trot and praise him.

Be careful about walking and giving him sugar every time he does it right. I have had horses that are so smart, they do a few good strides in the test itself, and stop and whip their head and neck around for the sugar. Pretty embarrassing!

Remember, this is all trot—it is just different types of trot (see fig. 21.1, p. 184). The horse

Tools and Their Correct Use

I have never had an issue with a tense horse when the horse has been started correctly and has been given rewards and confidence by the rider. But if the horse has been forced or whip-trained, he will get uneven or unlevel. The quality of a whip-trained horse will show with grounded front legs and the croup bouncing up and down. The tension of a horse that has been rushed is also obvious.

Remember, to finish this movement it will take at least two years of concentrated work and strengthening. Don't rush it! Use your tools correctly, and watch the whip, whatever kind it is. Incorrect use of the whip will cause Problems 2, 3, 5, and 7—see p. 173.

BAMBOO

A sensitive horse will be just fine using a long whip, but for a horse that is not as sensitive, bamboo will work better. The noise of a hollow bamboo also can encourage the horse to be more active. I have had good success with bamboo in my left hand (horse on the left rein) to help hold the horse more in place and a long whip in my right hind to encourage activity from the hind legs or to encourage a bit more sitting from the horse.

Most garden shops or hardware stores will have bamboo in the spring and summer. The very light type won't work well, because you need a bit more substance for the horse to "feel" the bounce of the bamboo and also the noise of the bamboo on the croup is helpful sometimes. When the bamboo is too big it is very difficult for the ground person to hold. You need to find the right weight and feel in your hand; you should be able to tell if your wrist will be able to support the weight or not.

LONG WHIP

I am not a fan of the "whippy" whip; I like to have a stiff whip that is long enough for me not to get kicked if the horse has such a plan in mind. The stiffer whip also gives me more control, and I won't tap the horse unless I really want to.

I prefer to use the whip on top of the croup in order to avoid all of the uneven and unlevel strides that can develop by using the whip on the hocks. I believe that if you have done your homework, and your horse will lift either leg when you touch him with the whip and will also hold the leg up in the air and stand (engage) on the other hind leg as long as you want him to, you will have won most of the battle.

LONGE WHIP

I only use this tool when the horse is very fast and not too happy with me on the ground. I rather like to stand in the middle of a canter pirouette with a longe whip and have the horse do a few schooling pirouettes around me where I can touch him with the lash of the longe whip if I need to encourage more activity. But for the piaffe, I prefer either the bamboo or the long driving-type whip.

needs to understand you are asking him to "trot smaller" or "trot bigger" with more suspension. Be patient.

Exercise Six:
Helping the Rhythm Out of Piaffe
This exercise will help deal with Problem 1—p. 173.

Review the aids for the piaffe. Just as in rein back, when you want to go forward again, you sit a bit deeper and move your legs forward. This aid, which the horse learned back in Second Level, should now help this transition. The key is to not drive the horse forward but rather allow all of that energy that was working on the spot to move forward. Once the horse has taken a step you can use your legs again. If you try to "drive" the horse out of the piaffe, he will get confused and only piaffe faster and harder—and get very tense. So practice just sitting down and moving your lower legs forward to the girth. You must allow the energy to go through the reins as well.

Don't do too many steps of piaffe in the beginning. Get your reaction, do two or three steps, and go forward again. The piaffe must have all the power on the spot, but wanting to go forward.

Exercise Seven:
Walk Pirouettes to Piaffe
This will help Problems 5, 6, and 7—p. 173.

Walk pirouettes used to be performed in the old Grand Prix tests. I could always tell as a judge if the horse would piaffe or not. If the pirouette "stuck," then I knew the hind legs were too lazy to really show an active piaffe.

Your walk pirouettes can help the horse understand that when you ask for collection in the walk, you also mean activity. Think a little about asking for a simple, almost-piaffe aid prior to the walk pirouettes. We are told as judges that if the horse overreacts in this pirouette not to be as strict with your score as the horse who ignores the aids and sticks and screws his hind legs into the ground!

By using the turning aids and moving the shoulders around the hind legs, you will help elevate the shoulders, which will help a horse who wants to ground the shoulders and bounce the croup up and down. By starting the walk pirouette and then asking for a few steps of piaffe, you will help encourage the horse to lower the hindquarters.

And for the naughty horse, you may be able to trick him into a few steps, as he is not thinking about piaffe, but rather a pirouette.

21

Passage

*The horse needs to understand that piaffe, passage,
and the transitions are all trot—just different kinds of trot!*

The passage is a majestic and highly cadenced trot. Watching a good passage performed in competition reminds us what an amazing partner the horse can be. The power and elevation is supple and totally in control of the rider. Think of a horse snorting around the pasture, with tail and head held high, nostrils flaring, and yes, passaging! This movement is truly loved by the horse in nature.

Imperfections and Evasions

As with other movements, here, too problems can occur. The horse:

1 Lacks cadence or elevation (trot-like).

2 Is too "free," lacking collection, or not "closed" enough.

3 Has unlevel strides.

4 Has uneven strides.

5 Shows resistance.

You can find solutions to these issues beginning on p. 185. But first let's turn to the USEF Rule Book for a definition of the passage (see sidebar, p. 184).

How to Ride and Train

In the previous chapter I mentioned that piaffe does not feel like much is happening. However, a good passage will feel amazing and take a lot of strength from the rider's core and upper leg to stay with the movement. If the horse correctly sits and engages the hind legs, they will act like springs and thrust the horse up in air with a lot of power!

I still have muscle cramps just thinking of a clinic on Halloh with Uwe Steiner. Uwe would walk behind me with two longe whips, one in each hand. These "German training tools" (I nicknamed them this in honor of Uwe and Bodo!) would remind Halloh to stay active. Then he would help us with our tempo with his "Ein, zwei, ein, zwei." It seemed that this went on for hours, which of course it didn't. Halloh scored very high in his passage. I kept going to the gym to stay fit and strong so I would not gasp for air after this schooling.

To be a Grand Prix horse, the horse must be able to perform the piaffe, the passage, and

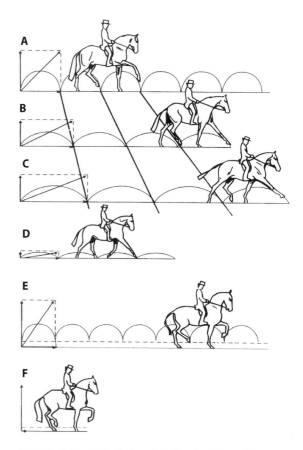

21.1 A–F The Principles of Collection: These illustrations show the relationship between degrees of collection, length of stride, and impulsion in the different paces, including collected trot (A), medium trot (B), extended trot (C), working trot (D), passage (E), and piaffe (F).

USEF Rule Book
PASSAGE

1 This is a measured, very collected, very elevated, and very cadenced trot. It is characterized by a pronounced engagement of the quarters, a more accentuated flexion of the knees and hocks, and the graceful elasticity of the movement. Each diagonal pair of feet is raised and returned to the ground alternately with cadence and has a prolonged phase of support compared to the phase of suspension.

2 In principle the height of the toe of the raised foreleg should be level with the middle of the cannon bone of the other foreleg. The toe of the raised hind leg should be slightly above the fetlock joint of the other hind leg.

3 The neck should be raised and gracefully arched with the poll as the highest point and the head close to the vertical. The horse should remain light and soft on the bit and be able to go smoothly from the passage to the piaffe and vice versa without apparent effort and without altering the cadence, the impulsion being always lively and pronounced.

4 Irregular steps with the hind legs, swinging the forehand or the quarters from one side to the other, as well as jerky movements of the forelegs or the hind legs or dragging the hind legs are serious faults.

the one-tempi changes. (As I've mentioned, I see quite a few horses in the show ring with one of these elements missing. I am not talking about a horse with mistakes in these movements, but rather an obvious omission.) Of these three elements, the horse that is not very elastic and a bit more earthbound with a "plain" type of trot will have most difficulty with the passage.

In this chapter I will give you some of the exercises that have helped this type of trot develop into a passage in my experience. You may have to settle for only a "6" for this movement, however.

Remember, when you work with your different trots, whatever you take away in length, you should add in height. So the passage is actually the shortest and highest trot you perform, and the extended trot is the lowest to the ground but the longest and most ground-covering trot you perform.

Rider's Aids

1 Inside and outside rein: In this movement, both hind legs are carrying equal weight and the horse is totally straight, so you do not have an inside or an outside rein. The rider maintains a soft and supple contact on both reins and, if a half-halt is needed, the rider can use a soft release on both reins at the same time.

2 Inside and outside leg: Both legs will move to the girth position. There are two systems: One is to use an alternating leg in the rhythm with the hind legs; however, this can cause a sensitive horse to swing the hindquarters. The other system is to use both legs at the same time at the girth.

3 Seat: Sit equally on both seat bones.

Training Exercises and Solutions

Exercise One:
Medium Trot to Passage
This will help deal with Problems 1 and 5—see p. 183.

The medium trot is the trot we use to help develop the passage. When I teach new judges

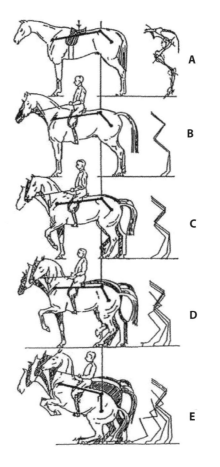

21.2 A–E The Principles of Increased Engagement and Elevation: These illustrations demonstrate how, through dressage, the horse is trained and prepared to carry with his hind legs, which increasingly bend and flex at the joints as movements become more difficult.

and want to give them an idea of how the medium will look compared to the lengthening, I tell them to think of passage. Ask yourself: Does my horse's medium trot make me think of passage? And for the judge: Can I *see the possibility* of passage in the medium trot?

If you have the ability to ride your horse into a medium with elasticity and power, you will have the ability to develop passage. It is important to remember that if you think about "shortening" the medium rather than using it for power, your passage will turn out to be short and expressionless. It's really a matter of learning to send the power a bit more up in the air for a longer period of time. If your horse is limited in the medium trot, you will have to try some of the other exercises I recommend.

One of the most important aspects of this exercise is the suppleness of the horse's topline. The horse may need to be ridden with the neck a little bit lower and rounder in order to keep the belly muscles lifted. In piaffe, the horse doesn't need to stay so round. Actually, demanding this in the piaffe may ruin the rhythm in the beginning. In the passage, however, the suppleness is of the utmost importance if there is to be any elasticity.

We have talked about different half-halts throughout this book. For half-halt from extended trot, medium trot to passage, or collected trot to passage, I like to use alternating legs in the half-halt to differentiate to the horse that this is not a transition to collected trot. Once the passage is established, I will go back to using both legs at the same time. This will serve you well later in the Grand Prix Special when you have many transitions from extended trot to passage.

Exercise Two: Work In-Hand

This will help with Problems 1, 2, 3, and 4—see p. 183.

Remember the first rule of passage and piaffe. Slow hind legs will get you in trouble. So, you may need to go back and review chapter 7 on the in-hand work and make sure the hind legs are active and "awake" (see p. 61). If the horse becomes too slow in the tempo, you will need to ride forward and activate the hind legs prior to attempting your passage again.

Just a word about *tempo.* The passage and piaffe are both trots. Two beats separated by a moment of suspension. There is some evidence that the piaffe might lose this moment of suspension, but the rhythm is still two beat with diagonal pairs. The piaffe will have the quickest tempo in the trot rhythm. (Remember, tempo is the repetition of the rhythm.) The passage will have the slowest tempo in the trot rhythm. This is because it is the trot with the largest amount of "hang time" between the beats.

It is important to have a ground person to watch the function of the hind legs when you begin your passage work. If the horse does not bend the joints and keep the hind legs in front of the tail, he is not engaged. It can still feel "passagey" and correct to an inexperienced rider when the hind legs "escape out the back door," pushing the horse along but not carrying any weight. A ground person will be able to help you assess this problem. If you don't have one available, then set up your video camera, video your ride, and watch it later to see if you are working with the correct feeling.

The ground person should be experienced if he or she is going to use either bamboo or a whip (see sidebar, p. 180). It is helpful now to have a longe whip and be able to use it to activate the hind legs every so often. Don't overdo this or you will create uneven or unlevel steps. Try first using the whip on top of the croup, as this method will not create the same issues.

If your horse is too "free" or needs more collection, ride a few strides of medium on the long side on the left rein. The ground person will have a barrier (either bamboo or a whip) in the left hand and a whip in the right hand. The horse will start to lift the shoulders when he sees the front barrier. Keep riding forward into the barrier for a few strides to help you and the horse get the feeling you need.

The passage takes a lot of strength so again, don't overdo it at the beginning. Test your reaction and while the horse is still working well, leave the movement and praise him.

I use a different "noise" for passage, and I want to save the "cluck" for only the piaffe. Note: Some of you who cluck all the time you are riding…*stop this now!* You will need this later as an important tool to associate aids. For the passage, I use a popping noise or a "schussing" noise.

Then when you are ready to train your transitions you can come from passage with a little clucking and put on your aids. If you're watching the top levels, you won't hear riders using their voice in the ring. This voice aid is helpful but again, don't depend on it, just as you don't want to depend on the whip to create the piaffe or passage.

I must say I was not amused when the FEI

Training Tools for Passage

CAVALLETTI

Always use an uneven number of cavalletti so the horse doesn't think of them as an "in-and-out" jump. Start with them on the ground and just long enough for the working trot stride. Allow the horse to gain confidence first. Next, put them a bit closer together for the collected trot, then raise them to the lowest height off the ground and trot through again, several times.

Again, do this just a few times—*not* for 30 minutes or you will make your horse muscle sore. Once the horse has confidence, put the cavalletti still closer together so you will get more suspension. If you need your horse to use his joints better and get more height, you can raise them one more time.

Gwen Blake and I used this system for the Friesian Tjesse (see photo 7.4, p. 61). Gwen's eyes got very big when we started as jumping is not really something most FEI dressage riders like! However, after the first time through—when Tjesse just thought they were Tinker Toys to be knocked about— he figured it out. It only took a few times and he had it. Smart boy!

WHIP

As I mentioned earlier, I like the long but stiffer whip at the beginning of the in-hand work for piaffe and passage. You have more control with it. The longe whip can be useful for the passage as you can let it bounce on top of the horse's croup. I find the longer whip easier with this movement, as I have to move faster to keep up with the passage.

BAMBOO

I discussed the use of bamboo in the last chapter on piaffe, but it is also a good tool in developing the passage (refer to p. 186 for details).

changed the Intermediate II test to start the first piaffe right in front of the judge at C. Why? Gosh, I hate to admit it, but with a green horse, I had found that a little clucking could be quite helpful for that first piaffe!

Exercise Three:
Using "Tools" to Your Advantage
This exercise helps with all the imperfections listed on p. 183.

You may need to experiment with the different tools at your disposal if you are having trouble teaching the horse the passage. Once the horse understands the aids and feeling, he is generally fairly willing to try.

When your horse's personality is a bit hot, try a trail ride. Take a few friends along, and ask them to go on ahead. Keep your horse back a bit and hope that he gets a bit excited—he may start to passage on his own. Reward him immediately. Seeing a deer in the woods also can work wonders, but deer aren't always available on cue when you need them!

A small tin can filled with rocks can be helpful, too. Someone on the ground can shake the can a bit as you come back from your medium trot. I once even used a plastic bag on the end of a longe whip to fire the horse up, and yes, we did get some passage steps, and it wasn't long until the horse understood what we wanted and did it on his own. Note that the intention is to gently excite the horse, not make him fearful, so use sound judgement.

Work with cavalletti. Try the bamboo (see p. 186). Sometimes one has to be a bit creative to find the right response from the horse.

Exercise Four:
Don't Rush It
This helps Problems 3, 4, and 5—see p. 183.

I find most of my students don't want to be patient. I want them to be able to perform the passage with willingness and regularity with equal-length strides behind and no "hitching" of the hind legs. It goes without saying: *without too much tension.*

Once the horse is working well in the "baby" passage, the rider and the person on the ground can challenge the horse with a good result.

So take your time and make sure you have the correct reaction 90 percent of the time. Once the horse has enough strength to go halfway around the arena with no problems, I would start to encourage him to give a bit more effort. Again, use only a few steps and then reward, go forward, and then try a few more.

I do not like to put the passage and the piaffe together until both movements are fairly confirmed and consistent. If they are not clear in the horse's brain or body reactions, you will have trouble with the transitions. Use your collected trot as a segue for a while: Collected trot/piaffe/collected trot. Then: collected trot/passage/collected trot. Or, medium trot/passage/collected trot.

Remember you are building strength as well as confidence. As I've mentioned before, think of that figure skater. He first learns a waltz jump. He lifts off one foot and does a half-turn in the air and lands on the other foot. Then he adds one full rotation. Then two. Then three—and a few in the world can do four. If you fall on your butt too many times as a figure skater, you go back down the ladder and work on the simpler jump. Dressage riders need to work in the same manner.

Canter Pirouettes

*In a wonderful canter pirouette, the horse will sit
and stay sitting throughout the turn. Novice riders will think
there is a problem as they won't feel anything happening!*

I love canter pirouettes. Of course, part of that is because I am good at training and riding them. (I do not have the same love for the Grand Prix zig-zag.) In this chapter I can give you some great tips and exercises to help you develop your horse, as well as your feel as a rider for the pirouettes. It seems some riders just have a knack for this movement. I have often told Steffen Peters he could make a pig do a great pirouette!

Please review chapter 12 on the walk pirouettes—Exercises One, Two, and Three can all be done first in walk and then in canter to help the horse's understanding of your aids (see p. 97). It is also a good idea to review chapters 7 and 13 and to make sure your horse understands the Pendulum of Elasticity (see pp. 58 and 103).

Imperfections and Evasions

Your horse:

1 Performs a pirouette that is too small (or has *too few* strides).

2 Performs a pirouette that is too big (or has *too many* strides).

3 Loses rhythm.

4 Loses bend.

5 "Rears around" the movement (has topline issues).

Solutions to these problems can be found starting on p. 190. In the meantime, as we saw in the chapter on walk pirouettes, the USEF Rule Book provides our standard definition for reference (see sidebar, p. 191).

How to Ride and Train

Rider's Aids

When riding a pirouette to the right:

1 Inside rein: Bends the head and neck and slightly positions the shoulders in the direction of the turn.

2 Outside rein: Supports the collection and helps to maintain the size of the pirouette.

3 Inside leg at the girth: Is the active leg and keeps the horse actively cantering. It also helps support the bend.

4 Outside leg behind the girth: Keeps the horse trapped on the inside hind and helps create the turning aid along with the rider's weight aid.

5 Seat: Sit in the direction of the turn or to the inside.

Training Exercises and Solutions

Exercise One: Perform Haunches-In on a 20-meter Circle

This helps Problems 2, 3, and 4—see p. 189.

The first exercise in the USEF dressage tests that asks for a *very collected* canter comes in Fourth Level. The exercise is ridden on a 20-meter circle with six to eight steps of very collected canter over the centerline. You will hear instructors ask for "pirouette canter," and this is the same thing (review Point 6 in the USEF Rule Book sidebar on p. 191).

Do a little bit of travers in walk just to make sure the horse is submissive to the outside leg.

22.1 Lauren Sammis and Sagacious HF in a pirouette. Sagacious is showing the ability to take weight onto the inside hind leg and stay laterally and longitudinally supple at the same time.

USEF Rule Book
PIROUETTES

1 The pirouette (half-pirouette) is a circle (half-circle) executed on two tracks with a radius equal to the length of the horse, the forehand moving round the haunches.

2 Pirouettes (half-pirouettes) are usually carried out at collected walk or canter but can also be executed at piaffe.

3 At the pirouette (half-pirouette) the forefeet and the outside hind foot move round the inside hind foot which forms the pivot and should return to the same spot, or slightly in front of it, each time it leaves the ground.

4 At whatever gait the pirouette (half-pirouette) is executed the horse, slightly bent in the direction in which he is turning, should remain on the bit with light contact, turn smoothly and maintain the cadence of that gait. The poll stays the highest point during the entire movement.

5 During the pirouettes (half-pirouettes) the horse should not move backward or deviate sideways. In the pirouette or half-pirouette in canter, the judges should be able to recognize a real canter stride although the footfalls of the diagonal—inside hind leg, outside front leg—do not occur simultaneously.

6 In executing the pirouette or the half-pirouette in canter the rider should maintain perfect lightness of the horse while accentuating the collection. The quarters are well-engaged and lowered and show a good flexion of the joints. An integral part of the movement is the canter strides before and after the pirouette. These should be characterized by an increased activity and collection before the pirouette and, the movement having been completed, by the balance being maintained as the horse proceeds.

7 The quality of the pirouettes (half-pirouettes) is judged according to the suppleness, lightness, cadence and regularity, and to the precision and smoothness of the transitions; pirouettes (half-pirouettes) at canter are judged also according to the balance, the elevation and the number of strides (at pirouettes 6 to 8 strides, at half-pirouettes 3 to 4 strides are desirable). When the turn is too large and the hind steps come off the prescribed line of travel, the correction is to take a straight line back to the track. Correction by use of half-pass or leg-yielding may result in a deduction of points.

8 The Quarter-Pirouette. As a preparatory exercise, the quarter-pirouette is usually executed on the track at a given letter, the horse being highly collected for 1 or 2 strides before and then through the execution of a 90-degree turn around the haunches in 2 or 3 strides, maintaining a correct canter footfall.

9 The Working Pirouette and Working Half-Pirouette. The pirouette (half-pirouette) is a turn of 360 degrees (180 degrees) executed on two tracks, with the forehand moving around the haunches. The size of the working pirouette should be approximately 3 meters. The requirements for a working half-pirouette are identical to those of a regular half-pirouette, except that the allowable diameter is increased to approximately 3 meters. A working half-pirouette is to be judged like a regular half-pirouette except that full credit must be given for a well-performed, but larger (3-meter) half-pirouette. Full credit should also be given for a well-performed regular-sized half-pirouette. A significant deduction should be made if a rider attempts but performs poorly a regular half-pirouette.

Also check that your weight is to the inside. When you ask for a travers position in the canter for this exercise, you are not asking for as much bending or angle as you would if you were performing a travers in the trot. Think of having the horse positioned slightly to the inside in the neck, with perhaps a bit more submission to the bending behind the saddle. Too much bend in the neck can cause a problem with control of the outside shoulder and later the turning aids.

Pick up your collected canter and push the haunches slightly to the inside. When you feel the shoulders coming up, think about keeping the shoulders up in the air for a few seconds longer with your half-halt. As you develop the strength of the horse, be careful: You must not overdo this exercise. Try to only ask for two to three strides before you straighten and go back to collected canter.

Exercise Two:
Riding a Square
This exercise helps with Problems 2 and 5—see p. 189.

Once the horse is successful on the circle, move the exercise to the square. Take as much time as you need to supple the horse, position the haunches slightly to the inside, collect, and do a square turn. There will be about two strides in the actual turn and a few strides of preparation. If you need to skip a corner and ride a bit farther down the straight line to organize, do so.

Exercise Three:
Riding a Triangle
This exercise also helps with Problems 2 and 5— see p. 189.

Once your square is working well, move on to a triangle, which will increase the number of turning steps. Come out of the diagonal and ride toward X. Before X, ask for your pirouette canter

22.3 Salope and Caryn Vesperman show the "sitting" behind in the canter pirouette, but the horse's topline has become stiff and he is using his neck to help maintain the balance.

and then turn toward the other diagonal marker. The pirouette will be about two to three strides of turning with this triangle.

Exercise Four:
Half-Pass into Pirouette into Half-Pass

This exercise helps Problems 2 and 4—see p. 189.

If your horse is pushing against your outside leg or is not maintaining the bend, then ride a few steps of half-pass in canter across the diagonal. Collect and ask for a half-pirouette, and then proceed in your half-pass.

JUDGING TIP

Note that this is *not* a legal movement in FEI freestyles. You must have at least three straight strides prior to and after your canter pirouette. Why? Because this exercise makes the movement easier, of course!

Exercise Five:
Counting Steps

This helps solve Problems 1 and 2—see p. 189.

Counting is important. Why? In a full pirouette, there should be six to eight strides; in a half-pirouette three to four. So, your horse must be strong enough to be able to "sit" for the number of strides needed to perform either a half- or a full pirouette, as well as the strides needed in the preparation and the finish of the exercise.

Let's think Pendulum of Elasticity for a moment. If I come onto the diagonal line for a half-pirouette, I must first make a transition to very collected canter. In Fourth Level there is a

score of 10 points awarded for this transition. The horse should sit and collect. This may take three to four strides to accomplish in the beginning. Perform the half-pirouette, which should be another three to four strides, then you must gradually come out of the very collected canter back into your collected canter, and actually ride a bit more forward for a good, expressive flying change.

In my opinion, for a chance to have a high mark in the half-pirouette in a test, your horse needs enough strength to perform pirouette canter for at least 10 strides on a straight line. Trying to do a half- or full pirouette before your horse has enough strength will only end in frustration for yourself and the horse!

So, as you work on your pirouette canter, start counting. Start with "one" when you begin the collecting. Count how many strides your horse will sit and stay under your seat. Then count again as you return to collected canter. Most riders do not have this concept in their heads; they only think of the pirouette, not the preparation or the finish of the exercise.

Total the strides for a successful full pirouette and you will have 12 to 15 strides of pirouette canter.

JUDGING TIP

The judge will also count your strides. Why? If there are too few strides, we feel the horse is "escaping" the difficulty of the exercise. If there are too many strides, we feel the horse must be more submissive to the turning aids. Just like in piaffe and the first half-pass in the zig-zag, judges give the rider a *little* leeway, as we are not 100 percent sure where you start the movement!

Exercise Six:
"Drop the Anchor"
This exercise helps fix Problem 2—see p. 189.

For a successful pirouette, you must feel like you "drop an anchor" from your inside shoulder through your inside hip, down the horse's inside leg, to the ground. This anchor must keep the horse on the spot, some say the size of a large dinner plate. Each horse will have a different circumference, in my opinion. An Arabian of 15 hands will have a much easier time making a smaller circumference that an 18-hand Warmblood. As a matter of fact, there have been a few times I have been asked to buy a horse for a client but I have said "No" after I looked at the huge canter and could not see how I could ever create a canter pirouette from it and still keep an elastic quality about it.

Exercise Seven:
What Comes First
This helps with Problems 3 and 5—see p. 189.

When the horse is learning, he must understand that he needs to "sit." When he sits, the tempo of the canter will slow down, as the inside hind leg is staying on the ground longer. Most riders will freak out at this moment and kick the horse, making the strides quicker, which unloads the hind leg.

Work on these exercises so that *first* comes the sitting and the lowering of the haunches. The inside hind leg must show a clear articulation in the joints. Once the horse understands this and is stronger, *then* the rider can worry about the activity. Don't try to get it "all" at the beginning. It won't work!

Exercise Eight:
The Cone Exercise
This exercise helps solve Problems 1 and 2—see p. 189.

I developed this exercise from my lessons with Uwe Steiner. He would stand in the middle of the arena with a longe whip. I had to come into a canter pirouette and stay exactly the same distance away from him at all times. He would be close to my inside leg and would use the whip to tap the horse's inside hind leg if I needed more activity. I would stay at this distance two to three times around and go out.

Sorry, Uwe, but when you were not there, I would replace you with a road cone! A nice tall one works well—this gives you a visual indicator as to how much control you have. It is hard when you are in the middle of the arena to really feel how much the horse can leave the line of travel.

I like to do two or three working pirouettes (not as small as performed in competition) and then go out and leave the movement. Why? To strengthen the horse and gain submission! With enough strength and control I am more confident in the show ring when I only need one rotation in the regular competition or two or three in my freestyle. With a greener horse, I often would walk a few strides, then canter, and when I lost control, I would walk again and reinforce the aids the horse was not listening to.

Exercise Nine:
The Pop-a-Wheelie Half-Halt
This exercise helps Problem 2—see p. 189.

My husband in his retirement (or is it midlife crisis?) has become a motorcycle guy. I am sure all of

you have seen a motorcycle rider lift the front end of the bike off the ground, or "pop a wheelie." The canter pirouette is about this same feeling. The rider cannot, at the beginning, do a small or subtle half-halt. The horse must understand you mean business. You need to be strong for a stride or two and then release.

Think about your half-halts and tension in your own body. We have discussed tension in the horse's body throughout this entire book. If you think of tension in the rider on a scale from "0" to 10—with "0" being the rider in a Lazy Boy recliner having a nap and "10" being where the rider is so rigid there is no suppleness in the muscles at all—then for me, riding should feel like a "7" most of the time. You have some supple tension in your core and your upper thigh to support your position and give you some leverage. In this moment you prepare for the pirouette, you may need to feel the tension of an "8" or "9" for a bit, and then go back to your "7." As the horse becomes more schooled and stronger within his own body, you will be able to use less strength yourself.

Exercise Ten:
The Five-Pointed Star
This exercise helps with Problems 1, 2, 3, and 5—see p. 189.

I find changing up the movement is good for the horse and keeps him sharp. I will collect and find my pirouette canter. Then I use my turning aids. Next, I use my inside leg to make the pirouette larger. Think of riding a five-pointed star. You will turn for two strides and then ride a bit forward to the point of the star with your inside leg. Then again, turn and ride forward to the next point of the star.

For the ultimate control, you must be able to make the pirouette smaller or make it larger whenever needed. This exercise helps ensure this ability.

Exercise Eleven:
Turning Toward the Wall
This exercise helps solve Problems 2 and 5—see p. 189.

In the beginning, when you collect in preparation for the pirouette, the horse may jump sideways one stride and then do a rather good pirouette. The problem is you are no longer on the line of travel. And, the judge will know when you are using the pirouette to develop more collection, rather than having the ability to collect the horse prior to the movement.

Ride in counter-canter down the quarterline. There will be 5 meters from the quarterline to the wall. Develop your pirouette canter and turn toward the wall. The first few times you will fail to complete the turn as the horse has likely jumped sideways as I described above, and now you are only 3 meters away from the wall.

Work with this exercise until you develop the control you need in the first turning stride and can complete the turn toward the wall.

Exercise Twelve:
Add More Activity
This helps solve Problems 3 and 5—see p. 189.

Finally, once your horse is submissive to the bend, the collecting aids, and the turning aids, you are ready to add more activity on the inside hind leg. You may first try by putting the whip in your outside hand. I find that using the whip in the inside hand confuses the horse and he often does a flying change. It can also make the horse a bit stiff and "stabby" with the inside hind. If you can tap the horse on the croup with the whip in the outside hind and perhaps add a little "cluck" from your voice, it generally allows the horse to understand your request.

If he seems confused or doesn't react correctly, you will need a ground person with a longe whip to help. Spiral down around your ground person, and have him quietly tap the inside hind leg or perhaps the top of the croup on the inside.

Again, you may need to experiment to find out where your horse will react in the right way. This varies from horse to horse. Some hotter horses will start hopping on the front legs when you touch the hind leg. A lazier and duller horse will react in a better way. Try tapping the inside hind, then the back of the loin and then, the top of the croup. One of these places will usually give you the correct reaction.

Exercise Thirteen:
Piaffe Steps Followed by Canter Pirouettes

This exercise helps with Problems 2, 3, and 5—
see p. 189.

At this level, many times you will need to "link" exercises. One will help the other. In the piaffe work or half-step work, the horse should now understand the aid to "get quicker" from the hind legs. Do a few steps with this reaction, then canter and ride a pirouette. Association is a good way to help a horse understand a movement.

I hope that you will come to love the canter pirouettes as I do!

CHAPTER

Have Fun!

*This is not brain surgery; no one will die if you
make a mistake. No one has had their life ruined over
an incorrect half-halt. Have fun!*

It's Okay to Smile

Dressage is a journey. I wish I had the body and stamina I had when I was 20 and the knowledge I have now. I often joke that in my next life I will be tall, blonde, and my thighs won't touch! We all have a dream, but in the meantime, we need to make do with what we have been given.

This "make do" refers not only to our own riding ability but also to the physical and mental ability of our "not-so-perfect" horses. As a judge, I love to see happy faces at the end of a ride.

The photo of Tiffany Busch and Forest leaving the ring is a good example (fig. 23.1). The horse looks happy, knowing he has performed well for his rider, and Tiffany has also enjoyed the partnership they exhibited during the ride.

I, too, often, see a horse that is stressed, with a nervous or "afraid" look in his eye at the end of a test. Why? Often the rider has overfaced the horse. Or the horse is a schoolmaster, but the

23.1 Tiffany Busch and Forest. Forest was trained to Prix St. George and Tiffany bought him as a schoolmaster. Tiff's goal was to qualify for the North American Young Rider Championships!

rider has not yet learned the demands of the movements and is constantly giving incorrect aids that are confusing and scaring him.

Praise Your Horse

I love to see riders reward their horse for his efforts. Not just at the end of the test, but also during their training sessions. I don't see enough of this rewarding, but I see lots of demands from riders! The photo of Chelsea Pederson and Baxter is a wonderful example of the fun and joy that can be had with dressage (fig. 23.2).

Age Doesn't Matter!

Dr. Jane Rutledge and her horse Gandalf the Gray rode their Century Ride in 2010. Their ages totaled 100. "Mr. G" was 28 and still going strong! The photo of "Team Rutledge" during the awards says it all. Even my dog Britta shared in the applause with happy barking. Judge Maryal Barnett stood in her judge's booth and gave Jane and G a standing ovation at the end

23.2 Chelsea Pederson and H.S. With Honors. Chelsea was one of my favorite young riders in Region 6. She loved her horse and always treated him with kindness. She is now married with a young child, and she has matured into a lovely young woman.

23.3 Team Jane, left to right: Jennifer Gage, Dr. Jane Rutledge (mounted), me with my dog Britta, and "Mr. G." I found Mr. G for Jane when he was eight years old. He and Jane have had a wonderful life together. Jane has suffered through many surgeries and has a knee and hip replacement. The "Century Ride" was a team effort—Jennifer rode Mr. G in the warm-up, and I read the test for Jane.

of the ride. The score did not matter. The experience was outstanding and inspiring for all who watched. All riders at the show were invited to a celebration at the show office with a huge cake served by Jane.

Broaden Your Horizons

Keep riding interesting by trying different things! Melanie Johnson on her Dutch stallion Pietro loved to dress up and ride side-saddle. They did many exhibitions this way at our stallion shows. During one clinic, Betsy Steiner asked to ride out with the cowboys who were rounding up the calves for branding. Looking simply elegant in her powder blue, off she went! The lead wran-

gler told me later that Betsy could not come with them again. I asked why, and he replied, "She wouldn't gallop after the cows. She kept saying something about the rocks and the footing."

Remember, "dressage" is not the French word for "afraid to jump." Wide Awake and I enjoyed doing a baby pair pace at Abbe Ranch. I jumped my horses from time to time…there's no reason you can't, too. Just open your mind, broaden your horizons, and give it a shot. You might be

23.4 Don't be afraid to try something new…like maybe ride sidesaddle! Here Melanie Johnson and Pietro enjoy themselves during a demonstration.

23.5 Jump! Wide Awake and I compete in a pair pace event.

surprised how much fun it can be to experiment a little.

Don't Give Up Hope

Julie Forman started working with me when she had a very large and not too cooperative Dutch mare who we nicknamed "Big Ears." Julie is only slightly over 5 feet tall, and Big Ears was 16.3 hands. The mare started working well at home but show time was a disaster. She spooked, she refused to enter the ring when the bell rang, and when she did enter, after about three movements she stopped, and that was it for her. It was one heartbreak for Julie after another.

So, Julie finally bought a small Warmblood gelding named Garand Paradox ("Solo"). He is so happy to do his work and they are just the right size for each other. As you can see from the photo, Julie and Solo are winning quite a few championships, too (fig. 23.7)!

23.5 Betsy Steiner rides the roundup! You can see from the big smile that Betsy had a wonderful time.

Sometimes, when you don't have the right horse, it is time to move on. It took Julie two years to make the decision to part ways with Big Ears, and now she wonders why she waited so long.

Ride a Freestyle or a Pas de Deux

Suzanne Sailor, a clinic student of mine from Houston, Texas, competes at Prix St. Georges with her Warmblood mare. For fun, she and a friend compete in the Pas de Deux (fig. 23.8). Her friend's horse is not at the FEI level but they both have tons of fun. And they were first place for

23.7 Julie Forman and Garand Paradox all smiles! This is so great for me to see as one of Julie's coaches. (I have also seen her eliminated and in tears.) Solo has been a joy to train and show, and after a successful season at Third Level, Julie is ready to move up to Fourth.

23.8 Riding a pas de deux with a friend can be a lot of fun.

the USDF Pas de Deux year-end award.

I remember two favorite freestyles with my horses. Maroon and I did Second Level freestyle for Dr. Edgar Hotz. I got a very high score. It was to music from Fiddler on the Roof and fit Maroon's light way of going. I came up the centerline and did a shoulder-in right, a travers right, then at X changed to a shoulder-in left, to a travers left. The freestyle was difficult but it was also short. I still do not like judging lower-level freestyles that have eight leg-yields—the shorter it is, the better.

Lago and I had a Fourth Level freestyle that wowed the judges and the crowd. We won a Regional Championship with it. Lago's owner, Dr. Dennis Law, was on the board of the Denver Opera. He had the Denver Symphony director put together the music. It was all from La Travi-

ata. The canter was ridden to the drinking song, called the "Brindisi." Many of the judges actually sang along!

Find Humor in Every Situation

This is not as easy as it sounds. I rode in and choreographed a FEI Quadrille that was performed in the "Pegasus" event, held in Denver, Colarado. This was held for several years and raised money for the St. Anthony Hospital's Flight for Life program. Dr. Dennis Law organized this great event.

The second year, Dennis and I invited Emil Jung to bring his four-in-hand team and wagon. Emil arranged for the now-famous dressage horse Corlandus to be shipped over from Germany and brought to our event. He was only a small tour horse at the time, but we had never seen anything like him in Colorado! Hans Peter Mohr, the Verband rider, came along to ride him. When he arrived in my barn he was immediately padlocked in his stall. This was required for insurance purposes.

During the black-tie dinner the excitement grew. The equine show included Arabian costume, reining, barrel-racing, jumping, the quadrille, the four-in-hand racing madly about the arena, with the highlight being Corlandus. It was the most stirring and inspirational freestyle I have ever seen!

The next day, the van was loaded and Corlandus headed back East to be flown back to Germany. Or so I thought. Four days later, I received a call from Germany. Corlandus had not been returned to them. Could I please find him and send him home right away?

I was in a panic, of course, but (thank goodness) soon found out that Emil's dressage rider was taking the scenic route home, through Michigan, where Corlandus was competed in a local show. There was a happy ending of course. The Verband got Corlandus back, and they sold him to Margit Otto-Crepin who competed with him for France and won many medals.

Final Thoughts

I hope this book has been helpful to you in your dressage journey. I hope you are excited every time you train with your horse, whatever his strengths and challenges might be. And, I hope your partnership is growing stronger and more consistent through your work together.

It's been my pleasure to join you on your journey. I hope to see you in the show ring. However, the most important part of your partnership is your daily bond with your horse. So, as you move along in your dressage life, working with your wonderful animals, remember to stop along the way and have some fun!

Meet My Horses

I was blessed to have so many wonderful horses and clients in my life. I would like to thank everyone who has helped me along my journey. Now I would like to you to meet some of my "professors"!

You have already met many of my horses in the previous chapters of this book. Here are a few I would like to thank, not for being "perfect," but for teaching me so much along the way!

A.1 Ta-Aden.

Ta-Aden

This purebred Arabian gelding, owned by Cariellen DeMuth, was a super good boy. He truly could go from Western pleasure one day to dressage the next. "Freddie," as he was known, was shown through Second Level. He did well for me and for his owner.

I was a good size for Arabians, and due to my success with Freddie, I became the local Arab trainer. I had some lovely Anglo-Arabians in my string as well. Bright Owl who showed through Third Level (barn name "Hootie"), and Strawberry Mousse owned by Foss Arabians. Both horses were out of good Thoroughbred mares from Kit Strang's ranch. Sires Little Owl and Mustafar were both US National Champions.

Two purebreds owned by Bonnie Rickel and Bara Farms were shown successfully through Prix St. Georges. Ravenwood Hairoy was also the Canadian National Champion over fences. Count Salah was the most wonderful and trainable horse. He was the Crabbet line, which I always love!

Malene

Malene was my first Warmblood in training. She was a 16.3-hand Holsteiner mare imported by

A.2 Malene.

Cornelia Millholland and sent to me for training. I could clock through the tests and get nothing but "8s" and "9s" on the trot work. The walk work wasn't too bad either. The canter was totally wild and not very balanced, but it mattered little, as US buyers were buying "super trots," probably because they were used to seeing the more average Arabian and Thoroughbred trots. (Seems we were forgetting about the canter, at the time!)

I remember one show; it was raining and hailing like mad. I was hoping the judge would just stop my ride. But no, I had to continue. Malene was really cantering well in this test, as the hail was beating her on the croup. Then, *disaster*. The flower pot at E blew into the ring just as we were coming down the long side for a medium canter. A huge leap and we cleared the sucker! The judge did not like our style, however, and gave us a "4." (Rather not our fault, I thought.)

Grande

Conversano Grandioso was my first Lipizzan. Drs. David and Nancy Markle from Steamboat Springs sent me to Tempel Farms to buy a horse for them. I knew of Karl Mikolka who was the head trainer at the time. He looked me up one side and down the other and was obviously not very impressed. I rode several of the young horses for sale as he watched but said nothing. I agreed to buy "Grande" for my clients.

Then, he finally spoke. "Come with me," he said. Uh-oh. He took me to the performance barn and told me to pick out a stallion—he would give me a lesson. Wow! I thought this was pretty cool! So, I picked out a stallion (they all looked pretty much the same to me), and all the male riders started to chuckle. I figured, oh great, I picked out a "killer" or something…

I never knew why they laughed at me, but I had a magical lesson that I can still vividly remember. I was able to ride all the Grand Prix movements with Karl coaching me the entire time. What a dream!

No one knew that I could understand German, and after my lesson he told the other riders, "You see, the little girl rides him better than you all!"

I thanked him in my best German!

Lago

Lago was purchased for me to ride by Dr. Dennis Law from Emil Jung at Locksley Farm in Virginia. At the time, this was the only place in the United States where you could go and look at 50 or more horses on one property. Emil was a former German four-in-hand driving champion. He offered horses for sale that were sent to the United States by the German Holsteiner Verband. I first met Scott Hassler here, while he was still a young rider. Tucker Johnson, our USET four-in-hand champion driver, was also started at Locksley.

Lago was fun and easy to ride when we tried him. After about a week at home, he decided he did not really want to play my game anymore. He would take off, bucking like a rodeo horse and try to unseat me. He never did, but I do admit I was pretty afraid. I let this go on for about a week. Then I decided he would never stop this behavior if I never did anything to make him know it was wrong.

I put a stronger bit in his mouth, put on spurs, and grabbed my whip. I decided when he took off this time, he was going to learn it was wrong, and if I went off in the process, I went off.

Well, I stayed on, and Lago decided that the bucking spree wasn't nearly as much fun anymore now that there were consequences. He never tried the bucking again, but he did develop another little quirk: on the left lead medium or extended canter, and only when it went toward C, he spun and bolted.

A.3 Conversano Grandioso.

A.4 Lago.

At this time, the Prix St. Georges test had the medium canter on the left lead, and it headed to C. Problem. The first time we rode it we made it to the end, but instead of collecting where we should have, Lago spun and bolted out of the arena.

The next time I rode the Prix St. Georges, he tried it again, but I was faster than him this time. We stayed in the arena, but it wasn't pretty. The third time I had my left spur close to his heart and all went well.

Years later when I was no longer riding Lago and another rider had taken up the reins, I warned her about this quirk. She felt she knew

better than me, and much to my delight, during her first Prix St. Georges, ridden at the Los Angeles Equestrian Center, Lago's quirk returned and she was eliminated. Let this be a lesson to all those riders who have been advised by another rider regarding a particular horse and his habits, likes, and dislikes—when someone with more experience with the horse than you tries to share some important information, pay attention!

I had many highlights with Lago. We won every Regional Championship (this was when there were only three, one in California, one in the Midwest, and one on the East Coast) from First Level to Prix St. Georges. I was also invited to compete at Insilco in Kansas City. He was schooling all the Grand Prix when I moved out of state. Jan Ebeling took over the ride and won the Grand Prix Freestyle at Dressage at Devon with Lago.

Ballad

Ballad was not a horse I thought I would ever own. As I told you in my introduction to this book (see p. xiii), I went to California to buy Electus while also looking for a schoolmaster for Dr. Dennis Law, a new client at the time. I bought Electus for myself and found a wonderful Prix St. Georges horse for Dennis. When I called Dennis, he asked what I had bought, I told him, and he asked how much I had paid for Electus. I told him and he said, "Well, something must be wrong with my horse; he is too cheap." He asked if there was another horse I liked, and I said yes! Ballad! So Dennis bought him, even though he was only five years old and about First Level. Ballad was not "cheap."

I was a nervous wreck when the van arrived from California as Dennis was going to see his horse for the first time! It was love at first sight. I won many championships with Ballad and was invited to compete at Insilco in Kansas City with him.

Ballad unfortunately got cast in his stall and tore up his hock. Dennis was a surgeon and with our vet Dr. Steve Long, worked many hours stitching layer upon layer trying to make it right. Ballad was sound, but had troubles with the flying changes one direction. I did not compete him again; rather my assistant, now USEF S Judge Janet Hannon, took over the ride and did some eventing. Dennis also rode him in all of his lessons.

Electus

Electus was a three year old when I bought him, and not yet under saddle. He was a Furioso II son, and I found out once I started riding him, he held quite a lot of tension in his topline. I have since found this to be true of most Furioso or Beau le Mexico (full brothers) offspring. Today, most of these bloodlines are more than two generations back, and these problems are not as obvious.

Another lesson I learned was not to buy a horse that you could not at least sit on, feel how he would react to your leg, and feel how he would react to your rein aids.

I had to go through the process of getting Electus approved by the Swedish Warmblood Association. Eric Lette (former Dressage Committee Chairman and FEI 4* judge) was on the committee. Eric was wonderful, and he stayed on as an inspector until he became a famous O judge and head of the Dressage Committee!

A.5 Ballad.

Electus tried very hard; he was very willing. But there was tension. The sand would hit the PVC pipe arena rail at the show and a big spook would result. He was 16.3 hands and had quite a long neck, and once we hit the FEI levels, keeping him collected was not so easy for me. But overall he was not a hard stallion to ride—he did not have attention issues and was not always on the lookout for girls.

I had him at the Los Angeles Equestrian Center to work with Robert Dover one spring when we were showing the small tour (PSG/Intermediate I). Robert had some jumper friends watching, and they were impressed with Electus. They asked me if he jumped. I said he should as he was a Furioso. They asked if I would sell him, I said yes, they offered me a lot of money, and that quickly, the deal was done.

Electus was thrilled with his new home and rider. Christine Shaw rode him in hunter classes, and he never lost an under saddle class. He loved

the new "frame." Electus could do most of the Grand Prix movements but he never would have been a happy horse at that level. Instead, he enjoyed his life as a hunter and sired some wonderful foals.

Halloh

You met Halloh earlier in this book (see p. 22). His real name was Ronaldson, but he came from Rosemarie Springer's barn "Gut Halloh," hence his nickname. Halloh was five years old and had been imported to the United States by Emil Jung. Emil called me and said, "I have the perfect horse for you." I thought that was wonderful, but I also was getting divorced and had no money at the time.

Like the horse addict I was, I decided to fly to Virginia to see him. When my flight was cancelled from Denver, I took that as a sign I should not have this horse! But as I was leaving the airport, I had a change of heart, and went back inside and got on another flight.

As soon as I entered the arena and saw Halloh, I was determined to have him. I told Emil I would buy him. On the flight home, I wondered where I would get the money.

I had an amazing Holsteiner mare named Optima that had been trained to Grand Prix, but she had been rushed, and her brain was fried. I currently had my assistant Kris Montgomery riding her out on the trails. I had another client, Nancy Winegard, who was a breeder of Holsteiners and wanted this mare. I had always said, "No," but now I needed money and I needed it fast. Nancy purchased Optima. She became a great mommy and never had to face the stress of training again. The balance I needed I borrowed from the bank.

A.6 Electus.

A.7 Halloh.

Halloh came with his own baggage. I think in the 1980s, every talented horse in Europe was asked to perform most of the upper level movements, whatever the horse's age. If a movement looked like it would be difficult or the horse exhibited some mental issues, he was sold to the United States.

The other problem was that it didn't look like Halloh had ever been wormed. I learned quickly that when you buy a horse from Europe, first you take a fecal sample. You do not start with Iver-

mectin. At the time, this product had just come out and was injected by the vet; it was not yet available in paste. There were so many worms that Halloh colicked badly and had to spend two days in the hospital hooked up to IV fluids. After this episode, he colicked regularly about once a month, but never seriously enough for surgery.

Halloh was the second horse I trained to Grand Prix. He did his first Grand Prix at age ten. When I say "myself," you have to realize that a project such as this really takes a village. Robert

Dover helped me with the tempi changes. Uwe Steiner helped me with the piaffe and passage, which were Halloh's highlights. Jo Hinneman rode him one day and showed me what my horse could really do! Wow! If only I were a 6-foot, German man! I usually received high scores on the extended trot, but the one Jo showed was worth a "10"!

I rode Halloh in Grand Prix for several years. One of my students was an excellent rider but had done mostly eventing, and now wanted to learn more dressage. So I leased Halloh to Rick Reed from Idaho Falls, Idaho. They had a great year at Prix St. Georges, and Rick shipped him to Florida with the hopes of showing, but Halloh tweaked a tendon on the trip down and did not get to compete.

Halloh came home and taught many students the art of sitting the trot, and about sitting straight (with his out-of-control one-tempi changes). His nickname around the barn was our "little birth control machine."

My favorite Halloh story, however, is his trip to the North American Young Rider's Championships with a para-athlete. The pair put in a wonderful performance, with the highlight being their freestyle.

Halloh lived in a "retirement home" until he was almost 30 years old.

Constitution

I hope that you have had or will have in your life a horse that just makes you smile! Constitution ("Condo") was one such horse. I bought him as a three-year-old from Emil Young. I had a good breeding program at the time, but most of the outside mares I bred were Thoroughbreds.

Condo was 17.2 hands with a lot of bone and great common sense.

The first day after his arrival to Colorado I heard loud screams of, "Help! Help!" coming from his stall. The barn help was huddled in the corner with Condo facing him, a 1,500 pound immovable object! Little did the guy know that Condo was just curious and being friendly. I opened the door, slapped my horse on the rump, and he gave a sigh and moved on to his hay.

Condo loved to play a game we called "slap lips." He would pull back his lips and ask us to slap his gums. He never tried to bite, but loved having his gums "spanked."

He had only been under saddle for three months when I took him to California for the AHSA Regional Championships. He was only entered in the stallion parade, and I thought it would be a good experience for him to go to the big city. To my surprise, the stallions had to be ridden—I had just planned on bringing him in and showing him in-hand.

I was training with Dennis Callin at the time, and I had Gaspadin, Raubritter, Electus, and Constitution at the show. Denny had Zorn, Laylock, and Damon. Our grooms were going crazy, as the stabling was quite a ways from the arena, across a parking lot and past a trade fair. I told Denny there was no way I was going to ride a horse that had only been under saddle for three months over to the arena. Luckily, Denny was a lot braver than I was.

We braided Condo up and Denny jumped on, trotted through the parking lot, past the trade fair, and into the arena. It was at night, the lights were on, music was playing, and the crowd was noisy. We laughed and said because of the

A.8 Constitution.

braids Condo thought he was in "bondage." He never came off the bit. He took both leads and was a superstar.

Condo loved to show. He usually won his classes with scores in the 70s. I had to make a hard financial decision in the late 1980s and I sold him. Karen Johnson from Fox Island, Washington, bought him and started a breeding program. She stood him for several years and he sired several Grand Prix horses and approved stallions, including Conquistador.

Sadly, Condo's life was cut short when he went into anaphylactic shock after a penicillin injection. Karen had not yet frozen any semen.

I still see grandchildren of his that I can recognize immediately. He stamped his offspring with good gaits and a great, trainable mind.

Image Credits

Photo Credits

Illustration Credits

Acknowledgments

When I started writing this book, I did not know it would take a village. Nancy Jones organized the manuscript, and without her, this project would never have taken shape.

Collecting all of the photographs and stories made me realize what a wonderful life I have been given. My students have become my friends. Their horses became my professors. I am blessed to have many mentors. They have graciously given of their time and their own talents in my quest to be a better rider, trainer, and judge. Bodo Hangen, Robert Dover, Uwe Steiner, Betsy Steiner, Kay Meredith, and Hilda Gurney were my early "eyes on the ground," and all of them have a special place in my heart.

In order to achieve my dream of riding and training horses to Grand Prix I needed top quality equine partners—thank you to Dr. Dennis Law and my mother Betty for providing them.

I have to mention those who have patiently helped develop my judging eye: Eric Lette, Stephen Clarke, and Uwe Mechlem are amazing! Linda Zang pushed me forward even when I was holding back. Steffen Peters and Debbie McDonald have allowed me to share their stage with our symposium series. It is a gift to me to be able to work with two of the best riders and trainers in the United States.

Thank you to everyone who has contributed to my career. For those of you reading this book, don't forget, when you think you know it all, you will, in fact, wither on the vine.

Index

Page numbers in *italics* indicate illustrations.

Hollowness. *See* Sidedness, in horses
Horses
    abilities and limits, 7–8, 148–150
    training pyramid for, 11–17, *11,*
    108
Hot horses, 21
Hotz, Edgar, 201

Impulsion, 15–16, 70, 81, 87–88, 122.
    See also Forward movement
Indirect rein of opposition, 15, 93
Inside aids, 8–9, 29, 70, 80
Insilco, xiv–xv
Instincts, of rider, 6–7
Instructors, 3–4, 8
Intermediate I/II level dressage, 59,
    103, 105, 148–150

Jogging, at walk, 76
Johnson, Melanie, 198–199, *199*
Joint supplements, 106
Jones, Nancy, 117, *117*
Judging tips. *See also* Scoring
    canter pirouettes, 193
    extended gaits, 153, 155
    free walk, 70, 74–75
    freestyles, 153, 193
    half-pass, 123, 126
    leg-yield, 55
    lengthenings, 67
    medium paces, 106
    stretchy, chewy circle, 46
    transitions, 66–67
    turn-on-the-haunches, 97, 98, 100
    walk, 73
    zig-zag, 159–160, 164
Jumping, 54, 199
Jung, Emil, xv, 201

Kicking, 27, 140
Kyrklund, Kyra, xvi, 106

Lago, xv, 64, *64,* 201
Late behind, in flying lead changes,
    143
Lateral bend, 47
Lateral movements, pyramid of, 50, *50*
Lateral reach, 55, 123, 160, 161–162
Lateral suppleness, 15, 16, 23, 46, 81
Lateral walk, 74
Law, Dennis, xiv, 64, 201
Laylock, 28
Lazy horses, 21–23

Lead changes. *See also* Flying lead
    changes
    exercises/solutions, 20–21, 42
    simple, 39, 63–64, 136, 142, 169
    unwanted, 155–156
Left-side short/long. *See* Sidedness,
    in horses
Leg-yield
    "bendy," 128
    defined, 51, *51*
    half-pass and, 126–127, 128
    imperfections/evasions, 49
    riding/training, 50–51
    shoulder-in and, 79, 80
    types of, 51–53
Lengthenings, 58, 65–67, 152–153.
    See also Extended paces; Medium
    paces
Lette, Eric, 70, 106
"Lightness," 15
Line of travel
    in canter pirouettes, 195
    controlling, 87
    in counter-canter, 117
    in half-pass, 122–123
    spooky horses and, 23, 26
    straightness and, 16
    in tempi changes, 166
    turn-on-the-haunches and, 100
Longe whips, 180, 183–184, 187, 194,
    196
Longeing, 27, 30
Longitudinal suppleness, 16, 23, 31, 47
Loriston-Clarke, Jennie, 159
Low-necked horses, 23

Mares, kicking by, 140
Maroon, 125, *125,* 201
Mathews, Mike, 125
McDonald, Debbie, 91, *91*
Medium paces, 104, 105–106, 108–
    114, 153
Mental aspects, of dressage, 6–7
Meredith, Kay, xv, xvi
Mighty Aphrodite, 140
Mistakes, learning from, 6–7, 20
Moshne, 106, *106*
Mukpo, Dianna, 64
Muscles. *See* Strength, building of

Neck
    balance role, 34
    bending of, 81, 116

curling up of, 46, 76
dropping, 42
shortness in, 154, 155
stretching of, 43–48

Ohlson, Linda, 106, *106*
One-tempis, 167, 169, 172
Open leading rein, 100
Otto-Crepin, Margit, 202
Outside aids, 9, 29, 31, 80, 86–87, 109

Pace events, 199, *199*
Paces. *See also* Collection; Extended
    paces
    defined, 57, 59, 104
    lengthenings, 58, 65–67, 152–153
    medium, 105–106, 108–114, 153
Pas de Deux, 28, 200–201, *201*
Passage
    defined, 184, *184*
    exercises/solutions, 185–188
    imperfections/evasions, 183
    vs. piaffe, in training order, 174,
    188
    riding/training, 183–185
Patience, 20, 188
"Pattern trained" horses, 161
Pederson, Chelsea, 198, *198*
Pendulum of Elasticity, 57–60, *58,*
    114, 147
Peters, Steffen, 60, 150
Physical aspects, of dressage, 6–7
Piaffe, *175, 176, 177*
    canter pirouettes and, 196
    defined, 174, *184*
    exercises/solutions, 148, 176–179,
    181
    flying changes and, 143
    imperfections/evasions, 173–174
    vs. passage, in training order, 174,
    188
    riding/training, 174–176, 180
    tempo of, 173
Pietro, 198–199, *199*
Pirouette canter. *See* Very collected
    canter
Plaisted, Taffy, 46
Poll suppling, 24–25, *24,* 80, 129
"Pop-a-Wheelie" half-halt, 193–194
Popeyed Chief, x, 135, *135*
Posting trot, 67
Praise, 198
Prix St. Georges level dressage, 59